Christianity According to Christ

John Monro Gibson

BIBLIOLIFE

Copyright © BiblioLife, LLC

This book represents a historical reproduction of a work originally published before 1923 that is part of a unique project which provides opportunities for readers, educators and researchers by bringing hard-to-find original publications back into print at reasonable prices. Because this and other works are culturally important, we have made them available as part of our commitment to protecting, preserving and promoting the world's literature. These books are in the "public domain" and were digitized and made available in cooperation with libraries, archives, and open source initiatives around the world dedicated to this important mission.

We believe that when we undertake the difficult task of re-creating these works as attractive, readable and affordable books, we further the goal of sharing these works with a global audience, and preserving a vanishing wealth of human knowledge.

Many historical books were originally published in small fonts, which can make them very difficult to read. Accordingly, in order to improve the reading experience of these books, we have created "enlarged print" versions of our books. Because of font size variation in the original books, some of these may not technically qualify as "large print" books, as that term is generally defined; however, we believe these versions provide an overall improved reading experience for many.

CHRISTIANITY ACCORDING TO CHRIST.

A SERIES OF PAPERS

BY

JOHN MONRO GIBSON, M.A., D.D.

AUTHOR OF "THE AGES BEFORE MOSES," "THE MOSAIC ERA," "ROCK *VERSUS* SAND," ETC.

"One is your Master, even Christ."

Second Edition.

LONDON:
JAMES NISBET & CO., 21 BERNERS STREET.
MDCCCLXXXIX.

Lisa

My memorable thoughts go with you, as we served our Lord together.
And of our Lord.
Matthew 28 v 20
and, lo, I am with you alway, even unto the end of the world.
Also John 14 v 20
At that day ye shall know that I am in my Father, and ye in me. and <u>I in you.</u>

Yours in Christ
Keith

THE several papers of which this volume is composed —some of which have appeared before in fugitive publications—are related to each other, and follow an order of thought which to some extent appears in the Table of Contents. The leading idea throughout is that of the Title; but the book makes no pretensions to be a treatise, nor has any special effort been made to avoid those occasional repetitions of thought which are to be expected in papers prepared at different times and for various occasions.

The increasing disposition to revert to "the simplicity that is in Christ" is one of the most encouraging signs of the times. That it is in this direction we must look most hopefully for the manifestation alike of the unity of the Church and of the power of the Gospel, has long been the writer's belief, and is the aim of these pages to show. Those who are in sympathy with this view will need no explanation of the prominence given to the Lord's Prayer, and the frequently recurring reference to it. If only the deepest desires of all the followers of Christ were such as find expression there, the Church would speedily "look forth as the morning, fair as the moon, clear as the sun, and terrible as an army with banners"—the visible embodiment of Christianity according to Christ.

LONDON, *September* 1888.

CONTENTS.

CHAP.		PAGE
I.	CHRISTIANITY ACCORDING TO CHRIST, AS EXHIBITED IN THE LORD'S PRAYER	1
II.	EVANGELICAL APOLOGETICS	28
III.	THE SCEPTIC'S QUESTION ANSWERED BY HIMSELF	53
IV.	GOD KNOWN IN CHRIST	68
V.	THE TRINITY AS TAUGHT BY CHRIST	78
VI.	UNION WITH CHRIST	88
VII.	UNITY BY THE WAY OF THE CROSS	98
VIII.	WISDOM PERSONIFIED AND LOVE INCARNATE	109
IX.	THE INCARNATE WORD AND THE INDWELLING SPIRIT	120
X.	ELEMENTAL EMBLEMS OF THE SPIRIT	130
XI.	THE DEMONSTRATION OF THE SPIRIT	154
XII.	THE VITALITY OF THE BIBLE	165
XIII.	THE SPIRIT OF THE AGE	175
XIV.	THE SOUL OF BUSINESS; OR, THE LAW OF CHRIST AS APPLIED TO TRADE AND COMMERCE	187
XV.	THE PROPHET HOSEA ON THE CAUSE AND CURE OF SOCIAL EVILS	208
XVI.	LAY HELP IN CHURCH WORK	220
XVII.	THE MISSIONARY OUTLOOK	232
XVIII.	THE GOSPEL ACCORDING TO CHRIST	251

CHRISTIANITY ACCORDING TO CHRIST.

I.

CHRISTIANITY ACCORDING TO CHRIST,
AS EXHIBITED IN THE LORD'S PRAYER.

IT is a true instinct that has led the Church of Christ to select the Lord's Prayer from the New Testament and place it side by side with the Ten Commandments from the Old, to be imprinted on the memory, impressed upon the heart, and treasured as a "form of sound words" beyond all price. For it is much more than a prayer-model. It teaches us not only how to pray, but what to pray for; and, inasmuch as prayer is the lifting up of the desires of the heart, out of which "are the issues of life,' by teaching us what the desires of our hearts should be, it shows us what our life should be; so that in these few memorable words we have our Lord's own presentment of the Christian life in its leading outlines and proportions. Here, in fact, we have an authoritative presentation of practical Christianity. The Lord's Prayer exhibits Christianity according to Christ.

Considering the importance which has always been attached by Christian people to this compendium, one would think that it must represent the Christianity of Christians as well as of Christ: their ideal at least, if not their actual life. However far short they might fall in attainment, one would expect that they would surely reach out towards the state of mind and heart represented by a prayer which most of them are offering day by day continually. But has it been so as a rule? We think not. We question if the majority of even earnest Christians have steadily set before them this ideal.

There are three classes of desires represented in the prayer: desires relating to God and His cause, desires for the supply of bodily wants, and desires for the supply of spiritual wants. Of these different classes of desires the place of supreme prominence and importance is given to the first, the earlier half of the prayer being wholly occupied with them; while the latter half is devoted to personal wants, being divided between the body and the spirit in the proportion of one to two. Now, it would seem that the great majority of Christians are content to dwell in the second and lower hemisphere, with only an occasional visit to the first. They do honestly try to subordinate temporal to spiritual wants; they do honestly try to attach at least double the importance to salvation from sin which they do to matters of bread; but their strength and zeal are almost all absorbed in this endeavour. They have only a fraction of energy left, if any, for the other and sunward hemisphere of the Christian life. The great struggle seems to be to reach a life corresponding to a prayer like this: "Our Father, which art in heaven, Forgive us our sins, and lead us not into temptation, but deliver us from evil; give us a comfortable living; and may Thy kingdom come."

All this is the more remarkable from the fact that the summary of the Ten Commandments which our Lord has given us follows the same order, and accentuates quite as much the superior importance of the Godward hemisphere. Just as in the Lord's Prayer we have the soul first lifted up to God once, and again, and again,—" Thy name," " Thy kingdom," " Thy will,"—so in the summary of the law "the first and great commandment" is, " Thou shalt love the Lord thy God with all thy heart, and with all thy soul, and with all thy strength, and with all thy mind." Furthermore, in the Lord's Prayer, after having poured out our hearts in longings for the Divine glory, when we come down to our own wants, we are taught to give our neighbour an equal share in each petition : " Give *us*," " forgive *us*," " lead *us*," " deliver *us* ; " thus following in the second part of it the second great commandment of the law, " Thou shalt love thy neighbour as thyself." Thus the commandments and the Lord's Prayer mutually confirm each other in regard to the relative proportions of the Godward and selfward sides of the Christian life.

We have spoken of the two parts of the prayer as two hemispheres, the two together making up a full-orbed Christianity. Perhaps a better idea of their mutual relations may be had by changing the figure. It is evident that in the first part and in the second part of the prayer we are in entirely different regions ; similarly in the first and in the second great commandments of the law. The former in each case may be regarded as the heavens, the latter as the earth of the Christian life. In calling upon us first to love the Lord our God supremely, and then our neighbour as ourselves ; likewise in asking us to pray first for the Divine glory, and then for our own and our neighbour's good, our Lord sets before us " a new heavens and a new earth, wherein dwelleth righteousness ; " first a new heavens, and then a new earth ; first a new heavens in order that there may be a new earth ; for it is only through the heavenly love that we can reach the earthly love and life to which our Saviour calls us. And yet how many are there who, though they do honestly try to live the Christian life, yet occupy themselves almost exclusively with the earthly part of it, only occasionally mounting up with wings as eagles, only now and then extending the horizon of their vision beyond the limited sphere of their personal and family interests. They dwell habitually in the lower regions; they only on rare occasions visit the heights.

It will of course be understood that it is only Christians who are called to set their hearts first on the cause of God; it is only those who have learned to say "Our Father," who are taught to make their first petition, "Hallowed be Thy name." The very first thing for a sinner is, of course, to be "reconciled to God." To him Christianity must first be a personal matter, a personal coming to Christ for pardon and "newness of life." In this personal acceptance of Christ he learns his primary lesson; so that he is able to join with all who, like him, have been reconciled to God in saying, "Our Father, which art in heaven." But now he is a child of God; his sins have been forgiven. He still will need cleansing from the stains contracted in his pilgrimage; but he no longer needs to seek bare life as one who is "dead in trespasses and sins." He no longer needs to make his own personal salvation his first care; he may now enjoy

'A heart at leisure from itself."

Christ's now, by willing self-surrender, he may—nay, he will—forget himself, "deny himself," for his Redeemer's sake; and thus he will set his heart, above all other things, on the hallowing of the Divine name, the coming of the Divine kingdom, the doing of the Divine will on earth as it is in heaven.

But some may be inclined to question whether the

order of this prayer should be the order of Christian endeavour: "Is it not, after all, the true way to begin with that which is easier, and proceed by degrees to that which is more difficult? and, inasmuch as it is a great deal easier to subordinate temporal to spiritual blessings, than to subordinate both to a desire for the Divine glory, is not that the more natural and the more practicable course which Christian people seem to be in the habit of taking? So long as we do not lose sight of the first half altogether, there surely cannot be any harm in putting our main strength into the second half until we have attained it; and after we have measurably attained it, after we have fairly learnt to put the spiritual before the temporal, then it will be time not only to give some place in our thoughts and lives to the first three petitions, but to try to give them the place of prominence which we acknowledge to be their proper place in a fully developed Christian life." Now all this would be reasonable enough if attainments in the Christian life were to be had on precisely the same conditions as attainments in other departments,—scholarship, for instance. If it were simply a question of our native powers *plus* our own personal efforts, then it would be only reasonable to take the easier first, and postpone the more difficult for later and more mature effort. But it is not so. We cannot accomplish even the easiest part of it by our own efforts. We need the Holy Spirit to teach us even to cry "Abba, Father." We need the Holy Spirit to enable us to seek the higher in preference to the lower blessings for ourselves. And seeing that without the Holy Spirit nothing can be done, and with Him all can be accomplished, the question of relative ease or difficulty is not a serious element in the case, and certainly affords no sufficient reason for departing from the order our Lord has Himself marked out for us. It is vain for us to enter on the struggle without the Holy Spirit; and with Him we need not fear to set before us the highest ideal. It is the very work of the Spirit to take of the things of Christ, and show them to us; and can any one suppose that He will be more willing to respond to our call if we invite Him to begin to help us in the second part of the Lord's Prayer, with the implication that if He only help us well through that, we shall then proceed to the first part of it? No, no; that is not the way to honour the Spirit; it is not the way to honour Christ. Let us take the ideal our Lord Himself has given us, in all its fulness, in all its grand proportions, and remembering His promise of the Holy Spirit to all who ask, and not forgetting that the Spirit is able and willing to "help our infirmities" in great things as well as small, let us by all means, from the very outset, aim at nothing short of a life which will embrace in it all the glory of the heavens, as well as all the gladness of the earth: which will put "Thou," "Thine," "Thee," in the first place; "we," "ours," "us," in the second; while from beginning to end "I," "mine," "me," pass out of sight,—lost in God in the first, merged in man in the second.

In proceeding now to look more closely into the heart of the prayer, it will of course be impossible to attempt anything like an exposition of the separate petitions. All I propose to do is to bring out and enforce those considerations which will serve the main object before us, namely, to vindicate the claim of what may be called the missionary petitions to the first place in every Christian heart.

The illustration already used may help to such a comprehensive treatment as may suit our purpose. We have spoken of the first three petitions as the "heavens" of the Lord's Prayer; but we must not forget that these heavens bend all around the earth, and touch it at every point, and that the interest of these petitions for us, and the possibility of a healthy and sustained enthusiasm on our part, will depend on our keeping this in mind. If we allow our thoughts to wander away off into a distant heaven,—away off, as it were, into the cold ether of the interplanetary and interstellar spaces,—there will be no warmth in our hearts and no life in our prayer. The need of this caution will appear when we consider that there has been a constant tendency to remove each of these three petitions from the range of the present and practical to that of the remote and impalpable.

In regard to the first petition, it has often been forgotten that it is the "*Name*" of God which is spoken of, and not God Himself; and hence a great deal that has been said and written in the old theologies as to making the glory of God the chief end of man has been unreal and intangible. When Christian people, guided by these representations, wished to test themselves on the question whether they were supremely desirous for the Divine glory, the test was apt to take the form of some severe abstraction, as, for instance, in the oft-raised question, "Have I such a supreme regard for the Divine glory that I would be willing to be lost for ever if that were to promote it?" Can anything be imagined more futile and unnatural than this?

The Name of God is that by which He has made Himself known to us, specially in the course of revelation; above all, the two great names of "Jehovah" in the Old Testament and "Jesus" in the New. As to the name "Jehovah," it has been rationalised away into the thinnest and coldest abstraction, through the influence of

This is the best channel in which personal enthusiasm for God and for Christ may flow. We would say nothing to disparage such outpourings of personal devotion as find expression in many of our modern hymns; and yet there is a danger of being carried away in the direction of something like sentimentalism, by which we mean the outflow of feeling without consequent action. The form of this petition guards us against any danger there may be in this direction. "Hallowed be Thy Name" does not translate itself nearly so readily into utterances of personal endearment as it does into such a grand and manly enthusiasm as that of "the sweet singer of Israel" when he cried: "His name shall endure for ever; His name shall be continued as long as the sun; and men shall be blessed in Him; all nations shall call Him blessed. Blessed be the Lord God, the God of Israel, who only doeth wondrous things; and blessed be His glorious name for ever; and let the whole earth be filled with His glory. Amen, and Amen." This first petition should by all means have as its animating spirit intense personal enthusiasm for Christ; but this fervour will not narrow itself to the mere personal relation of the saint to his Saviour, but will go out, with a grand sweep of missionary enthusiasm, to the very ends of the earth, according to the true suggestion of the paraphrast—

> "For ever hallowed be Thy Name
> By all beneath the skies."

The second petition has suffered somewhat in the same way as the first. Some think of "the kingdom of heaven," of which our Saviour is so constantly speaking, as if He meant a kingdom *in* heaven, whereas He makes it as plain as language can make it that He is speaking of a kingdom which He has come to establish on the earth; the expression "of heaven" referring not to its geography, but to its heavenly nature. And others, though recognising that the reference is to the earth, have nevertheless allowed themselves the habit of looking forward to some grand demonstration in the future, forgetting what our Lord was so careful to teach, that the kingdom of heaven of which He spoke came not with observation, and that, instead of expecting to be able to say, "Lo here!" or "Lo there!" His disciples should recognise it as already established, and having its sphere in the hearts of men. When our Saviour teaches us to pray "Thy kingdom come," He is not leading our thoughts away from the present, away from the sphere of our own proper activity and hourly interest; He is teaching us to pray for a kingdom which is as much a present reality, and as little in the clouds, as the kingdom of Great Britain and Ireland; for a realm whose concerns are as definite and as practical as those of the urgent politics of the day, and infinitely more important and farther reaching. It is a prayer the answer to which we should watch for day by day and hour by hour, not only in the subjection of our own wills to the blessed sway of the "King of kings," but in the growing consecration of believers, in the conversion of sinners, in the overthrow of tyranny and all iniquity, in the amelioration of human sorrow and suffering, in the progress of enlightenment amongst the people, in the dissipation of the fogs of doubt and the darkness of infidelity, and above all in the progress of "the Gospel of the kingdom" in all lands. True indeed, the eye of the Christian's hope should always be fixed upon the goal; we should look through all confusions of the present to the great future, when Christ Himself shall come in the clouds of glory; but while our eye is fixed upon that point in the future, our thoughts whose name is a guarantee for high excellence of work, there is a series of hymns founded on the Lord's Prayer, and of all the hymns, in number twenty-four, set under the third petition, there is not one which has the slightest reference to the main substance of the petition. They are all hymns of personal resignation; the pronouns which run through them all are "I," "mine," "me;" the prayers in them all are for personal blessings; there is not a single reference to the earth at large. I should not think it proper to refer to this if it were a solitary or an exceptional instance; but I do so because it is an indication of a common tendency of Christian people to turn this grand universal petition for blessing to the earth on which we live, into a matter of personal religion merely. For once that the sacred words "Thy will be done" are used in Christian language for a missionary aspiration, they are probably used a hundred times in reference to circumstances of personal history which call for resignation. This is probably to be accounted for by the influence of our Saviour's memorable words in the garden, "Not My will, but Thine, be done." There we have our great lesson in resignation. There we have a passage which will serve as a sufficient inspiration for one of the sweetest and most difficult of the Christian graces. By all means let the sacred words be used for this sacred purpose, and let hymns be written on the touching theme to guide and cheer the troubled souls of God's afflicted ones. But when there is so lovely and perfect a text for the important subject of Christian resignation (and there is no scarcity of similar texts throughout the Bible), why should an inroad be made upon the Lord's Prayer for another? why should this wide and grand petition be robbed of the grandeur of its meaning as a missionary prayer, and made a mere duplicate of another text, however beautiful and precious that text may be? It is true, indeed, that the grace of resignation is *implied* in this third petition. When we say "Thy will be done on earth," we of course include the few inches of the earth on which we stand. But it is one thing to remember that personal matters are included in the grand whole, and quite another to make personal matters the "be-all and end-all" of a petition which manifestly was intended to soar far above and stretch far beyond all mere personal considerations, and take the whole world in its wide embrace.

To illustrate the practical difference between the plain and obvious sense of the petitions, and that other meaning which too often takes its place in the thoughts of Christian people, let us look at it in relation to missionary funds. A man may pray for God's glory in the abstract, day after day, and year after year, and all the while it may cost him nothing. How can the glory of Him, who "dwelleth in light which no man can approach unto," be either advanced or hindered by any effort or sacrifice of mine? Similarly a man may pray for the coming of Christ in the clouds without his prayer disturbing the clasp of his purse. What can money do to bring Christ down again from above? And for the same reason it need not cost him anything to sigh and long for the holiness of the heavenly country; and as for resignation to the troubles of life, though it is one of the most difficult of all Christian duties, it does not tax any financial resources. But let a man pray that God's name may be hallowed by all beneath the skies; that Christ's kingdom may come here and now, all around him, and to the uttermost ends of the earth; that holiness may prevail among the men that are his own contemporaries; and, unless he be a hypocrite, and deceiving himself, he will be constrained both to work and to give for the proclamation of that Gospel which makes known the blessed name; for the heralding of the good news of the kingdom to all the nations of mankind; for the making known to all men of the presence and grace of the Holy Spirit, who alone is able to secure that the will of God shall be done on earth as it is in heaven. In the one case there is an impulse to the exercise of grace, undoubtedly, but it is the passive grace of contemplation, adoration, or submission; in the other case there is a mighty impulse, as well, to the highest and most devoted activity, to the consecration of all we are and all we have to that great cause which is enthroned in our hearts. The life to which the one points is like that beautiful ideal in Thomas à Kempis; the life to which the other points is that quite as beautiful and far grander life of the apostle Paul, who could say in a far higher sense than the other, "To me to live is Christ."

We have seen that it is necessary, for the sake of the heavenly part of the Lord's Prayer, that its relation to the earth should be remembered; that the heavens of our thought should not belong to "a happy land, far, far away," but to this very earth on which we live. The next thing will be to notice that as the heavens cannot do without the earth, neither can the earth do without the heavens. If the heavens must have the earth beneath to make them our heavens, the earth must have the heavens above it to make it habitable and enjoyable. And accordingly we shall find that when the first three petitions of the Lord's Prayer are given their proper place of prominence, the last three, far from being hindered, are very much helped thereby.

This is sufficiently obvious in regard to the fourth

petition. As long as a man is living for himself, without any very great enthusiasm, without any very wide horizon around him, it is very hard to persuade him to be contented with daily bread. When a military officer is living in London he is as particular as any other subject of the Queen as to his quarters, and surroundings, and style of living. But let him set out on service in the field, and he scorns these things. He is willing to sleep, if need be, on the bare ground; to live on the homeliest of fare, and to submit to hardship and privations of all kinds. So will it be in the service of Christ. So long as our thoughts are confined to the narrow sphere of our personal life, we shall find it hard to restrain the desire for more and more comforts, conveniences, and luxuries; and only after these growing demands have been fully satisfied shall we be ready to take into consideration the claims of the world at large. But let us realise that we are not now living quietly at home, that we are out on service in the field, and therefore that loyalty to our Sovereign ("Hallowed be Thy Name"), patriotic devotion to our country ("Thy Kingdom come"), and thorough consecration to the enterprise before us ("Thy Will be done on earth"),—that these are the claims which take precedence of all others; and we shall scorn to seek our own ease or pleasure; we shall be contented with the humblest fare, with the barest surroundings, with scanty rations, if need be, if only success attend our efforts in the great campaign! We should feel the soldier spirit rise within us, as it did in Uriah when, in answer to a suggestion addressed to his natural love of ease and pleasure, he said, "The ark, and Israel, and Judah abide in tents; and my lord Joab, and the servants of my lord, are encamped in the open fields; shall I then go into mine house to eat and to drink? . . . As thou livest and as thy soul liveth, I will not do this thing." Give me only, day by day, my daily bread, and I will find my satisfaction, my luxury, my life, in the service of my King and country in the field.

There can be no doubt whatever that the growing luxury of the time is one great reason why there is so little enthusiasm for the cause of God. If we would be content with "bread" (by which we do not suppose that barest necessaries are meant, but only such a moderate provision for daily wants as does not involve our making it the main object of life to secure it), if we were content with a scale of living anything like as humble as that which satisfied our King when He was here on earth, how much energy, how much time, how much money would be at once set free from the mere ministration to the wants of the body, for the proclamation of the Name, for the advancement of the Kingdom, for the accomplishment of the Divine Will upon the earth!

The evil of the growth of luxury has been long recognised among Christian people, and much zeal has been shown in the endeavour to stem the tide; but it is doubtful if the zeal has been, for the most part, wisely directed. It has generally taken the form of denunciation and condemnation. But the difficulty has always been to draw any line that the common Christian conscience would or could approve. The complex conception of worldliness has been an indefinite and uncertain aggregate of many particulars, most of them of such a kind that they cannot be condemned as in themselves wrong; and the result has been that, as is generally the case, people have given the benefit of the doubt to that side to which they have been most inclined; and so the appeals of the Puritan have not really reached the conscience of the Cavalier. But the question comes whether there is not, in the order of the Lord's Prayer, the suggestion of a more effectual method of counteracting the evil. We generally think in this way,—If we could only cure the worldliness of the Church, what an impulse would be given to the cause of Missions! But what if the better and more hopeful order be rather this,—If we could only stir a proper enthusiasm for the cause of Missions, for the glory of God, for the advancement of His kingdom, for the doing of His will on earth as it is done in heaven, would not worldliness cure itself? Let Christian people first learn from the heart to pray, "Hallowed be Thy name; Thy kingdom come; Thy will be done in earth, as it is in heaven;" and the result will be that their souls will have been so filled with these higher longings that when they reach the lower plain of the fourth petition, they will be under no temptation to exceed its modest limits. It is the old cure of the Gospel, which, under the designation of "the expulsive power of a new affection," Chalmers showed to be the power of God unto the salvation of the lost, and which is equally applicable for the purpose of saving the Church from the blight of worldliness, the almost universal hankering for so very much more than can be fairly thought of when we pray, " Give us this day our daily bread."

The same considerations are manifestly applicable to the fifth and sixth petitions, and the spiritual wants of a personal kind which they express. It is a great mistake to think that personal piety will suffer by allowing it to fall into the place which has been assigned it in the Lord's Prayer. The principle which our Lord laid down so often and in such absolute terms is just as applicable in the spiritual sphere as anywhere else: " He that will save his life shall lose it; and he that will lose his life for my sake shall find it." What was the reason that the plicated and much-debated subject, presenting innumerable difficulties which it is easy to raise and hard to answer, by which he is discouraged and repelled at the very outset. It is true that the mischief has been, to a great extent, neutralised by the care which has generally been taken to remind the inquirer that, while the road is long, and toilsome, and difficult by the way of the intellect, it is not so by the way of the heart; that a sinner may come to Christ without any preliminary investigations about the Bible or Christianity, and, by a direct and immediate exercise of faith in Him, receive such inward light, and enjoy such an experience of saving grace, that many of his difficulties will be removed at once, and those which remain will not interfere with his peace and progress. But the question seems scarcely to have been raised whether it is actually necessary that the path of the intellect should be so much more circuitous. If an inquirer who, in addition to the belief in God which most men have, has a sense of moral need springing from a consciousness of sin, is at once pointed to Christ without any further preparation, why may not an inquirer who is intellectually convinced of the being of God, and the need there is of some further revelation, be at once led to Christ, without being required first to wrestle with questions about the authenticity of the books of Moses or the Gospel of John, or with the question whether the complex creed which enters into his instructor's or his own idea of "Christianity" be all the truth of God? Why may not the first and main inquiry be, whether Christ, the Christ of history, be the Revelation of God which the soul needs, whether He be not the Truth of which the man is in search? When we are asked the way of salvation, we do not say, "God has revealed Himself in the Bible, therefore believe the Bible;"

nor, "Christianity is the true religion, therefore accept it." No; we present Christ at once, using only so much of the contents of the Bible, perhaps only a few sentences, as may be necessary to get the Saviour before the mind and heart, knowing full well that, if once He is accepted, there will be no fear for the rest. Now, is there any reason why, in the systematic treatment of the evidences, we should have ever so much to say and to prove about the Bible as an inspired book, or Christianity as the true religion, before we have a word to say about Christ Himself? Is there any reason why our Apologetics, presenting the truth to the intellect, should be less evangelical in its method than our Homiletics, presenting the truth to the heart?

As an illustration of how little has been thought of this order in the past, we may refer to one of the ablest and most spiritual works on the evidences, that of Dr. Hopkins. The subject of method was before his mind quite prominently, as is evident from his third chapter, in which he gives excellent reasons for taking the "internal evidences" before the "external," thus reversing the order which had been previously in use—a change which was a great improvement in the evangelical direction. Yet even he elaborates nine arguments for Christianity before he presents "the condition, character, and claims of Christ;" and when he does reach this point, he does not give it a separate, substantive position, but simply brings it in as the tenth and last argument of the series of internal evidences of Christianity. And it is not only in the more formal treatises covering the whole ground, that the claims of Christ are postponed till those of the Bible or Christianity are considered; but even in those monographs where attention is restricted to the Christological part of the argument, the same order of thought will show itself. Take, as an instance of this, the admirable little work of Dr. W. Lindsay Alexander, of Edinburgh, entitled "Christ and Christianity." The title would certainly warrant the expectation that the order of thought would be, Christ first, afterward Christianity. But it is not. He begins by speaking of Christianity as "the one religion for man," and then goes on to say (p. 9), "Let it be remembered that Christianity comes to us in an *objective* form—in the form of a book;" and, further on, "It is not only to certain cardinal verities that the Christian must yield his cordial assent, but *to all things which are written in the book.* . . . It is only as he has satisfied himself on solid grounds that the book, as a book, is entitled to his homage, that he will be prepared to bow to it with that docility which is required." (The italics are his own.) It is not till the second part that the Person of Christ comes in at all. Dr. Bayne's "Testimony of Christ to Christianity" presents the claims of the personal Christ with great directness and power; but is not the title he uses significant? The idea evidently is that Christianity is the thing to be proved, and that Christ is a witness to prove it. The question does not seem to have suggested itself, whether Christ Himself be not Christianity, and what we call Christianity a witness to Him rather than He to it.

The method for which we contend is to present Christ, and the claims which He makes on our confidence, *first*. Let the first effort be to lead the inquirer to believe in Him. Let Moses and Joshua stand aside, till a greater than either is introduced. Let even the Evangelists be nothing more than good, trustworthy witnesses, to begin with. Few candid men will stumble at that, and even if they do, they are more likely to be captivated by the wonders of the life and character of Him to whom they bear witness, than convinced by any argument for their inspiration that can at that stage be presented. It will be time enough to consider the less obvious arguments for the divine authority of the witnesses, after the more obvious arguments for the divine authority of Him, to whom they witness, have been presented in all their strength. It is important that the mind of the inquirer be directed to Christ as speedily, and kept there as steadily, as possible. After His claims are felt and acknowledged, it will be easy to satisfy him as to the divine authority of the Scriptures, and of all that can be fairly included under Christianity as a system.

On behalf of this method we have to urge, first, that it is the scriptural method. The apostles had to deal with intellectual doubters, as well as with those who were morally averse to the Gospel; yet they invariably presented Christ as the first object of faith. They made frequent use of the Old Testament Scriptures, it is true, especially in dealing with those who were already grounded in the belief of them; but we never find them urging belief in the Scriptures as the first thing, and faith in Christ simply as the result of their acceptance. When Paul preached on Mars Hill, he did not try first to convince his heathen audience of the divine authority of the Jewish Scriptures, but passed at once from the common ground of the truths of natural religion, to the setting forth of Jesus and the Resurrection. No one, indeed, would gather from anything in the apostolic writings that their idea was that God had revealed Himself in a book, and that, by receiving that book, a Saviour would be found in its pages. It was rather that God had revealed Himself in His Son, who is therefore urged on the acceptance of men; and when the testimony of the should be reared. And, when he has occasion to speak of the authority and value of the Old Testament, in that passage which has been considered the *locus classicus* of the doctrine of Inspiration (2 Tim. iii. 15, 16), he is careful to urge the central importance of "faith which is in Christ Jesus."

While little attention is called by the inspired writers to themselves or their writings, there is still less said of Christianity as a system. There is a striking absence of all those abstract terms with which all modern Christian literature, and especially our apologetic literature, is so profusely adorned. The word "Christianity" does not occur at all, and we can think of no expression which can be fairly considered its equivalent. We look in vain for any reference to "the Christian religion." The word "religion" occurs in only three places, and in none of them is it used in the comprehensive sense in which we use it now. It may seem to some strange, that the New Testament could have been written, from beginning to end, without any use of words which we find necessary on every page of our writings which refer to the same subjects. The explanation is very significant. Where we should write "Christianity" the apostles write "Christ." Instead of "the Christian religion," they write, "the gospel of Jesus Christ," or "the truth in Jesus," or simply "the faith," meaning the faith which has Christ for its object. From all which it seems sufficiently obvious that the scriptural method of presenting the truth to the intellect, as well as to the conscience and heart, is to put Christ Himself always in the front. The evangelical method of apologetics is certainly the scriptural method.

We shall now proceed to consider the working advantages of the method we are urging. And we shall find it of great value for the accomplishment of both the great purposes of Christian Apologetics, which are to guide the inquirer into the truth, and to defend the truth against its assailants.

The main advantage, for purposes of instruction, is one which has been already adverted to in explaining the method, viz: this, that it is the natural order of thought, from the simpler to the more complex. The importance of a simple and progressive order of thought can scarcely be exaggerated. It will be remembered that Des Cartes, who may be considered as the founder of modern philosophy in its critical development, began his investigations with the subject of Method, and published as the Introduction to his works "A Discourse on the Method of Rightly Conducting the Reason." In that discourse he lays down two leading rules, one negative and the other positive. The negative rule is the famous one about doubting everything to begin with, and so reducing the mind, so far as its beliefs are concerned, to a sheet of white paper. The positive rule is as follows: "To conduct my thoughts in such order that, by commencing with objects the simplest and easiest to know, I might ascend by little and little, and, as it were, step by step, to the knowledge of the more complex." Now, modern scepticism is so faithful in its application of the Cartesian negative that we cannot meet it to advantage without a faithful application of the Cartesian positive. But the positive rule of Des Cartes, obvious and obviously important as it is, seems to have been little regarded by the majority of writers on the Christian evidences. The inspiration of the Scriptures is one of the most difficult questions in the entire compass of theology. It cannot be discussed and settled without encountering a multitude of difficulties, many of which may prove serious stumbling-blocks in the way of an inquirer, who has as yet no solid ground on which to stand. On the other hand, no such difficulties lie in the way of the presentation of Christ. Even infidels, who have shown themselves most unscrupulous in attacking the Bible, dare not attack Him. His credentials, apart from the miracles He wrought, which being more difficult, ought of course to be presented later, are easily exhibited and easily recognised. His life and character shine out with such lustre that even the most strongly prejudiced will be unable entirely to shut their eyes to it. There are, of course, moral obstacles to the acceptance of Christ, which no method of presentation can overcome, which only the Spirit of God can remove; but, so far as the intellect is concerned, it would seem a much more hopeful course to begin with the revelation which God has given of Himself in the man Christ Jesus, and from that as a vantage ground, to advance to the belief of all that holy men of old, moved by the Holy Ghost, have written, than to attempt to reach the goal by the reverse method.

It is not forgotten, that there is a very wide interval between that admiration of Christ as a man, which no intelligent person can refuse, and that trust in Him, as the Son of God and Saviour of the world, which true faith in Him implies. But does not the one naturally lead to the other? And is not the inquirer far more likely to grow into this faith by the contemplation of Christ Himself, than to reach it by first assuring himself that the Scriptures are the Word of God, and then that they dogmatically teach the Deity of Christ? It is instructive to notice how our Lord Himself dealt in this matter with His disciples. It is evident that at first they had no adequate idea of His Divine dignity. But instead of dogmatically teaching them the truth in relation to His Person, He led them gradually up to it by manifesting Himself to them. After they had been some time with Him, we find them, in amazement at the calming of the lake, saying one to another, "What manner of man is this, that even the winds and the sea obey Him?" It was not till the critical interview at Cæsarea Philippi, well on in His ministry, that the pointed question was put, "Whom say ye that I am?" and the answer came, "Thou art the Christ, the Son of the Living God." In the same way the sincere inquirer (for it is only the *sincere* inquirer we are now thinking of) will be much more likely to reach the truth in regard to Christ's Divinity by being pointed to Christ Himself, and led to dwell upon His claims and credentials as the Messiah, than by having his attention diverted to the large question of the inspiration of the Scriptures, in order that after he is satisfied on that question, he may be constrained to accept the other on the authority of an inspired dogmatic statement.

But it may be objected here, that since in order to present Christ at all we must make use of the New Testament, or at least a part of it, it would seem more natural to begin with the Old, and thus follow the order which God Himself has followed in unfolding His truth to men. In order to meet this objection, it is only necessary to distinguish between the dogmatic and the historic use of the Bible. It is a great mistake to suppose that, by postponing the question as to the divine authority of the Scriptures, we preclude ourselves the use of the books either of the Old Testament or of the New. Time was indeed when there seemed to be only the two alternatives, when the prevalent infidelity represented the Scriptures as the work of impostors, who fraudulently invented the whole thing, history and all. But it is far otherwise now. The infidelity of the day accepts in the main the Scripture history. It takes great liberties with it indeed, especially in the way of "eliminating" the miraculous element from it; but it never attempts to do away with it altogether. After the most relentless of the literary and historic critics have done their worst, enough is left to show a providential preparation for the coming Christ; and that is all that is needed to begin with. After all, the framework of the Jewish history is all that is absolutely essential to the Christian Apologist, and that he can have without any controversy, and without encountering the storm of opposition which the attempt *ab initio* to establish the dogmatic authority of the Old Testament will inevitably raise. It is a significant fact, that even the evangelist Matthew, writing specially for the Jews, and having so prominently before his mind the idea of the fulfilment of the Old Testament Scriptures, should begin his gospel, not with a list of the books of the Old Testament, but with a genealogy; while the other evangelists make only the briefest references to the prophets who have gone before, and proceed at once to set the man Christ Jesus before their readers. What we contend for is, not that the Bible be closed, but that when it is first opened, it be used, not as a dogmatic revelation, but as simple history; and that only so much of it be used as may seem necessary in order to bring the Person of Christ before the inquirer's mind, so that his thoughts may rest upon Him, until he see His glory, "the glory as of the Only Begotten of the Father." Then the way is prepared for his receiving the Holy Spirit, Whose work it is to guide into all the truth—all the truth which is incidentally unfolded along the line of that historical development which is the main feature of the written Word.

Further, by following this method, we put ourselves

in a position to deal most effectually with certain *a priori* objections, in which the infidelity of the time intrenches itself. Chief of these is the alleged utter improbability of the miraculous. We shall come to this by and by. Let us first look at a more sweeping, though perhaps less deeply-rooted prejudice. We refer to the alleged improbability of God's revealing Himself in a book, especially a book which has grown up in the incidental, not to say accidental, way the Bible has, and which has been left to the ordinary chances of history for its preservation and transmission, without even the precaution which was taken with the Decalogue, of having at least one authentic copy engraven in stone—a book, moreover, which has, as a matter of fact, given rise to endless differences of opinion, even among those who thoroughly believe and truly love it, as to what its precise teaching is on many subjects that cannot be regarded as of slight importance. Now the way in which objections of this kind have been usually dealt with, has been to point out that we are not the proper judges as to the form or style or attendant circumstances of the revelation which God may be pleased to give us. All which is perfectly true. But is it not far better if we can take away the entire ground of the objection by showing that the Bible is not *the* revelation God has given, but the record of it; that the revelation which God has given, and which He calls upon us to accept, is not the written, but the Living Word; and that the main object of the inspired Scriptures is to point men to Him, which purpose they serve quite as well as if they had been engraven in stone and preserved in the pyramids, and far better than if they had dropped all stereotyped out of heaven?

By this method of reply not only is the alleged improbability disposed of, but it can be shown that the could be reasonably asked: superior wisdom, superior power, superior purity; and all these so immeasurably superior that they cannot be reasonably assigned to human genius, strength, and virtue; so much so, that those who will only look steadfastly at Him, as He is exhibited in the simple pages of the four evangelists, pages which bear the stamp of truth on them to the candid reader apart from any theory of inspiration, must surely be constrained to say with the centurion: "Truly, this was the Son of God!"

We do not, of course, deny that there are difficulties in the thought of "the Word made flesh," but they are difficulties of an entirely different kind from those which meet us when we make God revealed in the written Word the first thought. The difficulties connected with the manifestation of God in human likeness are difficulties which can be readily shown to inhere in the nature of the subject, difficulties pertaining to the necessary conditions of the revelation of the Infinite in terms of the finite. And, besides, these difficulties cannot be avoided on any method of presentation; whereas, when we take the more circuitous route, we have to encounter a whole array of Bible difficulties before reaching the Incarnation at all, and when we do reach it, it is not in the form of a substantive revelation, but as one of many miracles or one of many dogmas, resting with all the others on the authority of the book.

This is not mere theorising. The case of a very intelligent and earnest young man is here recalled, whose great difficulty was the story of the Incarnation, which he had been taught to look upon as one of the Bible miracles, to be accepted solely on the ground of its infallibility. Being troubled with difficulties about the Bible in the first place, to which was added his perplexity about the "miracle" of the Incarnation, he felt as if there were two great mountains between him and Christ, which he vainly tried to scale. But as soon as the thought was suggested to him to take the Incarnation first, not as a mere miracle, but as a substantive revelation, he was intelligent enough to see that, instead of being a stumbling-block, it was the very thing he was in search of; and then, with a clear and firm faith in Christ as the Son of God, it was, of course, much easier for him to deal with his difficulties in other parts of the Scriptures.

This leads us now to notice the vantage ground we may have in dealing with that bugbear of modern scepticism: the miraculous. When the Bible as a revelation is represented as the ultimate foundation of everything, all the miracles of the Bible are on the same evidential footing, and just as much depends on what you can say about the most difficult miracle of the Old Testament, as about the Resurrection itself. The sceptic may select his point of attack at will, because the position taken obliges you to maintain all. But when Christ is presented as the Revelation of God, we do not need in considering His claims to touch any of the miracles except those of the Gospels. Not that any doubt is cast on those recorded in other parts of the Bible, but simply that the consideration of these belongs to a later part of the subject. The question being simply concerning Christ as the Son of God, it would be manifestly irrelevant to take up the consideration of any other miracles than those wrought by Himself. And it is probable that few of those who have happily been well established in their faith from their earliest years, can have any idea what a relief it would be to many an inquirer to find that he can reach Christ without having to climb the mountain of Gibeon, or descend into the valley of Aijalon;

and what a luxury to hold his faith in the Son of God in such a fashion that a sneer about the burning bush or the lions' den may pass him as the idle wind. It *is* a great thing to meet the difficult question of the miraculous at a point where we are strongest, and our adversary weakest.

And not only so, but we meet it in such a way, that we can turn the tables on him in regard to probability. No one can deny that miracles, abstractly considered, are improbable. They would not be miracles if they were not. And no one can deny, that the presence of miraculous stories in a historical book, seems to render it unhistorical; so that when we deal with the miracles as a portion of the contents of a book, we have to face the question of their improbability. But when we take the other path: when we put Christ in the foreground, and show what He claimed to be, and what He was, instead of its being an improbable thing that He should perform those deeds of mercy which are recorded in the Gospels, it is in the highest degree improbable that He should not. And the absurdity becomes very apparent of making it a ground of objection, that He who lived as never man lived, and "spake as never man spake," should be said to have "done the works which none other man did." Ah, it is far better to lead men to Christ first, and then to the miracles; and not, as is so often done, to the miracles first, in the hope that thus they may be led to Christ. We do not deny, indeed, that there is a path that way; but we think the other better and more direct; and we seem to have the authority of the Master Himself for saying so, for this is the way He puts it: "Believe me, that I am in the Father, and the Father in me; *or else* believe me for the very works' sake." In former times the miracles were regarded as the mainstay of the Christian evidences, and hence they very naturally came in early and figured prominently in the argument; but now that they are more apt to be regarded as a burden than a bulwark, it is wise to postpone their consideration until we have advanced that against which even the most thoroughgoing infidel has nothing to say, the life and character of the Lord. And if we can only induce the inquirer to contemplate the person of the Lord Jesus, to drink in His words, to enter into sympathy with the plan and purpose and tenor of His life, to gaze on the beauty of His face, to fill his heart with the admiration which is due to the immortal loveliness of His character—in a word, to get really and truly acquainted with Him—instead of finding a difficulty in the wonders connected with His birth, or the deeds of mercy which He did, he will recognise in these the necessary complement of the other; and, instead of thinking it a thing incredible that God should raise Him from the dead, he will be prepared to enter into the true and deep philosophy of the apostle, when he said that God "loosed the pains of death" for Him, "because it was not possible that HE should be holden of it."

It need scarcely be pointed out that, for those who are satisfied as to the divine credentials of Christ, it is an easy step to pass, through His teaching on the subject of the Holy Spirit, both in relation to the prophets who went before, and the apostles to come after, to the acceptance of the entire Scriptures as given by inspiration of God; and, after being satisfied of the reality of the miracles wrought by the Lord Himself, to pass to the acceptance of those which stand connected with the names of the men whose office it was, either before or after His life on earth, to bear witness to Him.

This leads us to remark finally, under this division of

the subject, that, by following this method, the inquirer is kept in much closer contact with the Divine Personality. The order, in fact, is just the order of the Trinity. It is first God, then Christ, then the Holy Spirit From the contemplation of GOD as manifested in Nature and Providence, the inquirer passes to God as revealed in CHRIST; and, finally, in the third and last stage of his inquiry, advances to the consideration of God in Christ made known by the HOLY SPIRIT through the prophets and apostles, whose testimony and teaching are preserved in the inspired Scriptures of the Old and New Testaments. Thus the divine and heavenly is kept always in the foreground, and the inquirer is helped in the process of his inquiry to acquaint himself with God: the Father, the Son, and the Holy Ghost

But little space is left for considering the advantages of what we call the evangelical method, for purposes of defence. In doing so, the writer of these pages will take the liberty of using a few sentences from his own little book, entitled "Rock *versus* Sand," in which he makes the attempt to follow the order of thought recommended in this article:

"The vast accumulation of evidence for Christian belief has, to a large extent, hindered even Christians themselves from recognising where their greatest strength lies. Inasmuch as nine-tenths of all the attacks that are made on Christianity are attacks on the Bible, the attention of Christian apologists has been almost exclusively directed to its defence. And their success has been so great, that comparatively few have felt it necessary to go behind it. The Bible is such a wonderful book that, even if we could give it no place in history at all, it would commend itself to the careful consideration of every thoughtful man. Even though it set up no claim to inspiration, and could show as little connection with any remarkable name in history as the Book of Mormon can, it would be hard to explain it without some superhuman theory of its origin. If the defence of the Bible, as a whole, against infidel attacks had been more difficult or less successful than it has been, there would have been greater disposition to fall back on the foundations on which the Bible itself rests. Now, it is true that, so far as internal evidence is concerned, the position of the defenders of the Scriptures is stronger than ever. The objections against particular passages are, for the most part, the old objections that have done duty in every generation from the beginning till now, while deeper and more comprehensive study has brought out new beauties and glories, new adaptations and correspondences. But inasmuch as the inspiration of the Scriptures is now called in question even by those who admit the wonderful adaptation of the Bible to the spiritual wants of man, it is necessary, especially in these days, to make it evident that while we hold as strongly as ever that the Bible is its own witness, we decline to admit that it is its only witness; we maintain that, if the witness of the Bible to itself is challenged, we can fall back upon a Witness nobler still—One who stands acknowledged, even by the enemies of the Bible, as the culmination of earth's greatness, goodness, and nobility.

"Some even of the acutest and most learned of the opponents of Christianity have not really estimated the true strength of our position. Take the following passage from the introductory chapter of 'Supernatural Religion' as an illustration: 'Orthodox Christians at the present day may be divided into two broad classes, one of which professes to base the Church upon the Bible, and the other the Bible upon the Church. The one party assert that the Bible is fully and absolutely inspired; that it contains God's revelation to man, and that it is the only and sufficient ground for all religious belief.' Now, this is an entire misunderstanding and misrepresentation of our position. It is a confounding of the question as to the limits of inspiration with the question as to the grounds of inspiration. We are familiar with the standing controversy as to whether the Church rests on the Bible or the Bible on the Church. The latter is the Roman Catholic view, while the Protestant theologians have taken the position that the Church derives her authority from the Bible, not the Bible from the Church. Hence the famous watchword of Chillingworth, 'The Bible, and the Bible alone, the religion of Protestants.' Now, we are quite willing to stand by the motto, 'The Bible and the Bible alone,' when the question is as to *the limits* of that which is authoritative, when the controversy is with those who wish to impose decrees of councils and ecclesiastical dogmas and traditions as of equal authority with the Holy Scriptures; but it is quite a different thing, when the question is as to *the foundation* of our faith, and the controversy is with those who would take it away from us altogether. We do say that the Church rests upon the Bible, but we utterly deny that 'the Bible is the only ground for all religious belief.' We do say that 'we (the Church) are built upon the foundation of the apostles and prophets' (the Bible); but we do not stop there. With the apostle we go on and say, 'Jesus Christ Himself being the chief corner-stone.' And it is satisfactory to know that, while 'the foundation of the apostles and prophets' is so strong that it has resisted all attempts to undermine it for more than seventeen centuries, the corner-stone is so immovable that it not only stands secure in the estimation of all the friends of Christianity, but 'even our enemies themselves being judges,' as could be fully shown by quotations from many of the ablest of our opponents."

The general of an army, being vulnerable like other men, may not be exposed in the front of the battle. But it is different with "the Captain of our Salvation." He is general, army, fortress, and all. David knew how to put it: "The Lord is my Rock, and my Fortress, and my Deliverer; my God, my Strength, in whom I will trust, my Buckler, and the Horn of my salvation, and my High Tower;" and Solomon too: "The Name of the Lord is a strong tower; the righteous runneth into it and is safe." Just as the Saviour had to remind the Pharisees that "In this place is One greater than the temple;" and again, "Behold a greater than Jonas, a greater than Solomon is here"—so we have need to remember that, great as were those "holy men of old" who "spake as they were moved by the Holy Ghost," a greater than all is here; and we greatly weaken our position if, instead of resting their claims ultimately on His, we make His rest ultimately on theirs. We have need, especially in these trying times, to remember, that the chief corner-stone is our mainstay, that "other foundation can no man lay than that is laid, which is Jesus Christ." On the great underlying bed-rock of the Divine Existence rests the "Rock of Ages" (Is. xxvi. 4), which God Himself has laid in Zion for a foundation (Is. xxviii. 16, and 1 Pet. ii. 4-6); and on that foundation the apostles and prophets, and all the Church, is built "for a habitation of God through the Spirit," and it is to the Church as resting on that rock foundation of "Christ, the Son of the Living God," that the promise is given, "The gates of hell shall not prevail against it.'

We of the evangelical faith have learned to make our

preaching the preaching of Christ; we are learning to make our theology more and more centre in Christ, and we believe that as the combat thickens, our apologetics will follow in the same path, and in every department of Christian thought, Christ be acknowledged as Himself the Truth.

III.

THE SCEPTIC'S QUESTION ANSWERED BY HIMSELF.

"Pilate saith unto Him, What is truth?"—JOHN xviii. 38.
"Pilate saith unto them, Behold the Man."—JOHN xix. 5.

THE sceptic's question, answered by himself, unintentionally, unconsciously, but most admirably. No answer could be better. We thank thee, Pilate, for the word. It was meant for scorn; it has turned to praise. As out of the mouth of babes and sucklings, so, out of the mouth of a witness as unconscious as they, God has ordained strength because of the enemy. It is said that in nature the stinging nettle is closely attended by the healing blade, so here close to the sceptic's question lies its most appropriate answer. A little further on there is another unconscious answer. Pilate had asked in his undecided way, "What shall I do with this Jesus which is called Christ?" and out of his mouth comes the right answer: "Behold your King!" But one is enough at a time; we shall confine ourselves to the sceptic's question with its answer, and add Pontius Pilate to the staff of Cheshunt College* for the hour. It may be worth while, for once, to get a lecture from the Procurator's chair.

Though the speaker is ancient, the subject is not, for

* In its original form this was an address delivered at Cheshunt Anniversary, 1887.

the sceptical question which he answered so well is a question of the day. The truth doubted is the same which unbelief doubts now. For Pilate was no sceptic as to matter, or motion, or force; he believed in everything he saw; he did not doubt his senses or his reason or the reality of plain palpable facts of observation. That was not the kind of truth he suspected; it was the truth which Christ had been speaking, to which He had come to bear witness, the truth in regard to the permanent realities of life—those "high instincts," as the poet calls them, "which, be they what they may, are yet the fountain light of all our day," "a master light of all our seeing,"—the truth about God, and eternity, and duty, and destiny, the truth which underlies all changes and over-arches all experience. And his position was not one of denial, only of Agnosticism. He does not say "There is no truth," only raises the question whether it can be known, and thinks that by raising it he has justified himself in dismissing the subject from his mind; for immediately he goes out from the presence of Him who has been urging the claims of truth upon him. He asks the question and does not wait for the answer, a method of investigation which is by no means obsolete in the nineteenth century.

Well, now, let us look at the words which follow the question so closely that we can scarcely avoid connecting them with it, and see if they be not the very answer required. "What is truth?" he has just asked. "Behold the Man!" he now exclaims. Yes; and as we think of it, we remember what Christ Himself has said to His disciples the very day before: "I am the truth." We remember, too, how all through the Old Testament there are voices which seem to herald the coming of a man who shall satisfy the yearnings of humanity, and how all through the New Testament we are summoned and entreated to look unto this Man as one who has done it. Yes, Pilate, you are right, you are quite in the line of the true succession, of the prophets that went before, and the apostles that are to come after you, and in harmony with Him who stands before you, when, after asking the question, "What is truth?" you point to the incarnate Word, and say: "Behold the Man!"

First and foremost, there is the truth about humanity. What is man? What are we to think of human life; its meaning and value, its hopes and prospects, its duties and responsibilities, its nature and destiny? Come now, ye biologists, here is a life to study! Come, ye anthropologists, "Behold *the* Man" By all means study all kinds of men, savages and wild men of the woods, the most degraded specimens you can find; but do not consider your induction complete till you have given at least as much attention to the noblest and the best, and, above all, to the man whose life, by consent of all intelligent persons, is most of all worth looking into. You know the common reference to the play of *Hamlet* with Hamlet left out. Surely you do not intend to reach a conclusion as to man's place in nature with THE MAN left out, His name never mentioned, His great life never once referred to?

We have not a word to say against the investigation of the lower forms of life, the exploration of all that contributes to our knowledge of the meanest part or function of our complex nature; and if it is ascertained as a fact, that our bodies are closely connected with a succession of forms running down to the lowest organism, so let it be. Let us have all the facts, however mean they may be, or seem to be; but then let us have them all, however great they be; all the facts that point to what is grand and elevating, as well as those that point to what is mean and degrading. Why should attention be fixed so exclusively on the facts which belong to the lower phases of life? Why should the science of *life*, claiming, as it does, to include mind and heart and soul in it, be defined, as one of its greatest exponents defines it, as "the science of living matter," a conception which, however appropriate to the lower ranges of life, is utterly inadequate in the higher? Starting out with that conception, it is of course necessary to resolve all thought and feeling into modifications of "living matter," to make conscience and character, faith and hope, and love and righteousness, nothing better than so many varying movements of living matter; and, of course, when the living matter ceases to be living it is dead matter, and in that dead matter is to be found all that remains of faith, and hope, and love, and life, in the shape of ashes and water and gas. Now, so long as one keeps working mainly amongst molluscs or even among troglodytes, it is not difficult to think that all is only living matter. The mental phenomena are so very scarce and low in type that they are easily accounted for without spoiling the definition. But when we come to the higher ranges of life we reach a region where, if we deal honestly with the facts, we cannot dispose of them in so easy a way. It is impossible to do it honestly in dealing only with ordinary men; the difficulty is greatly increased when we are confronted with the great minds and noble souls, which have adorned the history of mankind; but when we look at the greatest of all, it becomes nothing less than an insult to reason to suggest it.

So long as we are looking at creatures in which the animal is clearly predominant, it is easy to think of them as mere animals, made up of living matter and nothing else; but as soon as the spiritual becomes manifestly predominant, as in the better sort of men, it is only by the most unworthy sophistry that the higher can be merged in the lower; and when you turn your attention to One in whom the *spiritual* so shines out as it does in this Man, in whom the spirit so manifestly lords it over the flesh—transfigures the common clay of its environment—gives it a glory which is manifestly not its own—it is impossible to believe that we are looking at a mere phase of animal life, flickering up for a moment, only to fall back again and be " cast as rubbish to the void.' It becomes manifest that in Him there is life quite out of the range of protoplasm and all possible variations of it, infinitely higher than any conceivable motion of living matter. See how the life shines out in contrast with the poverty and meanness of its setting, a demonstration that spirit and not flesh is the ultimate truth of humanity. " Behold the Man!" See Him in His humble home at Nazareth, to outward appearance only a carpenter. See Him trudging the dusty roads and climbing the steep hill-sides of Palestine, to outward appearance only a poor pedestrian. See Him despised and rejected of all the great of the land, to outward appearance only a deluded fanatic. See Him before Pilate, His form scarred with scourging, His face pale with anguish, the thorn crown upon His brow, mocking voices and scowling faces all around, to outward appearance a common criminal. Then think of that great soul of His, see it in its awful and majestic loneliness; compare the magnificence of the spirit with the shame of the flesh, the glory of the life with the abjectness of the living matter; and then say, if you can—if you dare— that the real truth of that manhood is to be found in the paltry matter of its flesh, and not in the magnificent, glorious Divine Spirit which shines out of that poor tenement of clay. No, no! my biologist friend, I do not think so very meanly of you as to suppose it possible that you can behold this Man, and not realise that you are hasty in your conclusion that matter is the substance, and spirit the shadow, that life is only passing breath, and death the Lord of all. Behold the Man, and see that spirit lords it over matter, and life triumphs over death. We are quite willing to reserve our judgment as to molluscs and apes, and we may not think it necessary to enter into controversy in regard to those poor wretches in human shape, that seem to be scarcely human at all, which so many think it so important to investigate. Perhaps the animal is so preponderant in them that it may swallow up anything that seems to rise above it, and carbonic acid gas be the crown and consummation of their life. But when we pass from those types which have the very least significance to those which are the most significant, and especially when we look at the One above all others, from whom there is most to be learned, we see—it is not a matter of faith; we see it—we see that the animal is merged in the spiritual, that mortality is swallowed up of life. And, accordingly, when we read a little further on of His resurrection from the dead, we cannot be surprised. Why should we be surprised? It is the survival of the fittest. Is He not, of all men that ever lived upon the earth, the very fittest to survive, and can we suppose that nothing in that noble soul survived after He bowed His head and gave up the ghost? It is not possible. The Apostle Peter was certainly right when he said it was not possible that He should be holden of death.

So far we have been thinking of the "Man" as the most significant type of manhood the world has ever had in it, and, therefore, best of all worth study if we would find out the truth of human nature and human life, with its meaning and purpose, its responsibilities and prospects. But as we continue beholding the "Man' we find very very much more in Him. He grows upon us wonderfully, even as He grew upon His first disciples, to whose early questioning about Him the wise and simple answer was only "Come and see!" and whose beholding ended in their seeing in Him "the glory of the Only Begotten of the Father, full of grace and truth." We find that that noble life is not only a type of humanity but a mirror of Divinity, reflecting all of the glory of God which it is possible and needful for us to see. Those who are " of the earth, earthy," who have allowed the faculty of spiritual discernment to die out or become obscure for want of use, will, of course, fail to see it, but they who are " of the truth," they who have that spiritual sympathy which is necessary to the recognition of beauty or glory anywhere, will certainly see in the Man Christ Jesus the face of God. Elsewhere in Nature we can, as it were, touch the hem of His garment, but we cannot know Him till we look upon His face. The face is nature's mode of revelation and recognition, and chief of all " the human face divine." Your face is not yourself, it is only the outward expression or incarnation of your spirit; but if I refuse to look into your face, and will not listen to your voice, I must remain unacquainted with you. In the same way, the Man Christ Jesus is the face of God to us. By looking at Him we become acquainted with our Father in heaven; not otherwise: "no man cometh unto the Father but by Me." Hence present day Agnosticism. The Agnostic is perfectly right in saying that God cannot be known by the pure intellect, but neither can we know one another in any such way. In our present condition the only way of certainly knowing spirits is by looking into faces and listening to voices: why, then, should we wonder that in order to know God we

should have a face to look at and a voice to listen to ? *
"Behold the Man" is the Gospel for the Agnostic. Ah! my good and learned friend, you are right in everything except in turning your back on Christ. It is perfectly true that you cannot find your Father God in earth or sea, with telescope or microscope, by alembic or retort; it is perfectly true that you cannot reach Him by soaring up on wings of speculation; but you can find Him by humbly sitting at the feet of Jesus and looking up into His face, and listening to His voice, giving special heed to those most weighty words of His, "I am the way, and the truth, and the life; no man cometh unto the Father but by Me."

These words remind us that the truth in Him is living, saving truth. It has a wondrous power on the beholder. As we look and listen we are humbled in the dust, brought to our knees, constrained to cry out for pardon and for purity. And as we watch Him, with the crown of thorns on His head and the cross upon His shoulder, and follow Him through the shame and agony of that awful day—wounded for our transgressions, bruised for our iniquities, crucified and slain for us—our hearts are won. Dead henceforth to sin, the hatefulness of which is seen in the awful sacrifice as nowhere else, we yield ourselves unto God and have peace, and hope, and life.

And as still we follow Him through the gates of death up to the throne on which He now is seated, we find as deep a meaning in the second word of Pilate as in the first—"Behold your King." Now we know Him as our Life, for His Spirit takes the throne of our heart, and as we still continue beholding in the Man Christ Jesus,

* "O Saul, it shall be
A face like my face that receives thee; a hand like this hand
Shall throw open the gates of new life to thee! See the Christ stand!"
—*Browning.*

as in a glass, the glory of the Lord, we are changed into the same image, from glory to glory by the Lord, the Spirit; and thus there is developed in us true life, not the mere agitation or fluctuation of living matter for a few years; but "life indeed," life which the truth has made free; life which rises above the animal, disengages itself from the transient and mortal, takes firm hold of the things that cannot be shaken, and so gives promise of at last emerging from its tenement of clay, victorious over death through the grace and power of Him from whom it came, and who is the Lord of life and glory. Such is the expected crown and consummation of the Christian's evolution, which begins by beholding the Man, and has the promise of ending by our being like Him, when we shall see Him as He is.

This, however, takes us somewhat beyond the region of our subject, into the region of hope rather than of visible truth. Let us therefore come back to the main conception of the truth as embodied in the Man Christ Jesus, and consider as briefly as possible how impregnable is the position in which Pontius Pilate places us. A very ignorant young man told me the other day that he understood that science had proved that there was no Christ. I could not understand what vague notions he had in his head, but evidently it was some confused idea of something he had heard about the Bible and science not being on the best of terms. Now, it is important to remember that we never hear of any conflict, real or supposed, between Christ and science; it is always "the Bible and science." Well, what is the Bible? It is the testimony of a long series of witnesses to Christ and His truth As a succession of witnesses to the greatness of the spiritual in man, and the reality of the love and grace of God, and in particular to the revelation of God in Christ, expected throughout the Old Testament and attested in the New, it is most impressive and most conclusive. But then, some people say, judging from some things that fall from them, these witnesses to Christ are not up to the standard of nineteenth century science. Are they not? What a pity! But what has that to do with the subject? We might say, indeed, that Christ is independent of all these witnesses, for that noble life of His, as we have seen, can speak for itself. But let that pass, and we have still to ask what worse witnesses are they to Christ, because they were behind, not their own age—nobody says that—but behind our age in geology and astronomy and biology? We really must remember that they had not access to the ninth edition of the " Encyclopædia Britannica," and therefore we must not think it so very terrible that they should be ignorant of some of its contents. Suppose we go somewhere else for our science, and make use of "all Scripture, for the purposes for which we are told it is given—for doctrine, for reproof, for correction, for instruction in righteousness," and especially for the chief purpose, signalised by the Master Himself, "Search the Scriptures, for in them ye think ye have eternal life, and they are they which testify of Me." The Scriptures were not given to lighten up the universe. Is it not enough that they lighten the path of life, and that from all parts there converge rays of light which are focussed on the face of Him who is the Way, the Truth, and the Life? If certain parts of the Bible and science are at variance, let it be settled between them, but whichever way it is settled, it will make no difference whatever, to an intelligent mind, in the force with which the truth impresses itself upon the hearts of those who take Pilate's advice and behold the Man.

But does not evolution, somehow or other, turn our flank? There is a vague idea in some minds, that the new genesis of all things, which has found so much favour with a large proportion of thinking men of our day, is unsettling the foundations of the Gospel. These fears would be dispelled if it were only remembered that, interesting and important as is the question " Whence ? " much more important and decisive is the question " What ? " Theories of origin are interesting, but facts of life are much safer guides to truth. Now the truth which we believe is grounded on no doubtful or difficult question as to how things came to be what they are, but on plain palpable facts—the great fact of sin, attested by the universal conscience; the great fact of the life of Christ; the great facts of the history which led up to Christ, and of that which has followed His death and resurrection; the great facts of experience, the experience of a vast multitude whom no man can number, out of every kindred and tongue and people and nation, who have found in Christ an ever-living, ever-present Friend and Saviour. We have not a word of disparagement for those interesting discussions as to the origin of all things; but it is surely manifest that they cannot set aside facts, nor can they compare with them in practical importance. There is a disposition in our day to attach far too much relative importance to the question of origin; and in nothing is this more marked than in the attempt to determine man's place in nature by inquiries as to the origin of species. Just think how apt we are to be misled in such estimates. What is a statue, for example? Could you get a satisfactory answer by visiting some marble quarry where labouring men are hewing out the raw material? Would not one visit to the Vatican, or one sight of the Apollo Belvedere, give you a better idea of what a statue is than a life-time spent in the quarries of Carrara? What would you think of the art critic who should insist on estimating the worth of some great painting in the Academy by the result of his inquiries into its material origin—the quality and cost of canvas, paint, and frame? In the same way, if you judge a man by his visible origin, you get a poor, degraded, and utterly wrong idea of him; whereas, if you judge him by the outcome of the great artist's work, you are much more likely to reach the truth. Let our friends dig away in the quarries; and we shall take interest in their work, and read their books, and rejoice in any true result they reach; but no result which they can reach by any such digging need at all diminish the appreciation and delight with which we contemplate the Man Christ Jesus, and open our hearts to the living power of the grace and truth which a million facts and experiences prove to be in Him.

Our position is quite secure, then, as far as science is concerned; but what of criticism? Here, too, we may possess our souls in patience, for here, again, it is not Christ and criticism which ever are at strife; it is the Bible and criticism, or, rather, current notions about the Bible and current notions about criticism; and the Bible, as we have seen, being a long line of witnesses, questions of date and authorship—interesting though they be as historical questions and Biblical questions—leave the grand witness to spiritual truth and to the coming Christ undimmed and undiminished in its power, whatever be the result. But, then, do not these critical questions affect the gospels themselves? No doubt, but they do not really affect the Gospel. How did the first preachers get on when there were no written gospels at all? We really do not need to discuss the gospels before finding the truth in them, any more than we need to analyse a loaf of bread before getting the good of it. It is simply a question of looking and listening, of seeing and hearing. As the Lord Himself said to Pilate: " Every one that is of the truth heareth my voice." The *life* shines out from the Gospel page, and any one who is of the truth can see, by simply looking at it, that it is genuine, that it cannot be an invention You might as well say the sun was an invention, a clever invention of four electricians, or, rather, to make the comparison just, of four men who knew nothing about electricity. I could as soon believe that, as suppose that Matthew, Mark, Luke, and John invented that life and set it blazing in the spiritual firmament these eighteen hundred years. There is the life, and we have only to look at it. Here is the Man, set before us as no other man has ever been, clearly, vividly, without adornment of language, with perfect candour and sincerity, with all the transparency of truth, with the glory of His spirit luminous before us. We have only to look that we may see. The message is not, Behold the Book, or, Behold the Books, but " Behold the Man."

And here all Christians are at one. There is no division among us in regard to the truth. The sneering question, " What is truth ? " has often been asked with the finger of scorn pointed to the different churches, as if each claimed to have the truth apart from all the rest. But such an imputation is utterly unjust; at all events, it is unjust now. The different churches may claim to bear witness to some small fraction of truth which others do not maintain, but in regard to *the* Truth—that which is central, vital, fundamental—all evangelical churches are at one. The time is happily past and gone when the unity of the faith was supposed to embrace a great system of the universe, in which the mind was expected to go back to the decrees of God in a past eternity, and to sweep on majestically to the consummation of all things in an eternity to come, picking up easily on the road such fragments of truth as lay in its path across the circle of the sciences, and if any luckless fact of science stood in the way, so much the worse for it! Unanimity of opinion through such a mighty range is no longer thought of. We have come, or are fast coming, back to the simplicity which is in Christ, to recognise that the unity of the faith towards which the growing Church is hastening, may be otherwise described as that of the knowledge of the Son of God, according to the Great Apostle who looked forward to the day when all should attain to that unity, and so reach the measure of the stature of the fulness of Christ. There are few things more hopeful than the growing disposition among Christians to make less of propositional truth, and more of Him who said, "*I* am the truth;" less of faith as a thing in itself, and more of it as a link which binds us all to Him; less of the dogmatic, "I know what I have believed," and more of the apostolic, "I know Whom I have believed;" to take as our greatest message to the world, not "Behold the Church!" or "Behold the Creed!" but "BEHOLD THE MAN!"

In this regard Cheshunt College has all along occupied a position far in the van. Where is there any of our Christian institutions that has borne clearer or nobler testimony to this unity, this genuine unity, of all true Christians in the Lord? Cheshunt has had a noble record written in the life-work of the men who have gone forth from its halls, and on this ground stands high among its sister institutions in its claims on public support. But it has also this peculiar claim upon us all—that it has been, and is, a standing witness to the reality of the Church's oneness in Christ Jesus, and, therefore, of its oneness in the truth, furnishing as it has done, and still continues to do, faithful ministers for all the evangelical churches of the land and for positions of influence in the great evangelical societies, and for service in the foreign field, far beyond the range of the devoted circle of earnest Christians, who first projected this noble institution on a basis so grandly catholic and apostolic. When we begin with Christ and make Him the centre of our life and thought, and from that centre work outwards towards the far horizon of truth in its widest sense, though we inevitably come to places where we must part company (for how is it possible for any two independent men to agree in all the boundless region of thought which opens out on every side?), yet there is so much, so very much, on which, as Christians, we are entirely at one, that we can work together side by side, with one heart and one soul, one earnest purpose and one glorious hope. Long may Cheshunt College flourish to be a witness to the unity of all true Christians in Him who is the truth, and to send out generation after generation of faithful heralds of the truth, who will not read essays, or spin theories, or elaborate arguments, but hold up to the eyes of men the thorn-crowned Saviour, and say: "Behold the Man! Behold your King!—the Man of Sorrows, the King of Glory, the tender, mighty Saviour of Mankind!"

IV.

GOD KNOWN IN CHRIST.

IT is quite understood, and fully admitted, that there can be no absolute knowledge of God. So far our Agnostic friends are right. But, though this is true, it is not new. In one of the oldest books in the Bible we have it quite forcibly expressed: "Canst thou by searching find out God? canst thou find out the Almighty unto perfection? It is as high as heaven; what canst thou do? deeper than hell; what canst thou know?" (Job xi. 7, 8).

This is manifestly true as regards God; but is not the same thing true on a small scale in regard to our fellow-man? Which of us knows even his most intimate friend right through and through? This is true, even though our friend may be below us in attainments; and it will be even more true of friends who are above us. Our knowledge of one another is in every case limited by two things: capability of expression on the one hand, and power of comprehension on the other. There may be much in the soul of my friend that is never expressed; never expressed in look, or tone, or word, or deed. There may be much in him that cannot be expressed; there may be much he would not express if he could, much he could not express if he would. And then, on the other hand, there may be very much of what is expressed that I cannot understand or catch.

To illustrate this still further—for it seems of very great importance in reference to the knowledge of God—let us consider what means we have of gaining a knowledge of such an one as Michel Angelo. There are fragments of revelation of the spirit of Michel Angelo scattered far and wide throughout the galleries of Europe, first in originals, then in casts, or copies, so that everybody has an opportunity of knowing something about him. Then there are poems of his which give a further revelation of the man to those who have an opportunity of reading them. These are all expressions of the spirit of the man, and it would not be an abuse of language to put them together and call them the Word of Michel Angelo. But it is quite evident that our knowledge of him will depend not only on our opportunity of seeing and studying these works, but also and still further on the degree in which our spirit is kindred with his, the degree in which we can understand that which is expressed in his works.

Suppose now that from such a study of his works we have learned something of the reality that lurks behind the great name of Michel Angelo, and we wish to learn still more about him, what do we do? We take up his life and read it. How much more knowledge have we now of the great artist? That will depend on what his biographer has been able to catch and set down of that which was expressed in his life, and also on what we are able to take in and understand of what is so set down. So in the same way if we look at his portrait, what we learn from it will depend first on what the painter has been able to set down on canvas; and second, on what we are able to see in that which is set down. Still further, the case would not be altered in principle even if we had lived in his time, and lived with him, and had the opportunity of seeing him every day. We should thus have had a far better opportunity of knowing him; but even then our knowledge of him would be subject to the same twofold limitation. First, it would depend on how much of the spirit within him ever uttered itself in his face or gesture, or word or deed; and, second, on our ability to comprehend and catch that which was thus uttered. And the point of view we have now reached is a favourable one for seeing of what immeasurable importance this second condition is; for is it not manifest that it would be quite possible for the artist's *valet de chambre*, if he had one, to know less of the true Michel Angelo than some kindred soul who had never seen him, never even read his life, but had paid one visit to the Sistine Chapel?

From all this it is evident that our knowledge of our fellow-man even under the most favourable circumstances, must be partial and inadequate. Why then should we expect a full and adequate knowledge of God? But then, even the imperfect knowledge we can have of each other is sufficient for the purposes of life; and why may not our knowledge of God, however imperfect and inadequate in an absolute sense, be not only real knowledge so far as it goes, but amply sufficient for all purposes of life? It all depends on whether God has expressed Himself at all, and whether our spirits are kindred enough with His to catch that which He has expressed. Thus the subject opens out into two great questions: first, Has God revealed Himself? second, Can we enter into the revelation so as to make out what is revealed of Him? The Scriptural answer to the first question is *the Word;* the Scriptural answer to the second question is *the Spirit*.

The *Word* is the whole utterance of God in nature, in providence, and in grace. God uttered Himself in creation; just as the artist utters himself in his works. He has uttered Himself in the whole history of the world. He has spoken to the fathers by the prophets. These are different utterances of the Word, but they are scattered and fragmentary, like the scattered work of a great artist. And the question still comes, Is there no possibility of getting nearer to Himself? Is there no personal revelation? Has no one looked upon a face with the very light of God upon it? Has no one listened to a voice that thrilled with the very love of God Himself? Is there no way of pressing in from the outer circle of His works, which are but the hem of His garment, to His very life, and soul, and heart? Yes, there is: "The Word was made flesh, and dwelt among us (and we beheld His glory, the glory as of the only begotten of the Father), full of grace and truth." "God, having of old time spoken unto the fathers in the prophets by divers portions and in divers manners, hath at the end of these days spoken unto us *in His Son*." There is the central point of the revelation of God: "He that hath seen Me, hath seen the Father." The rest are scattered rays of the Divine glory. Here is the central Sun. Here, in the face of Jesus Christ, is "the knowledge of the glory of God."

So much for the Word, the utterance, the expression of God: but that is not enough, as we have seen. There must also be a soul to comprehend it. We have seen that it is quite possible for a man to look at Michel Angelo's works, and even to live in the house with him from day to day, and know nothing but the mere shell of him; have no such knowledge of him as to be any better for having looked at him. What is wanted in such a case? The spirit of the artist; not in all its vastness necessarily, but some of it—enough to give sympathy, appreciation, delight in the artist and his work. And so here: it is necessary not only that God should utter Himself before us, but that God should give us of His Spirit, in order that we may understand what He has spoken. True, we may not have the Spirit without measure, as in Christ, but up to the measure of our capacity we may be filled with the Spirit; and that will be enough, even though our capacity be small, to secure sympathy, appreciation, and delight in Christ, and all that is His; and so the promise shall be fulfilled, "He shall take of Mine and show it unto you."

Thus it comes to pass, that the two natural difficulties that stand in the way of our knowledge of God are met in God's revelation of Himself, first in His Son, who in this relation is appropriately spoken of as "The Word;" and second, by the Holy Spirit. The one is the needed revelation without us, and the other the needed revelation within us. The two are present in one view in that magnificent utterance of the apostle, "God, who commanded the light to shine out of darkness, hath shined in our hearts [*the revelation within us*], to give the light of the knowledge of the glory of God in the face of Jesus Christ" [*the revelation without us*]. The two together give us every facility for knowing our Father in Heaven which it is possible for us to have. Even at the best and fullest, our knowledge will remain partial and inadequate. It will be very far from absolute knowledge; it will be wholly relative; but it will be trustworthy, trustworthy as the light, which of all material things about us comes nearest to the expression of the Divine nature; and it will be blessed, blessed as love, which of all that is within us is most akin to God Himself. The light of the glory of God in the face of Christ without, and the love of God shed abroad in our hearts by the Holy Ghost within—these are what are needed to give us that knowledge, which, however partial and inadequate at the best, is yet life eternal. And these, the light without us and the love within us, are all that are needed, for "God is light" and "God is love."

It remains to be noticed that the meeting-point of all is *in Christ*. We have seen already that in the Incarnate Word the scattered rays of the glory of God, which had been revealed in a fragmentary way before, were gathered together, concentrated as the soul of man is in his face; and just as in your intercourse with a friend you keep looking into his face, while you do not quite lose sight of his form or even of his garment's hem, so in order to acquaintance with God we should keep looking on Jesus, Who is the face of God, while we do not lose sight of anything in the works of God that may help to set Him more fully before us.

But, besides this, the other need of which we have spoken is met in Christ. Not only does He reveal the Father to us, but He gives His Spirit that we may understand the revelation. He promises to give the Holy Spirit to all who come unto Him. So the whole knowledge of the Father is provided in Christ. We are "complete in Him" He says, "All things are delivered unto Me of My Father: and no man knoweth the Son, but the Father; neither knoweth any man the Father, save the Son, and he to whomsoever the Son will reveal Him. Come unto Me." And long after, the beloved disciple, having found it all true, expresses it thus: "We know that the Son of God is come [*the revelation without*], and hath given us an understanding, that we may know Him that is true" [*the revelation within*].

From all this it follows that those who would know God must seek Him in Christ. "No man cometh unto the Father but by Me." Need we then wonder that very many of the most learned and patient searchers after truth never find God ? It is not that they are dishonest; it is that they do not look in the right direction It is not by the use of those faculties which are the glory of the learned and great; it is not by any process of induction, or labour of logic; no, it is simply by looking, by the lifting up of our souls to our loving Father,—the eye, the ear, the heart of faith all open to see His face, to hear His voice, to welcome His love. If our learned people would only give up dealing with propositions and with questions and with abstract truth, and would simply seek the Lord, they would soon find Him. If any one is minded to wrestle with questions, he can easily find a million of questions to wrestle with; but, alas! such wrestling will lead to no daybreak, and there will be no Peniel to keep it in memory. If, instead of wrestling with problems and questions, men would, like poor, weak Jacob, wrestle with God, then the day would dawn, their darkness would be dispelled, and the light of God would stream upon them. Then would they understand how it is that men in all ages who have walked with God, have learned to know *Whom* they have believed, however little they may have been able to expound fully, or justify wholly, *what* they have believed. "When Thou saidst, Seek ye My face, my heart said unto Thee, Thy face, Lord, will I seek." It is all there, the philosophy of it, the simplicity of it. Look at it! First, it is not the absolute essence of Deity that we are to seek; it is His *face*, what of Him is turned to us, so that we can see and recognise Him. Then, it is not elaborate searching, it is simple *seeking*. A wise man may search much and discover nothing; but even the child that seeks shall surely find. For, finally, it is a matter not of the intellect so much as of the heart and will: "When Thou saidst, Seek ye My face, *my heart* said unto Thee, Thy face, Lord, *will* I seek."

Perhaps a difficulty may occur to some who remember that it is an Old Testament passage we are quoting, and that at the time God had not been revealed in Christ. But had He not? Let us not forget that "in the beginning was the Word." Let us not forget that it was the Son of God all through who revealed the Father. "No man hath seen God at any time; the only begotten Son who is in the bosom of the Father, He hath declared Him." The incarnation is a great help to realise the personality of God; but it must never be forgotten that personality consists not in body, but in spirit Even when the Word was in flesh, a spiritual manifestation was necessary ("Flesh and blood hath not revealed it unto thee, but My Father which is in heaven"). And that manifestation of spiritual presence was possible before the incarnation, just as it is still our privilege long after it. The question put and answered when Christ was still on earth makes it clear: "How is it that Thou wilt manifest Thyself unto us, and not unto the world? Jesus answered and said unto him, If a man love Me he will keep My words; and My Father will love him, and We will come unto him, and make Our abode with him."

The essential point is this, that we must seek personal acquaintance with God, we must seek His face; there should be an outgoing of our souls to our Father in heaven, as He has manifested Himself unto us. Even in Old Testament times it was always in this way that God became known. Hence the prominence given to "the Name" of God. What was the Name of God? It included all of God that had been then exposed to view. It was all of His face that men had then seen or could see. We can see more of it now. We have "the light of the knowledge of the glory of God in the face of Jesus Christ," who is "the image of the Invisible God," "the express image of His person." But our attitude must be the same as theirs. There must be the lifting up of the heart, the outgoing of the soul, the spiritual act of which this is the simplest expression, "When Thou saidst, Seek ye My face, my heart said unto Thee, Thy face, Lord, will I seek."

The knowledge of God, as we have seen, begins by "looking unto Jesus." It grows by abiding in His presence, and keeping up communion with Him. As soon as we come to Him, we receive something of His Spirit, and are able to understand a little. As we stay with Him and walk with Him, we receive more and more, and are able to understand more. For the two processes go on together, the revelation without, and the revelation within; the light and the love; the shining in our hearts, and the vision of the glory on the face of Christ. The more we see of the Divine in Him, the more we receive of the Divine ourselves; and the more we receive of the Divine in ourselves, the more we see of the Divine in Him. By equal steps we "grow in grace and in the knowledge of our Saviour Jesus Christ." Or, as another apostle puts it, "We all with open face beholding as in a glass the glory of the Lord, are changed into the same image from glory to glory, even as by the Spirit of the Lord." And a third apostle (the apostle of love, as the others are of faith and of hope), putting the climax on it all, draws the veil a little aside from the glorious consummation, thus: "When He shall be manifested"—(not the mere limited and partial manifestation which is all that is possible now, but the fuller manifestation to which we are taught to look forward in glorious hope at the second coming of the Lord)—"When He shall be *manifested*, we shall be like Him, for we shall see Him as He is."

Oh, blessed knowledge of God, revealed in His Son, our Saviour Jesus Christ! O Thou who art Light, shine in our hearts, to give us "the knowledge of the glory of God in the face of Jesus Christ." O Thou who art Love, dwell in our hearts, and teach us to enter into the mystery of His cross and passion, and so to begin "to comprehend with all saints what is the breadth, and length, and depth, and height; and to know the love of Christ, which passeth knowledge." And then shall we understand better what the great Revealer and Redeemer meant when He said, "This is life eternal, that they might know Thee, the only true God, and Jesus Christ whom Thou hast sent."

V.

THE TRINITY AS TAUGHT BY CHRIST.

THE word "Trinity" does not occur in Scripture, nor is there anything to be found there corresponding to those complicated formulas by which (notably in the so called Athanasian Creed) theologians have tried to define the relations of Father, Son, and Holy Ghost. The doctrine of the Trinity is involved throughout in the language of the New Testament, but it is never defined, there is no attempt whatever to explain the mysteries which are inseparable from all thought as to the being and manifestations of God; when the subject is referred to it is always for practical purposes, not for the satisfaction of the speculative reason; hence not only the language but even the thought is simple. The simple practical thoughts are like familiar objects of nature standing clear and well-defined before us; but all around and behind and above there is the infinite azure with its measureless depths, and if men would only content themselves with seeing in sharp definition that which is capable of it, and leaving the atmosphere, as in nature, in vague illimitable profundity, they would see clearly all that it is necessary to see, while the invisible and unfathomable background would have all its value as an atmosphere without any attempt being made to penetrate it or set it bounds. If theologians had only followed the Scriptures in this respect, how many bitter controversies might have been spared, and how many needless difficulties and perplexities would have been avoided.

We cannot have a better illustration of our thought than is afforded by those striking words of our Lord, in which He speaks of Himself as the Way, the Truth, and the Life. There we see our familiar Friend and Saviour, the Lord Jesus Christ, set before us in a threefold relation. He Himself stands out clear before us in His human nature, in the midst of the sorrowful little company in the upper room; and what He says of Himself is perfectly simple in all its practical relations; and yet there is an atmosphere of mystery all around it, where the speculative mind may very readily lose itself. Yet there is no need to lose ourselves: Christ is speaking, not for the speculative mind, but for the troubled heart, which He longs to comfort with the assurance of a Father's love. "I am the Way," He says. The way whither? we ask, and the answer to this "whither" leads us back to "the Father —of an infinite majesty." But how can we know Him if He be of an infinite majesty? We cannot grasp the infinite. We cannot see Him. We cannot reach Him with our finite powers of knowledge. Alas, are we not lost? Listen again: "I am the Truth." Let not your thoughts roam in the infinite. Look unto Me. I am the Way; I am also the Truth; I not only show you how to reach the Father, I am Myself the revelation of the Father to you: "He that hath seen Me hath seen the Father." "I am the Truth" is simple and practical, and yet therein lies all the mystery of the divine Sonship. "No man hath seen God at any time; the only begotten *Son* who is in the bosom of the Father, He hath declared Him." But something more is necessary. There must not only be the objective revelation of the Divine, there must be a power to see the Divine in it. "Except a man be born again, he cannot see the kingdom of God." The way may be open, but without this new birth there is no desire to take it. The Truth may be clear, but without this inward light there is no power to see it. Not only love and light from above are needed, but life within, before the wants of man are fully met. Listen again: "I am the Life," says the Lord Jesus, claiming thus the special prerogative of the Holy Spirit; so that within the compass of these few simple words we have "the Father, of an infinite majesty, His honourable, true, and only Son, also the Holy Ghost."

Father, Son, and Holy Ghost, then, are all here; but in no perplexing separation or confusion; they are all in Christ Jesus; "I am the Way, the Truth, and the Life." The Father is here; but we do not see Him in His infinite majesty, we see Him as He is revealed in the man Christ Jesus; the eternal Son is here, but we do not see Him in His eternal glory, for it is veiled in mortal flesh. The Spirit is here, but only as the stream is in the fountain—the Holy Spirit is not yet given, but the promise of the gift is even now on the Saviour's lips, the promise of the Comforter, the Life Giver, ready to be sent as soon as His work as Opener up of the Way and Revealer of the Truth is done. Yes, Father, Son, and Holy Ghost are all here, each found in Him, so that our thoughts are not to leave Christ when they pass to the Father, or to the Holy Spirit—Christ is all—"In Him dwelleth all the fulness of the Godhead bodily."

Now this is manifestly the way in which we are intended to realise to ourselves the truth about God as Father, as Son, and as Holy Ghost—not by wandering away into the infinite, but by sitting at the feet of Jesus and looking up into His face. How simple this makes it all, if we would only be content with the simplicity of Scripture!

THE TRINITY AS TAUGHT BY CHRIST.

The reason why some get into difficulty and perplexity is their perverse determination—notwithstanding all the directions and cautions the Master has given—to seek a *separate* knowledge of Father, Son, and Holy Ghost. They wish to know God the Father, and in order to find Him they look away from Christ, instead of at Him; they gaze into the infinite unknown instead of looking at the face of Jesus. And when they think of the Spirit, again they must have this as a separate region of theological lore, so again they look away from the face of Jesus to find somewhere else God the Holy Spirit. If they could have what they are vainly seeking, they would have three Gods instead of one, as practically many puzzled Christians have. For they actually have great difficulty sometimes as to which of the Three to go to. What Christian minister has not again and again been consulted by good people, who were in some perplexity as to which of the Three Persons of the Trinity they should address themselves to. And what is worse, there are those who are afraid of praying too much to one Person, and too little to another, with the notion evidently in their poor confused minds that there is danger of jealousy between them!

It is very easy to show how utterly needless all this perplexity is, and how thoroughly unscriptural are all those notions out of which it grows. There is only one Person to whom any one can go, and that Person is Christ. We should go to Him always, under all circumstances—with our prayers, with our tears, with our longings, with our doubts, with our difficulties, with our troubles, with our innumerable wants.

But does not Christ Himself teach us to pray, saying, "Our Father who art in heaven"? Perfectly true; but when we say "Our Father," we must look to Christ, for He plainly tells us that we cannot reach the Father but by Him ("I am the Way"); and not only so, but we cannot hold the Father in our thought without filling our minds with Christ ("I am the Truth'). Christ Himself says, as plainly as tongue can express it, that it is impossible to know the Father apart from Him. "No man cometh unto the Father but by Me." And when, even after that plain statement, the still puzzled disciple says, "Lord, show us the Father, and it sufficeth us," what can the Master do but repeat the same truth in still more emphatic terms, as if He said to Philip, "You are seeking the Father, are you? And yet you are looking away from Me up into the unfathomable heaven; look not there, look here—do you not know Me yet?" "He that hath seen Me hath seen the Father." Who can suppose that Philip retained his perplexity after so clear an answer? Why should any one be perplexed now?

What has been the consequence of trying to know the Father otherwise than by going to Christ? Agnosticism. Let any man of clear intellect and strong logical power begin by rejecting Christ and he is sure to end in Agnosticism, which is only a confirmation of our Saviour's doctrine, "No man cometh unto the Father but by Me." There is no way to the Father through halls of science or academic groves. Christ is the only way, and those who turn away from Him set their faces to the outer darkness.

The same considerations apply to those who perplex and confuse themselves by trying to have a knowledge of the Spirit apart from their knowledge of Christ. Our Saviour is most careful to guard against this error. He had said indeed, "It is the Spirit that quickeneth;" but He feels under no constraint to say, "I am the Way and the Truth, *but* the Holy Spirit is the Life," as if the work of the Spirit were to be thought of as separate from His own person and power. With the same emphasis with which He claims to be "the Way" and "the Truth," He claims Himself to be "the Life." He speaks indeed of the giving of "another Comforter," but He is careful to say that the Father will send Him "in My name," and to tell them that when He comes He will not speak of Himself, but "He shall take of Mine, and show it unto you." And so complete is the identification that the Lord speaks of the Spirit's coming as His own coming: "I will not leave you comfortless, I will come to you." Still further, as if to anticipate any difficulty which might be felt as to the language which sometimes speaks both of the Father and of the Spirit as separate from Himself, He adds, "At that day ye shall know that I am in the Father, and ye in Me, and I in you.' " I am in the Father"—there is the doctrine of the Father. "Ye in Me"—there is the doctrine of the Son. "I in you"— there is the doctrine of the Spirit. That there is a great region of mystery is evident; but we do not need to explore it, for if we think of the Father, there is Christ, "I am in the Father and the Father in Me"—if we think of the Son, union to Christ is the practical thought, "ye in Me"—if we think of the Holy Ghost, the practical thought is Christ in us, "I in you," as He puts it here.

It comes to this, that practically Christ is all and in all. "*I am* the Way, and the Truth, and the Life." It is "I am" all the way through. The Divine name is all in Christ "Hear, O Israel, the Lord our God is one Lord." There need be no confusion. There need be no perplexity. The unsearchable God has made Himself known to us as Father, Son, and Holy Ghost. But all that there is for us in the Father—all that there is for us in the Son—all that there is for us in the Holy Ghost—is manifest in Christ. He is all and in all. All praise and glory to Christ the Son—the only Revealer of the Father, the only Fountain of the Spirit. Let our prayer always be to Him, whether we are looking at the Father as revealed in Him, or whether we are looking to Him as the source whence flow the streams of the Spirit's life.

Let us attempt a very simple illustration to make our meaning plain. When I speak to you or listen to you I always look into your face. But though I am looking at your face, I am not speaking to *it;* I am speaking to the invisible soul of which the face is the outward expression or incarnation; and again, when I am silent and listening to you I still look into your face, but it is not the face that is reaching me, it is the stream of sound coming from it and penetrating into me. But in the whole process there is no confusion between the invisible soul which seems at a distance, the visible face which is before me, and the invisible stream of sound coming from it as it were into me—the face is all I concern myself with.

And so, whether we are thinking of the invisible God quite out of reach, or of the invisible Spirit proceeding from Him and entering into us, the eye of our faith is ever directed to Him who is for us the face of God. "God who commanded the light to shine out of darkness hath shined in our hearts, to give the light of the knowledge of the glory of God in the face of Jesus Christ." Here is another of those passages where the Trinity is in the background: for light shining out of darkness, suggests the Father; shining in our hearts, suggests the Spirit; shining reflected from the face of Jesus Christ, there is the Son. But in all there is no confusion, for there is only one face to look at. Let us call Him Father by all means,

THE TRINITY AS TAUGHT BY CHRIST. 85

but as we do so we must look at His face; let us think of Him as Spirit and welcome Him as Spirit, but as we do so we still must look at His face. There is only one face—only one direction for the eye of faith to take—no confusion, no perplexity; all is simple as when a man speaks to his friend. "GOD WHO COMMANDED THE LIGHT TO SHINE OUT OF DARKNESS HATH SHINED IN OUR HEARTS, TO GIVE THE LIGHT OF THE KNOWLEDGE OF THE GLORY OF GOD IN 'THE FACE' OF JESUS CHRIST."

There are three great facts in the history, and factors in the work of Christ, which correspond to this threefold relation He sustains to the Deity and to us. These are His holy incarnation, His atoning death, and His blessed resurrection. In virtue of His incarnation He is the Truth. For—

> "So the Word had breath, and wrought
> With human hands the creed of creeds
> In loveliness of perfect deeds,
> More strong than all poetic thought;
>
> "Which he may read that binds the sheaf,
> Or builds the house, or digs the grave,
> And those wild eyes that watch the wave
> In roarings round the coral reef."

Thus by His holy incarnation He is the Truth.

By His atoning death He has opened up the Way; as it is put in the Epistle to the Hebrews: "Having, therefore, brethren, boldness to enter into the holiest by the blood of Jesus, by a new and living way, which He hath consecrated for us, through the veil, that is to say, His flesh; . . . let us draw near" to God.

And, then, by His resurrection and ascension, He has been exalted as the Fountain of Life; for thus it is that on the great day of Pentecost the inspired apostle explains the Pentecostal gift: "This Jesus hath God raised up, whereof we all are witnesses. Therefore being by the right hand of God exalted, and having received of the Father the promise of the Holy Ghost, He hath shed forth this." Thus the incarnation is specially suggestive of the Truth concerning the Father; the atonement, of the Way opened up by the Son; and the resurrection, of the Life brought by the Holy Spirit proceeding from the Father and the Son.

There is the same threefold relation in the familiar offices of Prophet, Priest, and King. The Lord Jesus came to earth as Prophet, bringing from heaven the Truth of God; He returned as Priest made perfect through suffering, opening by His death the Way from earth to heaven; He comes again as King, in the power of His Spirit, to reign in human hearts—all which is but an expansion of these most wonderful words: "I am the Way, and the Truth, and the Life."

Once more, see how in this threefold relation all the wants of our poor sinful humanity are met. To the poor bewildered *mind* in its darkness comes the great Prophet of humanity, the heavenly Apostle of our profession, bringing down to us the knowledge of God, which otherwise would have been impossible to us—bringing it down so as to be level to our capacities. It is perfectly true that none by searching can find out God; and that is the reason why God has sent His Son to search and find us, and so bring God within the range of our vision and our life. All this is included in the simple words, "I am the Truth." Thus the mind finds rest in Him.

Then there is the guilty *conscience*, which cries out for pardon and peace, for some way of reconciliation with an offended God; and again the same blessed Saviour steps forward as the High Priest of our profession, and says: "Come unto Me;" "I am the Way."

Finally, there is the disordered life, the weak will, the depraved *heart;* and once again the same Saviour steps forward, the risen Saviour now, and says, "I am the Life," "receive ye the Holy Ghost."

Yes: "It hath pleased the Father that in *Him* should all fulness dwell." So whatever perplexity there may be to the mind, that endeavours in the cold, dry atmosphere of intellectual speculation to solve the great mystery, to the seeking soul there need be, there is, neither perplexity nor confusion. Ye who are in doubt about your Father God, come to Christ as your Prophet, and you will find in Him the Truth you long for; ye who are burdened with guilt, come to Christ as your Priest, and you will find in Him your way to pardon and peace; ye who are weary of sin and long for victory over evil, accept Him as your King, and the power of the Holy Ghost will rest upon you, the power of an endless life. "Believe on the Lord Jesus Christ, and thou shalt be saved."

VI.

UNION WITH CHRIST.

"THERE is therefore now no condemnation to them which are in Christ Jesus." "Whosoever abideth in Him sinneth not." "Blessed are the dead which die in the Lord." These three declarations set forth comprehensively the immunities and privileges of believers in Christ. The first guarantees *peace with God;* the second, *purity of life;* and the third, *eternal joy.* It is, however, most important to observe that these immunities and blessings are all conditional on union with Christ, and that a union of a unique and peculiar kind. "No condemnation to them which are *in* Christ Jesus;" no sin in the case of those who abide *in* Him; and a blessed future for those who die *in* the Lord. None of the cases of personal union with which we are familiar could be expressed in this way. We may be united to one another in various ways, by ties of different degrees of strength and tenderness; but we never speak of being *in* one another. The ties which bind us to one another are ties of association, of connection, and of contact; but the relation indicated here is evidently more intimate than any of these. The first thing we have to do, then, in order to deal with this great subject, is to try to understand as clearly as possible the nature of the relation on which this security, power, and fruitfulness alone are based.

The texts quoted are all from the latter half of the New Testament; and this is no mere accident. Texts of the same kind might be quoted by the hundred between the one in Romans and the one in the Revelation; but not in the earlier part of the New Testament. How is this? How comes it that our Lord has so little to say on a matter so important? In the holy Gospels the relation of Christ to His people is set forth in a variety of ways. He is the Teacher, they the disciples; He the Master, they the servants; He the Leader, they the followers; and so on. Then there are also tenderer relations referred to; as, for instance, when He said, "Whosoever doeth the will of My Father which is in heaven, the same is My brother, and sister, and mother." But we read page after page of the Gospels without finding the intimate view of the relationship expressed by the preposition *in* · *in* Christ Jesus. To this rule, however, there is one notable exception found in our Lord's last words to His disciples in the upper chamber before His Passion—that wonderful last discourse recorded by St. John. In that discourse the thought is not only introduced but is brought into special prominence. It comes in, however, by way of anticipation. The Saviour is looking forward to the time after He shall have left them, and the Holy Spirit shall have come; and of that coming time He says: "*At that day* shall ye know that I am in My Father, and ye in Me, and I in you." A declaration this of very great importance, though it has received wonderfully little attention. The commentators for the most part pass it by, and one rarely hears it made a subject of discourse; yet there it stands, the very first passage in which the great thought is introduced of the Christian being *in* Christ.

"At that day shall ye know that I am in My Father,

and *ye in Me*, and I in you." From the way in which our Saviour thus introduces the idea, it is evident that the intimacy of this relation belongs to the dispensation of the Spirit. These striking words indicate the new way in which the presence of Christ must thereafter be realised in experience. As long as He was here on earth His presence with His disciples was manifested through the senses. He was with them just as they were with each other. Sometimes they were together, sometimes they were apart, and His nearness or distance made a very great difference to them. They were strong in His presence, and in His absence exceedingly helpless and weak. And now that His presence is to be entirely withdrawn, what will they do? The prospect seems hopeless in the extreme. Now sorrow, and not sorrow only, but something akin to despair, filled their hearts at the prospect of the removal from them of that presence in which they had found their safety, their strength, and their joy. It was in these circumstances that our Lord addressed to His disciples those comforting words to which we have referred. And the substance of the comfort He thereby gave them was just this: that His presence was to be withdrawn in one sense, but restored in another; it was to be withdrawn in an inferior degree, to be restored in a far better way; it was to be withdrawn after the flesh and restored in the Spirit; it was to be withdrawn as a human presence, and restored as a Divine presence; it was to be withdrawn as a local presence, and restored as omnipresence; it was to be withdrawn as an occasional and temporary presence, and restored as a perpetually abiding presence: all which is implied in the transition from the preposition *with* to the preposition *in*. We cannot go beyond the preposition *with* when speaking of a human presence. We can use the same, indeed, in speaking of the Divine presence, and our Saviour accordingly used the old and familiar expression when He gave the promise, "Lo, I am with you alway, even unto the end of the world;" for whatever of nearness is involved in the human presence is there too; but there is much more; so much more that the old *with* becomes inadequate: the intimacy is much greater: that which was nearness in the flesh becomes interpenetration in the Spirit; so that in effect He says to His disciples, "In that day, when ye shall know that I am in My Father, ye shall also know as a matter of spiritual experience, that ye are in Me, and I in you."

Inasmuch as this is a matter of spiritual experience, known only to those who have received the Spirit, it is exceedingly difficult to speak of it in the words of ordinary speech. Hence the need of illustrations from common things in order to help to a right understanding of it. Accordingly, our Lord presently makes most effective use of the illustration of the vine and the branches, the appropriateness of which can be seen almost at a glance. The relation of the branch to the vine is not simply that of association and simple connection. The branch is not *with* the vine; it is *in* it—it lives the life of the vine—it is absolutely dependent for all it is, and all it can ever be, and all it can produce, upon the vital currents which come to it from the vine. So the life of the branch is not the branch's life; it is the vine's life in the branch. So that when our Saviour, looking forward to the dispensation of the Spirit very soon to begin, says, "Abide in Me, and I in you," He explains Himself as meaning, Abide in Me as the branch abides in the vine, and I in you as the life of the vine abides in the branch. The illustration of the body and its members so frequently used by the Apostle Paul is to the same effect precisely. The hand is not *with* the body merely, it is *in* it; it lives a life which belongs to it only so long as it is in the body. If you were to sever it from the body, its life would cease. So our position in Christ is like that of the hand in the body, and Christ living in us is like the life of the body animating the hand.

But there is another of our Lord's illustrations which will perhaps come closer to the point of view suggested by His way of introducing the subject: "At that day" (evidently the day when the Holy Spirit shall have come) "ye shall know that I am in My Father, and ye in Me, and I in you." The illustration referred to is that suggested by the very word "spirit," which means breath or air, and also by the words addressed to Nicodemus: "The wind bloweth where it listeth, . . . so is every one that is born of the Spirit."

The nearest analogue that nature has to spiritual, as distinguished from bodily, presence, and omnipresence, as distinguished from mere local presence, is the air—that vast atmospheric ocean in which we live, and move, and have our being. It suggests the spiritual because we cannot see it, and, when it is still, we cannot feel it; and, therefore, it is quite possible to be surrounded by it, and yet not be conscious of its presence. And then, whither can we go from its presence? If we ascend the highest Alp, it is there; if we descend to the deepest abyss, it is there; could we take the wings of the morning, and dwell in the uttermost parts of the sea, there should we find it too. And then not only are we always in it, but it is no less true that it is always in us. It is just as necessary to our life that the air should be in us, as that we should be in it. In all this we have a very helpful

UNION WITH CHRIST. 93

illustration of what the presence of Christ with His people is under the dispensation of the Spirit. Now we know that He is in the Father. His human presence which was here on earth when, as Son of God, He veiled His glory in mortal flesh—that human presence is now withdrawn from us; it is, so far as our power to recognise it is concerned, merged in the Divine; so that, instead of being a local presence as before, it is now omnipresence; instead of being an occasional and temporary presence, it is now abiding; instead of being a human presence merely, it is a presence like this elemental air which fills all things, so that the old preposition *with* becomes inadequate, and that other becomes needful to express the intimacy, the interpenetration of the new relationship. We are *in* it; it is *in* us.

There is, however, one respect in which the illustration falls short. We are in the air, and the air is in us by necessity. But those who are in Christ, and He in them, are there by choice. They once lived in quite another element; they now live in Him: they formerly lived in the human element of selfishness; they now live in the Divine element of love: as the apostle has it, "God is love; and he that dwelleth in love dwelleth in God, and He in him." But even at this point we are not left without a parable in nature to help us. So far as our physical life is concerned, we have no choice of elements; we must live in the air or else not live at all: there is no option in the matter. But in the spiritual life there is an option: we may live in the world in the old element of selfishness, or we may live in Christ in the new element of love. Now, though we cannot find an analogue in the physical life of man, we may find one in other lives. God has given us many illustrations of spiritual things in the lives of the lower creatures. Look, for instance, at the history of the dragon-fly as an illustration of this point. It is born at the bottom of the water. For a considerable time it lives there, a narrow, low, greedy life; for that particular grub is said to be exceedingly voracious. It creeps about on the submerged parts of an aquatic plant, and lives on aquatic insects. It breathes air, indeed, but only as other inhabitants of the water do, by an apparatus which gets out of the water the small quantity of air that manages to filter into it from the atmosphere above. So it lives on and on in utter ignorance of any higher and better life, of any larger or more generous supply of that vital air by means of which it lives; until at last one day there comes a wondrous change, taking place it knows not how, a change which cannot be better described than in the words of the Laureate—

> "To-day I saw the dragon-fly,
> Come from the wells where he did lie.
> An inner impulse rent the veil
> Of his old husk; from head to tail
> Came out clear plates of sapphire mail.
> He dried his wings; like gauze they grew;
> Through crofts and pastures wet with dew,
> A living flash of light he flew"

The same animal as before; but how different the life! "Old things have passed away, behold all things have become new." And the change cannot be more comprehensively expressed than by saying that it now lives in a new element. Formerly it lived in the water, now it lives in the air. It is now dead to the water, and alive in the air. Its old grub life is gone; its new ethereal, heavenly life has begun. It is true that even when it lived under the water it could not get on without air; but it knew nothing about it: it simply took in so much water and got out of it the air which the water had absorbed. And so, in the same way, even those that know not Christ, and have no experience of the power of His resurrection, are not independent of the God whom Christ reveals. They are not conscious of His presence, and yet they could not live without Him; though they get from Him every breath they draw, they have no conscious relation to Him, while in works they utterly deny Him—are just as much strangers to Him as the grub living at the bottom of the muddy pool is a stranger to the glorious sunshine in the upper air. But when by faith they take hold of Christ they are lifted out of the muddy pool, drawn from the waters of sin which have submerged them, and then they not only owe their life to God, as all along in a dim unconscious way they have done, but now they know that they are in Him, living a new life in a new element, bathed in the sunlight of His presence, surrounded by the fresh breezes of His Holy Spirit—a life which is no longer bounded by the narrow limits of a little muddy pond, but which stretches out on all sides to the dim horizon of indefinite distance, and, when bounded at all, it is by the everlasting hills, over which, as over all, is spread the infinite of God's glorious sky.

And how different the temperature! There was, indeed, power to sustain life, such life as there was, in the air which was mixed with the water; but there was no genial warmth in it, and these gill-breathing animals are a cold-blooded race. But how different the upper air, the air that is warmed by the rays of the glorious Sun of Righteousness!

And the light! Here again we have a favourite illustration both of our Lord and of His apostles. The light of the world which seemed to go out on Calvary has been rekindled in the heavens. He who descended into the lower parts of the earth has now ascended above earth's horizon, as "the Sun of Righteousness, with healing in His wings." Who has not observed the force of that beautiful metaphor which the prophet Malachi employs in the last Old Testament promise? What wings are those he speaks of? They are the wings of the Holy Dove, that other Comforter whom our Lord promised to send from the high heaven, to which He was about to go, to wrap His disciples round with the light and the warmth of His own perpetual presence. See how beautifully expressive is the sacred emblem. Christ Himself is the Sun now exalted in the heavens. The Holy Spirit is the Light which streams perpetually from Him. The sun in the sky has its local presence in one particular place in the heavens, but is by no means confined to that spot, but with those wonderful wings of his fills every point of space wherever his rays are not cut off by intervening obstacles; and so, too, the Sun of Righteousness has His local habitation in the highest heavens, and yet is not confined to it, but by His Holy Spirit is present everywhere, except where He is shut out by barriers of wickedness erected against Him, or excluded by soul-windows fast closed within by those who love the darkness rather than the light.

"At that day shall ye know that I am in My Father." How do we know that the sun is shining in the heavens? Only by the light which streams down from it and reaches our eyes. In the same way, "No man can say that Jesus is Lord, but by the Holy Ghost;" or, as it is in the Revised Version, "No man can say Jesus is Lord, but in the Holy Spirit." "At that day ye shall know that I am in My Father."

"And ye in Me." On a bright but chilly day in early

spring a man sees his friend walking on the shady side of the street, as some foolish people will do. He calls over to him: "Come and walk in the sun with me." The sun is many millions of miles away, yet we speak of being in it, and walking in it, when we are bathed in the light and warmth continually proceeding from it. In the same way are we in Christ when we are surrounded by the gracious loving presence of His Holy Spirit. So, "Ye in Me."

"And I in you." Not only must the light be around us, but in us, before we can be said to live in it and walk in it. A blind man is surrounded by the sunlight as any one else is, but he does not live in it; he does not walk in it; he cannot enjoy it. Why not? Simply because it is not in him. We must have eyes; and these eyes must be opened to receive the light into the body, so that we may live in it, and walk in it, and enjoy it. And in the same way must the eye of faith be opened to receive the heavenly light into the soul before we can even be aware of its presence; and it must be kept open in order that we may "walk in the light as He is in the light." Christ must be in His people by His Holy Spirit in order that they may live in Him.

Such are some of the views given in the Scriptures of the nature of that spiritual union in which is found the security, strength, fruitfulness, and joy of those who are "in Christ Jesus."

VII.

UNITY BY THE WAY OF THE CROSS.

THERE is a unity of the Church which does not need to be sought after or prayed for, because it is already enjoyed. The oneness of all true believers throughout the world with their Lord, and with one another in Him, has already existed as a fact, and is for the most part acknowledged by those within its hallowed circle. To the reality and indefeasibility of this union all evangelical Christians count it a privilege to bear witness, inscribing on their banner the motto, "*Unum corpus sumus in Christo.*"

But we should not be satisfied with the recognition and declaration of this spiritual unity. We should pray and labour for a unity which will be recognised not only within itself, but by those that are without—the unity for which our Saviour longed so earnestly as He looked down the coming ages before He left the world: a unity so manifest that the world must see it, and, seeing it, cannot but be convinced that He around Whom all so lovingly gather must be in very deed the Son of God and King of men.

Where are we, now that we are nearing the closing decade of the nineteenth century? How far have we reached? Surely something has been gained, some progress made. This much, surely, at all events: that we have entered on the right path, so that there need be no steps retraced. If we do not yet see as clearly as we would wish how this visible manifest union is to be attained, we have had a good deal of quite demonstrative instruction as to how it is not to be attained. We have learned, for instance, that it is not to be attained by organisation, political or ecclesiastical—that it is a thing of the inner life, and not of the outer shell—that it cannot be attained by building a great house round about a divided family, so as to have them all within the same enclosure; but that its essence is to be sought in the one spirit pervading the family, whether they all dwell under the same roof or not. We have learned, by whatever slow degrees, the old lesson, that the union of which we are in search is a union like that which subsisted in all its fulness between the Father and the Son (John xvii. 20–23), even when one was in heaven and the other on earth.

It is not less obvious that unity is not to be reached through forced uniformity. To us now, who have learned the lesson, it does seem very strange that an attempt to reach it thus could have been made by those who had in their hands the New Testament, almost every page of which is a standing rebuke to those who attach vital importance to matters of form. The familiar illustration of the body and its members might have been a sufficient barrier against so foolish an error. What sort of bodies should we have if all the different members were reduced by some act of uniformity to the same shape? Then, indeed, might the hand say to the foot, "I have no need of thee;" and each of them to the head, "I have no need of thee;" for head, feet, and hands would be all alike, and quite too many of them! We may certainly now set it down as among the things surely believed among us, that true Christianity is not a thing of outward form but of inward life—that "in Christ Jesus neither circumcision availeth anything, nor uncircumcision, but faith working through love.'

And here again we are, beyond all question, in the right path.

But experience has proved that, even after learning that the unity required is a unity the essence of which is in faith, it is possible to take a wrong road to it. It has been found possible to replace faith which works through love by a faith which works through logic, and which, therefore, instead of making harmony, has multiplied divisions. In place of the simple faith of the Scriptures, which is the resting of the heart on the Lord Jesus Christ, there came a prodigious effort of intellect, exhausting itself in the attempt to grasp a great system of the universe; and the unity of faith was supposed to lie in absolute identity of opinion through all that mighty range! These days are, happily, past, and we have come, or are fast coming, back to the simplicity which is in Christ, and learning, with the Apostle of the Gentiles, to look forward to the day when we shall "all attain unto the unity of the faith, *and of the knowledge of the Son of God*, unto a full-grown man, unto the measure of the stature of the fulness of Christ; that we may be no longer children, tossed to and fro, and carried about by every wind of *doctrine* . . . but speaking truth in love, may grow up in all things unto *Him* which is the Head, even Christ; from Whom all the body fitly framed and knit together through that which every joint supplieth, according to the working in due measure of each several part, maketh the increase of the body unto the building up of itself in love."

There are few things more hopeful in the prospects of the cause of union than the growing disposition among Christians to make less of abstract truth, and more of Him who said, "I am the truth;" less of faith as a thing in itself, and more of it as a link which binds us all to

Him, in a word, less of creed and more of Christ. Oh, how much better than the "one Church, one creed, one mode of baptism," of the sectary, is the "one Lord, one faith, one baptism," of the Apostle,—one Lord, on Whom we all believe, and into Whom we are all baptized by the one Spirit into the one body; bowing alike in trustful adoration to the one God and Father of all, and looking forward in one hope of our calling to the Father's house, into whose many mansions shall gather from north, south, east, and west, out of every kindred, and tongue, and people, and nation, one ransomed Church, one family and "household of God."

This recognition of the personal Christ as the object of the Church's faith is far more satisfactory than the attempt which has also been made, in the interests of Christian union, while not abandoning what may be called the documentary idea of unity, to limit its difficulties by limiting the size of the document to which all should subscribe—to reduce, as we might say, the creeds of the churches to their lowest terms—to find some "least common denominator" for all the denominations, so that they might be added up by their numerators into one result. We by no means say that efforts in this direction have been fruitless, for it is plain that many of the divisions of the Church have been due to the attempt to include far too much in the Church's creed, and the movement in the direction of brevity and simplicity has been wholesome and hopeful in the main; but then there is always the fear—and not only the fear, but the danger—of reducing the creed too much, getting it down to terms so low that it ceases to be a Christian creed at all, and leaves room for a "Christianity" without Christ. On the other hand, when the scriptural idea of faith as a living link to a living Saviour is kept prominent, all that is essential in the creed of the Church is conserved; for there cannot be this outgoing of the soul to Christ without the most cordial acceptance of His teaching about Himself and the Father and the Holy Spirit, and the way of salvation, and the whole circle of saving truth. We do not say that more extended creeds have not been of service, and are not needed still, especially as a guarantee for the teaching in the Church; but as a basis of Christian fellowship and fully acknowledged brotherhood, we hold that nothing more is necessary than evidence of unfeigned faith in the Lord Jesus Christ. "*Unum corpus sumus* IN CHRISTO." That is enough: "Christ is all and in all."

But, so far, we seem to be getting farther and farther from a union that is manifest to the world. A great ecclesiastical organisation is a visible thing; uniformity, though less impressive, is yet quite easily observed; even a creed is something that can be made visible after a fashion by the use of the press; but this "faith in Christ" withdraws the essential unity so entirely into the spiritual region that the world cannot be expected to follow it there and find it out, and be any the wiser or better for it. It remains, then, to show how this unity of faith in Christ can be made manifest to the world.

And here it will be safe to go back to the Apostle again. "Neither circumcision," he says, "nor uncircumcision, but faith"—so far so good, and what next? "Faith *working through love*." Here we have the transition from the invisible to the visible. The faith which links each Christian to Christ is unseen by men, but the love which is the result of it, need not, cannot in fact, be concealed from them, if it is there in force And every effort should be made to promote love among Christians, and to induce them to avail themselves of all means within their reach, not only of cherishing it in their hearts, but also of expressing it in their lives. There has been progress in this direction too, very marked and happy progress, in recent years; but there needs to be a much larger development and fuller expression of this Christian affection before much impression can be made on an unbelieving world. It must, in fact, be so marked and remarkable as not only to compel attention, but to oblige those who observe it to ask the questions, How can it be? Whence has it come? No one can say that this point has yet been reached. The extent to which Christian love prevails is not yet so extraordinary as to raise any serious question as to its origin; still less is the phenomenon so startling as to manifestly call for a supernatural cause. It is a great thing that unnatural variance and bitterness of strife have in so many regions been replaced by what may fairly be called natural affection; but our Christian love must manifestly transcend the limits of natural affection before we can expect the world to be convinced that it is from above, that it comes out of heaven from God, and that He through Whom it comes is, *ipso facto*, proved to be what He claims to be—the Son of God and Saviour of men.

This brings us to the point we have mainly in view in this paper—viz., that while it is by love that the unity of the faith is to be manifested, it is not by love in its ordinary range, but in the extraordinary range which belongs to the faith in Christ—the love, that is, which finds its example and model in the Cross. It is by the Cross that the Divine love is commended to us; and in the same way must it be commended by us to those that are without. It will be remembered how even Christ Himself, pure and holy and loving as He was, failed on any large scale to draw men unto Him, until the light of the Divine love had been made, so to speak, to *blaze* before the eyes of men in the awful sacrifice of the Cross. It will also be remembered how distinctly this was present to His own mind, as when He cried, "I, *if I be lifted up* from the earth, shall draw all men unto Me." It was not till Divine love blazed out in the Cross that men were attracted in large numbers to Christ; and it will not be till the love of Christ blazes out in the same manner in His people that the world will be compelled to recognise their oneness with Him who gave His life for men who were His enemies.

The trouble with our love and its manifestation hitherto has been that while there has been quite enough of *sentiment* in it, there has been far too little *sacrifice*. It has not been conspicuously marked with the sign of the cross. It is easy to speak and to write of "our dear brothers and sisters in Christ;" but what do we give up for their sakes? There has, happily, been not a little sacrifice for the cause of Christ, as represented by the wants of the perishing heathen abroad and at home, but very little of it, as yet, for His cause as represented by the woes of the torn and bleeding Church. We put crosses on our churches still, and there is certainly no place where the tender but awful symbol is more appropriate; yet the church is often the last place where good Christian people think the cross in its reality ought to be. How many are there even of those who, as private Christians, show not a little of the spirit of their Master, self-forgetful, tenderly considerate of others, ready to make sacrifices for their sakes, who show none of it in their bearing and conduct as members of the branch of the Church to which they belong! In putting on the churchman, they put off the man, become haughty and exclusive, regardless of the feelings and interests of others, insist always on what they call their rights, and think little or not at all of what is certainly their duty—to love their fellow Christians as Christ has loved them. They justify their conduct to themselves by the thought that they are contending for the cause of Christ; but they forget that the cause of Christ cannot be identified with the interests of any part of His kingdom except in so far as its interests agree with the general interests of the whole; and they forget, besides, that what may seem to them, and may really be, a great advantage to the cause of Christ, may be secured at far too great a cost. Whatever we are striving after must be, indeed, of overwhelming importance, if it be not too dearly purchased at the expense of that unity of spirit among Christians, the longing for which was the great burden of the prayer which was in the Saviour's heart and on His lips as He advanced to His great sacrifice. The Church as a whole, and all its individual members, are called upon to make sacrifices for the good of the world; but no less is it the duty of the different parts of the Church to make sacrifices for each other. Yet how seldom is this ever thought of! Where two denominations of Christians are working in the common cause in the same place, how seldom does the one make any considerable sacrifice for the other's sake! How seldom is it made conspicuous that Christ is all and in all to the Christians of our towns and villages and country districts; that in very deed it is not so much, not nearly so much, a question whether this, that, or the other enterprise shall flourish, as whether the name of Christ shall be exalted and His cause advanced at whatever cost! "But our cause might die," says one. So be it, then, if thereby the cause of Christ be advanced. "But our enterprise is so essential to the progress of the cause; its life is too valuable to be sacrificed." Very well; but was not the life of Christ valuable, too valuable to be risked or sacrificed? Yet He gave it up—gave it up, indeed, for a purpose wider than the accomplishment of unity; and yet, as we have seen, this prayer for unity seemed to be deepest in His heart at the very time. But, after all, just as it was with the Master, so will it be with the servants; the ultimate issue will be not death, but larger, fuller, richer life. Christian enterprises are not likely to die by being carried on in a truly Christian spirit; and the principle our Lord so frequently insisted on is as valid for collective communities of Christians as for each individual member of them: "He that will save his life shall lose it, and he that will lose his life for My sake shall find it."

The crucifixion of self in every form is what is needed, including that most insidious form of it which says "My church," or even "Our church," in place of "The Church of the living God," "The Kingdom of Christ." We must beware of that subtle form of selfishness which takes such liberties with the Lord's prayer, saying from the heart, "Our name, our kingdom, our will;" while only on the lips are the very words the Lord has taught us, "Hallowed be *Thy* name, *Thy* kingdom come, *Thy* will be done on earth as it is in heaven." Ah! it often costs a great deal to get the word "Thy" down from the lips to the heart. The true Christian knows what it costs in private life, and why should it not cost something in Church life? Shall it be the plain duty of Christians to take up the cross at home, and in the street, and the market; and yet shall they be at liberty to lay it down and leave it outside when they enter the church porch, or sit in council in the church court? Surely not. It is there especially that the world looks for it; and it is for the want of it there, very largely at least, that the world will not believe that Christ, in Whose name churches are gathered and church courts meet, was sent of God (John xvii. 21). If there could only be this crucifixion of self through all the Church—far more of it in private life, and a fair share in church life too,—how speedily would our oneness in Him and with one another be manifested! Men would see everywhere "the marks of the Lord Jesus;" every doubting Thomas could put his fingers in the print of the nails, and thrust his hand into the wounds in the side. That would be the true *sign of the cross*, and again, with far deeper meaning and grander result, the Church might inscribe upon her *labarum* the old device: ἐν τούτῳ νικα, "by this conquer!"

Only let the Church be "lifted up from the earth" as her Lord was lifted up, and she will "draw all men unto her." Herein is her true glory, as it was the glory of her Master; a glory He refers to in that very prayer for unity—"The glory which Thou gavest me I have given them, that they may be one;" a glory which He has just explained in these striking and suggestive words: "For their sakes I sanctify myself" (devote myself as a sacrifice), "that they also may be devoted in truth." We must, not only as individual believers, but also as members of the Church, enter into the fellowship of the sufferings of Christ, if we would share in His glory. We must be willing to be put into the ground and die, if we would bear much fruit. The days for martyrdom are not past yet. We have no longer to give our lives in the same absolute way; we are not asked to give the whole of them at once; but we are asked to deny ourselves day by day—to give up what may be dear to us as life itself. There are large portions of ourselves that we must be willing even in these days to allow to be put into the ground and die, if we would not abide alone, but bring forth much fruit. We must take the way of the

Cross, which is the way of the Master, if we would reach the unity for which He prays.

It is no easy way. It cannot be reached by speeches, and resolutions, and expressions of endearment, and cultivation of brotherly relations, and so on. It cannot be attained without sacrifice. This love of ours for one another must be so *lifted up from the earth* that men will see it is not of earth, but heavenly and divine. People may turn away and say, "It is not in human nature to make such sacrifices." The answer is—that is the very reason they must be made. It is not human nature the world wants to see in order to believe; it has quite enough of that It is divine nature the world is waiting to see. It insists on seeing not mere human affection, but divine love, which can make itself infallibly known only by carrying on its front the sign of the cross.

It comes to this, then—that what is most wanted in order to the manifestation of the unity of Christians in their common Lord, is more, and more, and more of the spirit of the Cross throughout the Church. As it was put long ago, by one who, next to the Lord Himself, knew best what Christian love is: "Hereby know we love, because He laid down His life for us; *and we ought to lay down our lives for the brethren.*" Lord Jesus, who didst lay down Thy life for us, grant us, and all Thy people, Thy Holy Spirit, that He may teach us how we too must lay down our lives for the brethren! Give unto us more and more of Thy glory, that we may be one with Thee! Let the love wherewith Thou hast loved us, be in us, that the world may know as it looks at us and sees us one with Thee, that Thou in whom we trust art indeed the Son of God, the Saviour of the world!

VIII.

WISDOM PERSONIFIED AND LOVE INCARNATE.

IT is not our purpose to discuss in this paper the large subject of "Wisdom" in the Hebrew literature; but only to call attention to a sadly common perversion of part of the noble passage in the opening of the Book of Proverbs—an abuse of Scripture which has done and is doing incalculable mischief. It has long been a commonplace of popular evangelical exposition that "Wisdom" in the Book of Proverbs is Christ. The ground of this belief is the unquestionable fact that the greater part of the utterances of "Wisdom" in the Proverbs, especially in the eighth chapter, would come most appropriately from the lips of Christ, and some of them are striking anticipations of His gracious invitations and promises.[*] This is just what we should expect. Wisdom is one of the divine attributes; and Christ "is of God made unto us wisdom," as well as "righteousness and sanctification and redemption." We may surely expect, then, that up to a certain point the utterances of Wisdom and of Christ would coincide; so that in these passages in the Book of Proverbs we should be able to find, as we find throughout

[*] There is, however, a difference even here. For example, take that favourite text, "I love them that love Me." How far short does it come of the grace of the gospel in which "God commendeth His love toward us, in that, *while we were yet sinners*, Christ died for us." The order of grace is not, "I love them that love Me;" but, "We love Him, who first loved us."

the whole of the Old Testament, some portion of "the testimony of Jesus." But does it follow that because some or many of Wisdom's utterances may be correctly spoken of as the words of Christ Himself, therefore all of them may be so regarded? To see how utterly foolish is this way of reasoning, we have only to remember how many of David's words not only coincide with those of Christ, but are actually quoted in the New Testament as if Christ Himself had uttered them; and yet no one is so foolish as to insist that all the words of David can be safely put into the mouth of Christ. Suppose, for example, that some one should quote David's dying curse upon his enemies as the words of Christ, who would not resent it as a slander on Him whose dying word for His enemies was, "Father, forgive them, for they know not what they do;" and yet it could be justified on precisely the same principles on which so many put into the mouth of Christ the awful words: "I also will laugh at your calamity; I will mock when your fear cometh · when your fear cometh as desolation, and destruction cometh as a whirlwind; when distress and anguish cometh upon you. Then shall they call upon me, but I will not answer; they shall seek me early, but they shall not find me."

We have been moved to write on this subject by a recent sad experience. An earnest Christian lady visiting an infirmary found an old sinner in a very anxious and penitent state of mind. She pointed him to Christ, and told him the gospel of free grace and dying love. He listened with deep earnestness and great interest, and then dashed her hopes by telling her sadly that the gospel was not for him. Asked why he said so, he turned to the first chapter of Proverbs and read the awful sentences we have just quoted. She tried her best to point him to other passages; but he could not get beyond this one, which seemed so utterly to close the door of hope. The visitor reported the case to her minister. He pointed out to her that these were not the words of Christ, but of Wisdom; that if there were nothing but wisdom in God, there could be no hope for sinners; but that "God is Love," that that love has found expression in the gift of His Son Christ Jesus, and that, though sinners could not find salvation in any words of Wisdom, they could find all they need in Christ, Who can and will "save to the uttermost all that come unto God by Him." She went back joyfully with her message, delivered it to the sick man, with the result that his face lighted up, and he seemed about to find what he was seeking, when a man lying on the next bed interposed. He had been a local preacher, and had no doubt often preached fiery discourses on these awful words. He told the poor old man that the visitor was all wrong, that all who understood their Bibles knew that "Wisdom" was Christ, and in proof of it triumphantly pointed to some of those sayings in the eighth chapter which read like words of Christ. The result was that the old despair came back into the poor man's face, and the visitor surrendered too, and to this day feels constrained to treat this passage as an inspired declaration that the Lord Jesus Christ can—and *does*—laugh at calamity and mock at prayer!

This is no solitary case. It is a familiar experience, especially in dealing with the comparatively uneducated. And, besides the injury done to anxious souls, no one can tell how many have been driven into infidelity by the unwarrantable liberty which so many good people allow themselves with this passage of Scripture when they take out the word "Wisdom" and put in the word "Christ" or the word "God." Is it any wonder that those who know not the truth should say: "Better no God at all than one who would laugh at the calamities of His children, and mock them when in agony they pray to Him"?

It does seem, then, of the utmost importance that this passage should be expounded; and it is in the hope of inducing the readers of this paper to do what they can to dispel the popular misunderstanding on the subject that the attempt will be made to show, in as clear a light as possible, wherein the words of Wisdom coincide with those of Christ, and wherein they do not.

As we said at the beginning, Wisdom is one of the attributes of God, and therefore the words of Wisdom must be, up to a certain point, the expression of the Divine mind. We may say that Wisdom expresses the mind of God in creation, in providence, in the whole realm of law. And in this realm, as well as in the realm of grace, the Son of God has His place as the Revealer. As St. John sets forth in the prologue to his gospel, He is the λογος, without Whom nothing was made that was made; and as St. Paul tells us, "He is before all things, and by Him all things consist" (Col. i. 17). Closely parallel with this we have the remarkable passage in the eighth chapter of Proverbs, commencing "The Lord possessed me in the beginning of His way, before His works of old" (see the whole passage, verses 22–31). We may then regard Christ and Wisdom as identical *throughout the realm of natural law;* so that no error would result from the substitution of the one for the other within that range of truth: but when we leave the realm of law and enter that of grace, it is entirely different; then it may not only be injurious but fatal to take the utterances of mere Wisdom, and put them into the mouth of Christ. If Christ had been only

WISDOM PERSONIFIED AND LOVE INCARNATE. 113

Wisdom, He could not have heard the sinner's prayer; but He is also "righteousness and sanctification and redemption;" and that makes all the difference, for now that He has made an atonement for our sins and opened up the way of life, He can speak not only in the name of Wisdom, but of pardoning mercy and redeeming grace; and accordingly, far from laughing at calamity and scorning the penitent's prayer, which Wisdom, alone, must do, He can and will and does " save to the uttermost all that come unto God by Him."

Having thus considered the extent to which we may expect to find "the testimony of Jesus" in the words of Wisdom, let us now test the principles we have laid down by an examination of the passage. The paragraph begins with the bold and striking personification: "Wisdom crieth without; she uttereth her voice in the streets; she crieth in the chief places of concourse, in the opening of the gates; in the city she uttereth her words, saying"—and then follows the passage with which we have mainly to do. Let us then listen to Wisdom's cry, and observe how truthfully and powerfully it is translated into the language of men. We shall see its truth to nature better, if we first look back a little. She begins not with a cry but with tender words of counsel and of promise (vers. 8, 9): "My son, hear the instruction of thy father, and forsake not the law of thy mother; for they shall be an ornament of grace unto thy head, and chains about thy neck." These are the tender and kindly words of counsel in which she addresses the young man setting out in life. Following this are tender and yet solemn words of warning against the tempter whom every one must meet (ver. 10): "My son, if sinners entice thee, consent thou not," and so on. But now time passes on, and Wisdom's *protégé* begins to go astray, to forget the instruction of the father and the loving law of the mother, and so now she lifts up her voice and cries, entreating the wanderer to turn before it is too late (vers. 22, 23).

Time passes on, and the warning cry has been as little heeded as had been the tender voice of Wisdom at the first. The son, instead of being prudent, has been rash; he has been not economical, but extravagant; not temperate, but dissipated; and so he has gone on till his last opportunity has been thrown away, his patrimony squandered, his health gone, his last friend lost. Then once more his early monitor appears. The prodigal remembers the tender words of counsel and of promise, he remembers the solemn and kindly warnings against evil ways. He remembers how, when he was just beginning to go astray, before he had become hopelessly entangled in evil, Wisdom lifted up her voice and *cried*. For a long time his old counsellor has not been present to his mind at all. He has been hurrying on in courses of evil; but now his very wretchedness forces him to stop and think. And, again, there stands Wisdom before him. How does she address him now? Does she speak to him in soothing tones? Does she promise to restore him his money, or his health, or his friends? Alas, no; she cannot. All she can say is: "I told you it would be so. I warned you what would be the end; and now the end has come. You must eat the fruit of your own ways, and be filled with your own devices." That is positively all that Wisdom can say; and there is no tenderness in her tone. She seems to mock him rather. She seems to laugh at his calamity. It is in fact the old story of Wisdom come back as a spectre of Remorse, tossing her snaky head, shaking her bony fingers, flashing her scornful eyes, and muttering: "Ye set at nought all my counsel, and would none of my reproof: I also will laugh at your calamity; I will mock when your fear cometh; when your fear cometh as desolation, and your destruction cometh as a whirlwind; when distress and anguish cometh upon you."

Is it of any use to call upon Wisdom now? Had she been invoked in time, she would have responded as she always does to those who seek her early in life. But will she respond, can she respond, now that life's opportunity is used up, and its prospects utterly blighted? Alas, no. She can only upbraid; she cannot help. They may call upon her now, but she will not, for she cannot, answer; they may seek her now, both early and late, but they cannot find her. There is no place of repentance, however carefully they seek it with tears. Such is the voice of Wisdom in the end to those who have despised her counsel in the beginning. And is not the whole representation true to nature? Is it not patent to every intelligent observer of men and things? Yes, it is perfectly true that "Wisdom crieth without, she uttereth her voice in the streets," and says these very things so loudly that no listening ear can fail to hear them. It is no matter of deep philosophy. It is no ecclesiastical or theological dogma. It belongs to *the proverbs,* the proverbs of the streets. One does not need to go to church to learn these commonplaces of universal common sense. The merit of Solomon in this chapter is not in telling us something we should not otherwise have known, but in putting what we already know in a very striking form. The object of the passage is to bring a strong pressure to bear, specially upon the young, to listen to the voice of Wisdom while yet her tones are tender and full of promise, before the awful time come when the voice of grave and kindly monition shall have been altered into tones of bitter mockery and scorn. We question whether in all literature there can be found any more vivid and alarming description of the terror and despair of a remorseful conscience, as it looks back and recalls, when too late, the neglected counsels alike of earthly and of heavenly wisdom.

So far *Wisdom*, and if it were only with her that sinners had to do, it would go hard not only with the profligate and openly vicious, but with the most respectable. But He with whom we have to do is not known as Wisdom. He is wise indeed; and all wisdom is from Him. But there is that in Him which is higher than Wisdom. " God is Love." Wisdom is the expression of His will in the realm of law; but love is the expression of Himself. From His works in creation and in providence we can get glimpses of His attributes; but when we wish to know HIM we must look into the face of Jesus Christ, who is not only wisdom personified but love incarnate, and as such " the image of the invisible God "—and His word is, " Him that cometh unto me I will in no wise cast out." True indeed He is too wise to receive sinners into favour without genuine repentance. He could say, and often did say, the severest things in condemnation of those who hardened their hearts against God. But He never laughed at calamity,* and never refused to hear those who called upon Him.

The love of God is not a lawless love. It is not at

* Those who are anxious to make out that God laughs at calamity sometimes refer to Ps. ii 4 and Ps xxxvii 13, as if they expressed the same idea as in the passage before us. This is one of many instances of the danger of mistaking mere verbal coincidences for real parallels. The laughing in the 2nd Psalm is not at calamity, but at the feeble efforts of wicked men to frustrate the Divine purposes. The kings and rulers who are laughed at are not in calamity, but in the heyday of their power, and rejoicing in the supposed success of their rebellion. So, too, in the 37th Psalm the Lord is represented as laughing, neither at the calamities, nor at the prayers, but at the plots of the wicked—manifestly a totally different conception.

variance with Wisdom. The law which ordains that the sinner must eat of the fruit of his own way and be filled with his own devices, cannot be set aside by the mere emotion of compassion. Hence it was necessary in order to redeem man from the condemnation of sin that the Holy One of God should suffer. Hence, too, it is that, though by the suffering and death of Christ believers in Him are set free from the condemnation of sin, yet the natural consequences of the transgression of Wisdom's laws are not abolished. If health has been wasted, it will not be miraculously restored. If money has been squandered, there must be suffering from the want of it. If friends have been alienated, they must be won back by the slow process which the laws of Wisdom in such cases demand. If character has been forfeited by dishonesty or impurity, it may never be redeemed on this side the grave. The laws of Wisdom are not repealed or set aside, or set at nought; they remain in force. But such has been the ingenuity, so to speak, of the Divine love, that without infringing on the proper domain of Wisdom expressing itself in law, the way has been opened up for the full pardon and ultimate restoration even of those who have wandered farthest and sinned the most. And accordingly, a passage like this awful one in the first chapter of the Book of Proverbs, instead of obscuring the Divine love in the smallest degree, or interposing so much as a thread between the sinner and his Saviour, rather serves as a dark background on which to set forth the radiant form of the Saviour of mankind—

"Whose love appears more orient and more bright,
Having a foil whereon to show its light."

The foil is inexorable law, the god of modern infidelity, who shows no mercy. Force and law never show mercy.

They always laugh at calamity, and mock when fear cometh. When fear cometh as desolation, and destruction cometh as a whirlwind, men may call aloud to the gods of unbelieving science, but they will not answer. And that wisdom which deals only with such matters as law and force, and rejects the revelation of divine love, has no gospel for humanity. All it does is to spread a dark background which the more vividly sets off by contrast the glad tidings of a Father God, who "forgiveth all thine iniquities; who healeth all thy diseases; who redeemeth thy life from destruction; who crowneth thee with loving kindness and tender mercies."

Experience has convinced the writer that it would be too much to expect all those who have been in the habit of putting these awful words into the mouth of our Father in Heaven or of His Son Christ Jesus, to acknowledge that they have been wrong. But surely it should not be too much to ask even those who are most wedded to traditional interpretation and inferences to honour the Scriptures so far as to quote them correctly. If they will cling to the idea that when the Bible says "Wisdom" it means to say God or Christ, then why should they change the word? If it so obviously means God in the Book of Proverbs, it will have the same meaning when it is quoted. Let them tell the people that "Wisdom" says these things; but if they take away the Bible word and put in another, are they not taking the name of the Lord their God in vain? For either "Wisdom" in the passage quoted means God, or it does not. If it does, it is not necessary to make the substitution; and surely it is a vain thing to suppose that their word is better than the word in the Bible. If it does not, and there is no evidence that it does, then in a far more serious sense it is taking God's name in vain to thrust it in. It is not as if there were not passages enough to set forth the wrath of God against sin. No man who accepts the Scriptures as from God can honestly deny that there is a terrible doom for the impenitent sinner. But it is just as plain that God " delighteth in mercy," and " doth not afflict willingly," that there is infinite sorrow in His heart at the thought of the calamities of the wicked, represented throughout the Old Testament by the most pathetic appeals, and expressed with infinite pathos in the tears of Jesus over doomed Jerusalem. Let the vengeance of God be by all means proclaimed against impenitence; but let it be distinctly known that it is the vengeance, not of cruel exultation, but of Divine sorrow and love.

IX.

THE INCARNATE WORD AND THE INDWELLING SPIRIT.

THE God Whom we worship is represented to us in Scripture, not only as God the Supreme, but as Father, as Son, and as Spirit. The word "Trinity," though it is never used in the Bible, seems justified by this threefold representation. Great difficulties are encountered when the attempt is made to imagine how the one God can exist as Father, Son, and Spirit; but no greater than reason would lead us to expect, for "who can by searching find out God?" There are unfathomable mysteries in the complexity of our own constitution, and philosophers who have devoted the closest attention to the study of man, have come to the conclusion that there is a mysterious trinity in his nature, of body, soul, and spirit. This is not suggested as in any sense parallel to the Trinity in the Divine nature, but it may surely prompt the question—If we find that which is unfathomable in our own nature, why should it perplex us to encounter that which is utterly incomprehensible by us in the nature of God? The doctrine of the Trinity, indeed, is sometimes put in such a way as to involve a contradiction; never in Scripture, however; only in the vain attempts of men to put the incomprehensible into logical or arithmetical forms of expression of their own devising. Many are sorely perplexed, and some are decisively repelled, by the apparent irrationality involved in the very word "Trinity," especially when it is put in the arithmetical form, "Three in One, and One in Three;" but it is only necessary to bear in mind, first that the Bible is not responsible for that way of putting it, and next, that while God may be said to be Three as well as One, it is certainly never meant that He is or can be Three and One *in the same sense.* The doctrine cannot thus or in any way be relieved of incomprehensibility; but it is certainly relieved entirely of contradiction and absurdity.

The Father is preseted to our thoughts as God invisible, inaccessible; the Son, as God manifest; the Spirit, as God working. Some, beguiled by the apparent simplicity of the conception, have maintained that these are three successive revelations; that God revealed Himself as Father under the old covenant, as Son in the life of Christ, as Spirit on and after Pentecost. But this theory is at once set aside by the fact that the Son and the Spirit are found all through the Old Testament as well as the New. The Apostle John, looking back over the old dispensation, says: "No man hath seen God at any time, the only-begotten Son who is in the bosom of the Father, He hath declared Him." The Son was God manifest from the beginning. "In the beginning was the Word, and the Word was with God, and the Word was God." From the beginning, too, the Spirit is spoken of as exercising His divine energy, for do we not read at the very opening of the Bible, how "the Spirit of God moved upon the face of the waters"? And there are many passages in both Testaments, in which both creation and providence are attributed to the Son and to the Spirit; to the Son when they are regarded as manifestations of God, to the Spirit when they are regarded as works done by the divine energy. And not only are the Son and the Spirit spoken of as engaged in creation and providence from the beginning, but in the work of salvation as well. The declaration of St John above quoted is a proof of this, and it is fully confirmed by a careful study of the Covenant name Jehovah, and of those very numerous passages in which the Angel of Jehovah or the Angel of the Covenant is spoken of in such a way as to identify Him with the Word, Who in the fulness of the time became flesh and dwelt among men. For proof of it in relation to the Spirit, reference may be made to such passages as these: "My Spirit shall not always strive with men" (Gen. vi. 3); the prayer of David, "Cast me not away from Thy presence; and take not Thy Holy Spirit from me;" the message to Zerubbabel, "Not by might, nor by power, but by my Spirit, saith the Lord." It is plain then that the theologians have rightly interpreted Scripture, when they have spoken of Father, Son, and Spirit as alike eternal, without beginning and without end.

But, though the Word is eternal, the Incarnate Word had a beginning; and though the Spirit is eternal, the Indwelling Spirit dates from Pentecost. When Jesus was born in Bethlehem, the Eternal Word was made flesh and dwelt among us; when the 120 were all with one accord in one place on the day of Pentecost, the Eternal Spirit came as the Spirit of the Son to dwell in human hearts. The two events, the two great Advents, are most closely related; and it is of great practical importance to keep the relation between them clear and full in our minds. The Incarnation prepared the way for the Indwelling; the Indwelling crowned the Incarnation by rendering it practically universal and perpetual.

The connection between the one and the other is most

THE INDWELLING SPIRIT.

clearly and beautifully brought out in our Lord's discourse to His disciples in the upper chamber. We may say that the key to the right view of the subject is to be found in the great word "Comforter," which is used by our Lord so frequently and so significantly in giving the promise of the Spirit. It is a translation of the Greek word "paraclete," meaning literally *one summoned to our side*, a word frequently employed in ordinary Greek to denote an advocate in a court of law, and also in a more general sense, a counsellor, keeper, strengthener, comforter. The delightful old English word Comforter has been wisely retained by the revisers, with such marginal alternatives as to keep before the mind the fact that the word in the original is much wider in meaning than ours, and that the idea of Advocate especially (by which the same word is translated in 1 John ii. 1, and which is really the Latin equivalent of the Greek " paraclete ") must not be left out.

Is it not to be regretted that this title, which seems intended, by the way it is used in Scripture, to connect as closely as possible the Incarnate Word and the Indwelling Spirit, should have been so restricted in its use among Christians as almost to lose the connection? "The Comforter," "the Paraclete," is always understood of the Spirit; and it seems rarely to suggest itself to the minds of Christians that the Lord "Jesus" has equal claim to the title. Observe how the Saviour expresses Himself. The first form in which He puts the promise is this: "I will pray the Father and He shall give you *another* Comforter,' thus plainly intimating that He Himself was the one Comforter and the Holy Spirit the other. And that the title still belongs to Him, now that He has gone to the Father, is evident from the use of it as applied to Him in the Epistle of St. John. Let us then remember, not only that the word "Comforter" is one of the titles of the

Lord Jesus Christ, but that it is *His* first, that *He* was the Comforter of His disciples while He was with them on earth, and that, in order to console them in prospect of His leaving them, He promised to send them " another Comforter." Clearly, then, the idea of the word " Comforter," which is so pointedly used by our Lord to express the relation the Holy Spirit would thereafter sustain to His people, is to be found in the relation of Christ to His disciples—that close, tender, sympathetic, familiar, endearing relation which He sustained to them when He was on earth. This was manifestly quite different from anything that Abraham, or Moses, or David, or Isaiah, or any of the Old Testament saints ever experienced God was a helper to them, a counsellor, a friend, a comforter too, in the ordinary sense of the English word; but He did not stand to them in that very familiar, endearing, and brotherly relation which our Lord held to His disciples, and in virtue of which He called Himself their " Paraclete."

All this sets in a clear light what has brought difficulty and perplexity to many, the constant reference to the gift of the Spirit at Pentecost as something new. It is not simply spoken of as a larger measure of what had been enjoyed before, which is all that many interpreters make of it, but as something quite different from the previous visitations of the Spirit. It is spoken of as an advent, just as definitely as the advent of the Son of God into the world is spoken of; and the two advents are to be regarded in precisely the same light. When the Word was made flesh, it was not simply another added to the many manifestations of God which the saints of old had enjoyed; it was something entirely new. The newness, however, did not consist in the coming of a new Person, for it was the Son of God Who, as the Angel of the

Covenant, had appeared to the Patriarchs, to Moses, and to the Prophets. It was not then the mere coming which was the new thing, but the coming in the flesh, the coming as a Brother, the coming as a Comforter, one *summoned to our side,* to be always ready to guide and comfort, and help in every time of need. But now the question comes, How long is this relation of "Comforter" to continue? Only for a few years? Must the far off relations of the old dispensation be brought back again? When the Lord Jesus returns to His Father, shall His disciples no longer know Him as their Brother, their familiar sympathising Friend, their Comforter? The Saviour's promise proves that there are better things in store. It is as if He said, "I, your Comforter, must go, but another Comforter will come, one as tender, as sympathetic, as condescending, as brotherly, as truly a Comforter as I have been, and one, too, who will not leave you in a short time as I must do, but who will abide with you for ever. And Who is this Comforter to be? The Holy Spirit—He who has often visited the children of God from the beginning, even as I visited them before I came in the form of a Brother, but who will no longer come as He came before, a heavenly visitor, to gladden you for a time, but as a Comforter, to abide with you for ever."

What we have learned by an examination of the first form of the promise, is still further confirmed by the way in which it is put the next time that the "Comforter" is mentioned. "These things have I spoken unto you, while yet abiding with you. But the Comforter, even the Holy Spirit, whom the Father will send *in My name,* He shall teach you all things." He Who came before as the Spirit of God is now to come as the Spirit of the Lord Jesus, Whose human heart has beat like ours, Whose eyes have shed the bitter tear, Whose feet have trod the dusty highway, Whose arms have been outstretched to heal the leper and to raise the dead, Who took little children in His bosom, Who with the tender tones of His human voice called all the weary to come to Him for rest, Who hung upon the accursed tree and lay in the lonely grave for love of lost sinners of mankind. His coming is to be, to all intents and purposes, the coming of the Lord Jesus Himself; and accordingly He again and again puts the same promise in that simple way: "I will not leave you comfortless, *I* will come to you." (See No. V. p. 83.)

From this point of view we can readily understand why the " other Comforter " could not come till the Lord Jesus had gone to His Father. It was necessary that the manifestation of God in the flesh should be perfected before the Spirit could fulfil the promise, " He shall take of Mine and shall show it unto you." The death of Christ, His burial, His resurrection, His ascension, His intercession, were all parts of that truth which the Spirit was to use as His rod and staff for His people's comfort, and He must wait till all things are ready. Still more, it was only on the ground of the finished and accepted work of the first Comforter that the second could come at all. It is no light thing that the Spirit of the Living God, Who " is of purer eyes than to behold evil," should enter into such familiar relations with the sons of men; and, before it could be, it was necessary that atonement should be made and accepted—an atonement on the ground of which He would be entitled to ask the bestowment of the gift. "*I will pray the Father,*" He says, and He will send you the Comforter. But after all things had been accomplished; after the atonement which had been made on earth was accepted in heaven; after " God manifest in the flesh" had been "justified in the Spirit;" after He had "by Himself purged our sins," and "sat down on the right hand of the Majesty on high;" then the great promise was fulfilled, then the Spirit of the Living God came down to earth as He had never come before, came into relations with human hearts such as Eden itself had never witnessed, into relations as close, as tender, as brotherly as those which the Blessed Lord had held to the nearest and dearest of His disciples, caught up the features of that face which death had covered from His dear ones' eyes, to flash them in upon the souls of true believers with a steady light that never should be quenched—took up those tender tones which had passed so quickly into silence, to make them thrill for ever in His people's hearts—took these seeds of divine truth which the great sower had scattered around Him, to work them out to leaf and flower and fruit in human hearts—took that peerless, perfect Human Life, to set it all as if transfigured, bathed in heavenly lustre before the admiring eyes of those who had wondered what He meant when He said to them, "A little while and ye shall not see Me; and again a little while and ye shall see Me, because I go to My Father." In a word, the new gift was the gift of the perpetual and universal presence with all His people of the Lord Jesus, the Man of Sorrows, the kinsman Redeemer, by an entirely new manifestation of the Spirit, in like manner as the Incarnation had been an entirely new manifestation of the Son. Was not this something new indeed? Was it not something far better than Abraham, or David, or Moses, or any of these ancient worthies ever enjoyed? It is *the* unspeakable gift, sealed and made an heritage to the Church for ever. "God so loved the world that He gave His only begotten Son;" and that only begotten Son, having by His atoning death taken away the sin of the world, gave His Holy Spirit, full of grace and truth and tender human love, to abide with His redeemed ones evermore.

May we not say then that the Indwelling crowns the Incarnation by giving it universality and perpetuity? When the Spirit takes possession of the hearts of Christ's people, is not God manifest in them? The Apostle Paul at all events does not hesitate to put it so: " I am crucified with Christ, nevertheless I live; yet not I, but Christ liveth in me," and again, speaking in the name of all true believers: "We are members of His body, of His flesh, and of His bones." And from this point of view we see a new light in those words of the Saviour in reference to the coming of the Comforter· "At that day ye shall know that I am in the Father, and ye in Me, and I in you." This was a knowledge which the saints of old had not at all. Nor did the disciples of Christ reach it in the days of His flesh. It was with the greatest difficulty that they could rise even to a vague conception of the truth that He was in the Father, and they had as yet no experience of being in Him, and He in them. But to those who have received the Spirit it is a matter of familiar knowledge. Not that they understand these mysterious relations; but that they know them as facts of experience. As the Apostle John puts it: "We know that the Son of God is come, and hath given us an understanding, that we may know Him that is true, and we are in Him that is true, even in His Son Jesus Christ." The illustration of the vine and the branches comes home as a shadow of the true vine and its branches—they in Him by faith as the branch is in the vine from which it draws its life, He in them by His Spirit as the sap of the vine stalk is in the branch through which it flows. As there was a "body of Jesus"* in which the Spirit of God dwelt on earth, so there is a "body of Christ,"* embracing all who believe in Him throughout the wide world, in which the Spirit of Christ dwells. The Indwelling of the Spirit is, so to speak, the diffusion of the Incarnation, the consummation of which will be reached when "we all come in the unity of the faith and of the knowledge of the Son of God, unto a perfect man, unto the measure of the stature of the fulness of Christ."

* These expressions are never used as synonyms in Scripture. The first always means the natural, the second always the mystical, body.

X.

ELEMENTAL EMBLEMS OF THE SPIRIT.

AIR—WATER—FIRE.

ACCORDING to the Ancients, there were four elements —Earth, Water, Air, Fire. These formed an ascending scale, from Earth (which stood for all that was heavy, gross, dark—in a word, "earthy") to Fire, which seemed a thing of Heaven. Water and Air held an intermediate position between Earth and Fire, but had their associations with the higher rather than the lower. Earth alone was positively gross. All the rest were refined, and had, moreover, refining and purifying power. Water was much less gross in texture than Earth, more mobile, more alive, and had, besides, the power of giving to Earth whatever life it had; for waterless earth is always desert. Then, it was pure, except where Earth mixed with it and stained it; and it had the beneficent power of washing earth-stains away.

Air, again, was still more refined than Water, lighter, more ethereal, more mobile; invigorating, fresh, pure, except when charged with earthy particles—soot, or smoke, or dust, or something foreign to its native purity; and then it was specially associated with life—for man lives in the Air and by the Air, and only when he is ready for the grave, does Earth receive him to itself. Fire, as we have said, was highest of all. It seemed a thing of

Heaven come to Earth. Hence the old theory of Prometheus stealing fire from Heaven—a fable which, like many of its kind, is more than fable—for is not the Fire element heavenly in its origin as none of the others are? Our water, and our air even, are our own, all contained within earth's envelope or sphere; but our light and heat, our fire, comes to us from another orb, far away; is stolen, as it were, from Heaven. And this is even truer than it seems, as science has made plain by teaching us that the hidden fires of coal and all inflammable substances are "imprisoned sunbeams" of long ago. See, too, how much of the heavenly nature is in this Fire element. It shines with its own light, it is full of life and action—life and action not given to it, as when you throw a stone or set a stream of water running down a slope, but life and action which seem to come out of its own being; and see how it diffuses the warmth and light of Heaven through the darkness and cold of Earth; and, while all other things tend downward, it always soars, as if struggling to get back to its native Heaven.

We know, of course, that these old world ideas were not scientifically correct; but there was, and there is, a great deal in them. They give at least phenomenal truth; and they are full of poetry, which is, after all, deepest truth; and, so looked at, they help us to appreciate the wealth of Scripture imagery, especially in relation to the Holy Spirit and His cleansing, quickening, and refining power. Man as a sinner is "of the earth, earthy"—dull, heavy, dark, dead. God's Spirit comes to him like water, like the wind, like fire (for these are the three great symbols of the Spirit; the others are subordinate to these, as, for example, the oil which feeds fire, or the dove which is the visible embodiment of the light and air-like visitation of the Spirit), bringing life, and purity, and refinement, and all good things, from the heavenly sphere. Earth, dark as it is, and dead as it is when left to itself, is yet stored with abundance of life germs, remaining dormant and to all appearance quite dead till "the scent of water makes them bud;" and then up into the air they grow; on it and by the water they feed, every leaf a lung, and every rootlet a mouth, while by the grace of light and heat they come to lovely flower and luscious fruit. Is there not a whole world of wealth of poetic imagery in these old elemental emblems? We can do little more than show the way to some of it.

I. Let us begin with the wind or the AIR, as the first and simplest—first, for the very word for "Spirit" in the language of the Bible, as in almost all languages, means breath, or air; and simplest, as containing the most elementary conceptions of the Spirit's person and work, and therefore used by our Lord in giving to Nicodemus his first conception of the higher things of the new dispensation. At first, indeed, it seems disappointingly negative in its suggestions. Air cannot be seen, it cannot be felt, and when you seem to hear it coming as wind, it is only "the sound thereof," it is known only by its effects; and then it "bloweth where it listeth," having apparently no law but its own arbitrary will; and "thou canst not tell whence it cometh or whither it goeth"—all negative and disappointing—it starts in the unknown, it leads to the unknown, its ways are unknown, it is itself unknown; it is all unknown, unknown; must we then be Agnostics, and have nothing to do with it?

But we cannot. Notwithstanding all its mystery, there it is, and we cannot get away from it. Though we do not see it, and even when we do not feel it, it is all about us, in close relation to us, and our very life depends on it. It is true we are in the habit of treating it as if it were nothing. We use it as a symbol of unreality and emptiness; and yet nothing is more real, nothing more vital to our well-being, more necessary to our very being. And, again, we use it as a symbol of fickleness and inconstancy; and yet there is nothing in all nature on which we can more certainly and absolutely depend. Though we can never tell "whence it cometh or whither it goeth," we are always sure of it wherever we go, into whatever treeless desert or waterless waste—when everything else fails us, air fails us never—we are always sure of it just when and where and in what quantities we need. It amounts to this, that so long as we make a mere study of this subtle breath that breathes around us, it is full of mystery and of insoluble difficulty, and the more we try to enter into it and understand it, the more lost we are and ready to take refuge in the convenient retreat of the Agnostic; but when we cease to perplex ourselves as to whence it cometh, or whither it goeth, or what it is, and just take it as it is, open our windows and doors and let it in, or go out into the fields and let it blow around us, we find it all we could desire, and in it life, and health, and satisfaction.

"So is every one that is born of the Spirit." The Spirit cannot be seen, nor grasped by the hand, nor comprehended by the intellect; but He is near, He is all about us. It is seldom that His presence makes itself felt in any startling way. Once in a long time it seems as if there came from heaven a "mighty rushing wind;" but usually it is more like the soft wing and quiet footsteps of the dove. It is like the gentle breeze which finds a tongue in the murmur of the leaves, so that its voice is easily missed. But at any time we have only to get away from the noise and bustle of the world, and, having hushed to rest all the uneasy motions of our own spirits, to wake up our hearts to listen, and we shall certainly hear the voice of God—it may be in awful tones, like the moaning of the pine-trees in the dark, or even terrible, like the rush of the tempest, so as to compel the cry, "What must I do to be saved?" or in its more familiar tones of gentlest whisperings, like these: "Come unto Me, and I will give you rest;" "Thy sins are forgiven thee; go in peace."

"At any time?" But the "wind bloweth where it listeth," and how can I make sure of it when I list? Look at the symbol once again. Little as we know of the motions of the wind, and impossible as we find it to control its currents, there is one thing we know for certain, that wherever we make space for it, in it will come. The house a man lives in may be full of the most noxious gases, and so long as he keeps open drains beneath it, and these never cease to send up their noisome exhalations, there must be death in the house; but if only he will close these drains, or have them flushed and cleansed, and then open his doors and windows, death will be driven out, and life and health will come in. He does not need to know all about meteorology to be sure of this; he may be totally ignorant of ventilation, or even thoroughly sceptical about it; but common-sense will tell him that he has only to trust the wind; let it blow as it list, no matter "whence it cometh or whither it goeth," he has only to let it in; and presently the house will be clean, and sweet, and wholesome, and will remain so, if he in the first place has thoroughly cleansed it, down to the very foundation, and in the second place opens the windows often enough to let in a fresh supply. Is it not then a good thing, after all, that "the wind bloweth where it listeth"? So long as it always listeth to bring such blessings on its wings to all who make it welcome, let it blow on, however little we understand about it, however helpless we may be when we try to command it otherwise than as it listeth.

The supply is unfailing. For, while the air we breathe is the most valuable and indispensable of all the gifts of God to men, it is the one of all others that has been given in greatest abundance The supply is inexhaustible; and the poorest is as welcome to it as the richest. Men may buy and sell the earth on which we tread. Even water must often be bought with money; and there are places where it is not to be had at all. Light is bought and sold, heat is bought and sold; but atmospheric air never. Men have to purchase horse-power, water-power, steam-power; but the power of the wind is free to all. Free as the air we breathe, or the wind that blows around us is, the Spirit's quickening grace. None can buy it, none can earn it, but all may have it in rich abundance if only they will ask it—in unmeasured quantity, one might say; for it is true, just as it is true of the air, with this qualification, that the measure is limited only by the capacity of that which is open to receive it. "Open thy mouth wide and I will fill it." Blessed be the God and Father of our Lord Jesus Christ for the royal bounty of His Spirit's grace as set before us in the, at first sight disappointing, but in the end most satisfactory and encouraging, symbol of *the air*.

II. We now pass to the symbol of WATER. But before doing so let us endeavour to get some idea of how the two symbols of air and water stand related to each other. The research of modern science has brought out the fact that this air which breathes around us, even when it seems most utterly transparent, is laden with germs of life; and wherever there is susceptibility for their development, nothing more than contact is needful to secure it.

Take off the seal from the infusion, expose the surface, and life will spring up at once.

Now, the susceptibility for development of which we have spoken consists especially in the presence of water. Without water there can be no springing up of life. We know how absolutely necessary it is to all forms of vegetable life—waterless land is always desert; and we have learned from recent experiments that in the same way it is only when a watery surface is exposed to the air that the germs with which the atmosphere is stored awake to life. Bearing this in mind as the link of connection between air and water as to the development of life, let us now proceed to consider the truth concerning the Spirit as set forth in the water symbol.

There are so many passages in which the Spirit is set forth under this symbol that it is not necessary to refer to them, further than to call to mind that just as the word "spirit" suggests the symbol of air, the way in which the Spirit is most frequently promised suggests the symbol of water: "I will *pour out* My Spirit." Perhaps, however, one very definite passage may be referred to, that in which the Lord Himself, after speaking of Himself as the fountain, refers to the flowing of the waters, and adds, "This spake He of the Spirit." More of this anon.

We have seen that the emblem of the air applies readily to the universal presence of the Spirit of God in all places and at all times; but this one of water suggests some manifestation of the Spirit which is not equal everywhere and always, but is found here and there, like fountains and springs, and now and then, like dew and showers, and which, instead of moving hither and thither, like the wind, which "bloweth where it listeth," flows in certain channels, like our streams and rivers. Accordingly, we find that whenever the symbol of water is used, the reference is to the Spirit of the Lord, not as everywhere present, but always in relation to some particular man or men who have thus become fountains of living waters. The well-known prophecy, "A man shall be as rivers of water in a dry place," is fulfilled first in Christ (the anointed One, anointed with the Spirit), who received the Spirit without measure, and who is therefore the fountain-head of all living waters; and next in those who have received of His Spirit, and who thus in their turn become fountains or rivers.

The symbol is even more appropriate than at first appears. We have learned from chemistry that between air and water there is one element in common, and that the great life-giving element of each—viz., oxygen. But there is this difference, that the oxygen of the air is free —*i.e.*, uncombined with any other element; while in water it exists only in combination with another element. It is oxygen that gives value to water as well as to air; but in the air it does its work immediately and directly, in its own name, so to speak; in the other case it does its work mediately—not as oxygen, but as water. Now let us think, alongside of this, of the ways in which the Spirit of God reaches us. First, His presence is diffused everywhere, like the air, and we have only to open our hearts to Him to have Him come to us immediately and directly, as the Spirit of God, like the wind which "bloweth where it listeth." But besides this, He has entered into combination with the human spirit, so that human life and thought and feeling have been, so to speak, saturated with His grace. Thus it was that "the prophecy came not of old time by the will of man" merely, but "holy men of God spake as they were moved by the Holy Ghost." This "speaking in the Spirit" is the flowing of the waters; and hence it comes to pass that this water symbol is so constantly associated with the Word; as, for example, when the Church is spoken of as " sanctified and cleansed with the washing of water *by the Word.*" The Word is the water, but what is the oxygen that gives it its value? It is the Holy Spirit's grace. He comes, not in His own name, but through the medium of the Word; just as the oxygen, which in the air is free, comes, unrecognised perhaps, but really comes, through the medium of the water. Thus in the water, which, unlike the omnipresent air, springs from a particular point and flows in certain well-defined channels, we have a fitting emblem of the Spirit of God *as poured out upon men,* who become, as it were, channels of divine grace flowing forth from them to others. Then, just as oxygen in both its forms is necessary to life—for we cannot live without water any more than without air—so in order to spiritual life we must have the Spirit in both His manifestations: " Except a man be born *of water and of the Spirit* he cannot enter into the kingdom of God." It will not do for a man to shut his Bible, and turn away from Christ and His apostles and prophets, and say, " Why should I trouble myself about what Moses, or David, or Isaiah, or John, or Paul, or even Christ has said? Is not God's Spirit present everywhere, and cannot He speak to me directly? My temple is this great universe, my God is the God of great Nature, who can speak to me as well in the green fields, or on the purple hills, or in the light of setting suns, or in the moaning of the lonely sea, as He can speak to you in your little church, or from your Bible, or through the life and lips of Jesus of Nazareth." Perhaps that might have sufficed if it had not been true that " that which is born of the flesh is flesh," while only " that which is born of the Spirit is Spirit." It might have been sufficient if we had been not carnal at all, but spiritual, our souls in closest touch with the omnipresent Spirit of God, ourselves pure and holy, with no earthliness or sin to hinder our receptivity of the divine. But manifestly it is not so. None of us is thus receptive of the divine. Hence we must have the divine brought nearer to our capacities as men, mortal men of flesh and blood. So the Word must become flesh and dwell among us. We cannot reach God in any independent fashion. We cannot "by searching find out God." The result of any such quest must be, as we find in these days it is, the void of Agnosticism. We must find a point of contact, of vital contact with the Spirit of God, and this is found only in His Son Jesus Christ. He was filled with the Spirit of God, and when we are united to Him by a living faith, by the loving trust of the soul, the contact is established—and then, like the rush of healing, cooling, refreshing, life-giving waters, the Spirit of God flows in upon our souls.

We can now see why it is necessary to welcome the Spirit in both His manifestations in order that we may be quickened and refreshed. There must be first the Word, saturated with the Spirit's grace, the Holy Scriptures which testify of Christ the living Word; but this is not sufficient; for how often are the Scriptures read, even read with attention and interest, without any saving result; and that not only when the Gospel is scornfully rejected, but even when it is respectfully listened to. What is wanting? Is not the Spirit there in the Word? Yes; but He must also be welcomed immediately and directly, coming as the air or breath of God. As we read or hear the Word, we must lift up our souls in prayer for the coming of the Spirit directly to our own minds and hearts that He may quicken into life the seeds of truth it carries. "The Spirit breathes upon the Word," and it becomes living waters to our thirsty souls.

But the symbol of water carries us further than this. It has important teaching, not only as to the way in which life is received, but as to the way in which it is communicated to others. On that great occasion when the waters from the fountain of Siloam were poured out beside the altar, and, amid the rejoicing throng, Jesus stood and cried, "If any man thirst, let him come to Me and drink," He did not stop there, but went on to say, "He that believeth on Me, out of his inmost life shall flow rivers of living water. This spake He of the Spirit which they that believed on Him should receive." Already this had been realised in the case of those "holy men of old," who "spake as they were moved by the Holy Ghost;" but the time was coming when it should be a promise for all: "It shall come to pass in those days that I shall pour out My Spirit *upon all flesh.*" Every believer in Jesus was now called not merely to drink himself, but to become a fountain of living water to others. As the prophet Joel put it in a less known portion of his great Pentecost prophecy, "It shall come to pass in that day that . . . *all the brooks* of Judah shall flow with waters." In the olden time there had been here and there a man "like *rivers* of water in a dry place"—a Moses, a David, an Isaiah; but now "all the *brooks*" are to "flow with waters."

For an illustration of the fulfilment of the promise on the largest scale we cannot do better than look at the great change that passed over the disciples at Pentecost. They had been drinking of the fountain all the time of their discipleship; but only then did they become fountains themselves; only from that time did the rivers of living water begin to flow from them. And think what rivers they were! Think of John—his life saturated with the

Spirit of his Master, sending forth constant streams of blessing for nearly seventy years; his gospel, no mere record, as of a scribe, every sentence of it flowing, not from his pen, not from his fingers, not from his mind merely, but from the inmost recesses of his soul; his letters so instinct with the life of his Master, so full of His Spirit of love and tenderness; his Apocalypse,—what an opening of Heaven that has been, not to John himself merely, to make up for the shutting of earth, but to what multitudes since then! We get bewildered with the magnitude of that one man's influence for good; but take a little portion only as a sample. Suppose we could trace the history of the last two chapters of the Book of Revelation down the ages, and get some idea of the comfort and refreshment and revival they have brought to human lives, would it not be a most wonderful story, a new Apocalypse? Was not his own symbol a prophecy of it, " a river of water of Life proceeding out of the throne of God and of the Lamb"? God and the Lamb were enthroned in his heart, therefore from its recesses these rivers have flowed. And so will it be, in measure, with all hearts where God and the Lamb are enthroned. We cannot all be Johns, indeed; but according to our capacity and opportunity we may be fountains of living waters, and all of us to a much larger extent than we are apt to imagine. It might be presumption, indeed, for me to expect that out of my poor little life should flow such streams of living power. But it is not from me,* it is from the Christ-life in me that they are to flow. "He that believeth on Me, out of him shall flow." "This spake He of the Spirit." The man is only the channel. The Spirit is the living water, and though it might be vain for a man to think he could be a *source* of blessing, may

---

* "Behold THY POUND hath gained ten pounds"

he not be a *channel* of it? Look at John again; what could he have done as John? Probably no more than any John among us. May there not then be for any believer, not, of course, the special usefulness of the Apostle, but something, at all events, far removed from the commonplace or the poor; something really worthy of Christ, from whom the Spirit comes, and of the Spirit Himself; something far beyond what apart from the power that worketh in us "we could even ask or think"? And if it is still difficult to entertain such large expectations, we may be helped to it by remembering that our lives do not stand alone. Each life influences many other lives. There is no follower of Christ, however obscure, who might not be the means of bringing to life some other soul, from whom rivers of living water might flow. And why only one? Why not two, three, four, more, many more? And if so, at once we are launched on streams flowing out into the plain of the future, with ever larger possibilities as time passes on. Thus in grace, as well as in nature, the tiniest stream may in process of time become a very Amazon. "He that believeth on Me, out of his inmost life shall flow *rivers* of living water."

If individual life have such promise and potency, what shall be said of Church life? Recall the striking vision of Ezekiel in his forty-seventh chapter, of the waters issuing from the House of the Lord close beside the altar, rising first to the ankles, then to the knees, then to the loins, then to the depth of a great river to swim in, and so flowing on and on, carrying life and verdure and blessing all along its course, through the wastes of the wilderness of Judah, and at last sweetening the waters of the Dead Sea itself. What a grand ideal of the Church, and Church life and power—partially realised at Pentecost, where we can see the waters issuing from beside the great world-altar at Jerusalem, from beside the cross on which Christ, "lifted up," began to "draw all men unto Him;" we can see them flowing on through Judea, and Samaria, and Galilee, and Cyprus, and Asia Minor, and Macedonia, and Greece, and Rome, and westward, westward; we can see them even sweeten the waters of the Dead Sea of Roman corruption and barbarian brutality—we can trace it all in history; not that the vision is fully realised, but enough to give an earnest of its final accomplishment, as sketched in the Apocalypse of Patmos: "And he shewed me a pure river of water of life, clear as crystal, proceeding out of the throne of God and of the Lamb. In the midst of the street of it, and on either side of the river, was there the Tree of Life, which bare twelve manner of fruits, and yielded her fruit every month; and the leaves of the tree were for the healing of the nations. And there shall be no more curse."

That is the final fulfilment, the realisation of the true ideal of Church life and power. Meantime, why should we not approximate it, seeing the Pentecostal blessing is still at our disposal as fully as ever? It is hardly possible to overestimate the power for good even of a small community of Christians, if only they would make the promises of Christ their own, and yield themselves, emptied of self and sin, to be filled with the Spirit, so that it might be said of them as it was prophesied of the first little church in Judah: "It shall come to pass in that day that all the brooks of Judah shall flow with waters." And if such is the power of a single little community filled and flowing with the Spirit of Life, what might we not expect if the whole Church to-day were so filled with the Spirit? And why not? Why should there not be a general waiting on the Lord, "until the Spirit be poured out from on high, and the wilderness become a fruitful field, and the fruitful field be counted for a forest"?

III. The highest symbol of the Spirit's power still remains, that of FIRE The symbol of air belongs to all dispensations alike, but it was specially characteristic of the Old Testament. "Whither shall I go from Thy Spirit? If I ascend up to Heaven, Thou art there; if I take the wings of the morning, and dwell in the uttermost parts of the sea, Thou art there"—such utterances as this show how fully the Old Testament saints realised the omnipresence of the Divine Spirit, so well set forth in the air symbol, which is embodied in the very name by which He was known. Water is also frequently used in the Old Testament as a symbol of the Spirit, but almost always in the way of prophecy, pointing on to the time of the Incarnation, when it becomes prominent. The meaning of the symbol was not fully unfolded until Christ, first at "Jacob's Well," and then at Jerusalem in connection with the pouring out of the water from the pool of Siloam, set forth Himself as the fountain and His people as the rivers to convey the grace of the Spirit of God, the Water of Life, to a thirsty and sinful world. These waters were to flow on through the next dispensation; but inasmuch as they took origin from Christ Himself, they may be reckoned as pertaining to the time of the Incarnation But there still remains a symbol which is the special property of the dispensation under which we live, beginning at Pentecost, and is therefore known as "the dispensation of the Spirit." In the Old Testament the Spirit was known under the symbol of the air, and promised under the symbol of water. In the time of Christ the Spirit began to be known under the symbol of water, and was promised under a new symbol, as in these striking words of John the Baptist: "He shall baptize you with the Holy Ghost *and with fire.*" In accordance with this, the outward accompaniment of the Pentecostal baptism was the appearance of "tongues of fire"—*tongues,* the old idea of the Word, which, as we found, was symbolised in the water; but now it is not merely a word like flowing waters, but like spreading *fire.*

Fire had been from the beginning a symbol of the Divine presence, as every reader of the Bible knows; but now it is set apart as the distinctive symbol of the Spirit since the exaltation of Christ. We found in the beginning that while air and water belong to earth, fire is a thing of Heaven; they are of this little planet, it is of the great and distant sun. It seems especially appropriate, then, that after the Ascension the blessing of the Spirit coming down from the heavenly throne should be set forth under the symbol of fire. And we have now reached a point of view in which we can see also the naturalness of the order in which the symbols are developed in the Scriptures. If it had been a simple ascending scale, it would have been first water, then air, and lastly fire. But it is not an ascending scale. There is a deep descent into the valley of humiliation, followed by an ascent to the throne. Even in the Old Testament God humbled Himself to dwell among men in the spiritual sense—a presence which is fitly symbolised by the air which is all about the earth, but not at all of it. It was a much deeper humiliation when He "became flesh and dwelt among us," a presence which is, as we have seen, appropriately represented as living waters issuing from an earth fountain and flowing along earthy channels. But now He that first descended has ascended above all Heavens, and so His presence among us now is most fitly represented under the heavenly emblems of light and heat that come down to us from the sun, or, to put all in a single word—the emblem of fire.

At first sight, indeed, it does seem strange that the same thing could possibly be represented under symbols so utterly diverse as those of water and fire, which seem to be sworn foes, mutually destructive. But this is only to a superficial view. Modern chemistry and physics have taught us not only that the life-giving element in air and water is the same, but that this same oxygen, so potent in its life-giving power in the air and in the water, is equally potent in the fire. What is fire? It is the combination of this invisible, impalpable, ethereal element with some grosser substance. Take, for example, the familiar case of coal, which is dull, heavy, hard, dead, emphatically " of the earth, earthy," until this wonderful ethereal element combines with it; and then it lives, it leaps, it glows, it sparkles, it soars, develops latent power in the most marvellous manner—drives engines, sets whole factories to work, runs trains, does the work of a thousand men or horses—and then ascends into the unseen, claiming no credit to itself, "only remembered by what it has done." So is every one that is touched by the heavenly flame of the Spirit, every one who truly and fully receives the baptism of fire.

This baptism of fire implies both a new *element* of life and a new *energy* of life,—a new element, so that Christians are spoken of as living in the Spirit and walking in the Spirit; and a new energy, for we read equally of the Spirit being in them and working in them. In truth, all the different symbols of which we have been speaking lend themselves to this twofold conception. Air is the element in which we live; but it must enter into us, by the nostrils and lungs into our very blood it must enter, that we may live by it. Then, water, for purposes of cleansing, must be applied from without; but we must also drink it, take it within us, that we may live by it. So in the same way when we would heat a cold iron, we must first put it into fire, so that the heat may be all around it; but presently we find that the heat has entered into it, deep into the inmost recesses of its compact structure. Not only is the iron in the fire, but the fire is in the iron too. The new element around has developed a new energy within. So is every one that is baptized of the Spirit. By faith in Christ we are introduced into a new element of life. We see everything through a different medium—we see in the light of eternity, we judge by the measures of eternity. The temperature is changed; we have passed out of the winter of selfishness into the summer of love— from the region of the cold North and East winds, in which all living things wither and die, into that of the warm South and West winds, whose breath brings life and spreads dewy fragrance all around. Thus genuine faith in Christ changes the very temperature in which we live —it gives us a new environment. But we need not only a new environment, but a new life. When the warm South wind comes, it wakes new life in every bud—some warm germinating power is set to work within—and it is this unseen energy working in millions of life germs and buds which brings about the blessed change that ushers in the summer life and beauty. So is it in the heart of every one that truly believes in Christ. The fire without is answered by the fire within.

This fire within has a twofold energy. It is first a *cleansing* fire. This cleansing agency is, of course, very prominent under the symbol of water. But there is far more energy in this symbol, which suggests the idea of searching, penetrating, resistless agency. There are some stains that water cannot take out. It may be that they are so ingrained in the substance that water only passes over them; or that they are so far within the intricacies of its mechanism or constitution, so out of reach, that no mere washing can touch them. The only way to get rid of such stains is to have them burned out. For while water only affects the outside of a hard substance, fire penetrates the pores; it searches into the inmost recesses of the heavy, hard, compact iron, for example. Its work is thorough. When it changes a substance it changes it through and through, as when the hard rock becomes quick-lime. Such is the cleansing power of the baptism of fire. John's was the baptism of repentance, and when the soldiers asked him, "What shall we do?" he said, "Do violence to no man, neither accuse any falsely, and be content with your wages;" when the publicans asked the question, he said, "Exact no more than is appointed you;" when the people asked him, he said, "He that hath two coats let him impart to him that hath none; he that hath meat let him do likewise." All very good, most valuable, and necessary, but all belonging to the surface of the life, such as the baptism of water might reach. How different from Him that came after him, who searched down to the angry thought, the lustful look, the covetous heart, penetrating to the deepest thoughts and intents of the hidden life of the Spirit! Now, when the Spirit comes in the name of Christ, He carries His cleansing fires right in, in, in, to the deepest recesses of the heart, and burns out the impurity which had been there ingrained, even that which seemed to have become part of our very nature. Oh, are there not many that need this burning out? Do not all need it more or less? Then let us not shrink from it; let us welcome it, let us petition for it: "Come, Holy Spirit, come; come as the fire, the cleansing fire, and make us pure within!"

And why should any one shrink from it? It is no wasting, desolating fire with which He comes; it is the blessed fire of love—a love, however, which has for its counterpart a holy jealousy, keenly sensitive to anything that mars the union of the soul in marriage covenant with the Heavenly Bridegroom—a holy fire of love, which, even as the sun allowed with full ray to stream upon the fire in the grate is supposed first to pale it and then put it out, so, if allowed full play in the heart, will really cause the old wasting fires of lust and passion first to pale and then to perish, quenched in the blessed light and heat of Heaven.

But the energy is not of cleansing merely, but of *quickening* Here again we are on the old ground. We had it in the symbol of the air. We had it also in the symbol of the water. But here again there is an energy in the new symbol of fire which is lacking in the others. Water and air are restoratives. But fire does not merely restore an energy which belongs to the life already. It comes as a new energy altogether, where there was none before—a new energy working all through, making that which was dull before to burn and glow, causing that which before lay useless, only taking up room, like dead coals in a fireplace, to kindle up and live and send out rays of light and heat in all directions, scattering a benign warmth and radiance on all surrounding objects; for the quickening power of fire, while it acts first on the substance itself, making it alive and glowing, never stops there. From the very nature of fire it cannot remain where it is generated—it must give itself out. It is the very law of its being to scatter itself in all directions. We can confine earth in a vessel without any difficulty. With some difficulty we can confine water, making the vessel water-tight. With greater difficulty we can confine air, making the vessel air-tight.

But we cannot confine fire. That same penetrating power, by which it searches its way deep into the hidden structure of that which is exposed to its action, enables it to search its way out, so that, however walled in, with iron, for instance, your fire may be, as in a close stove, it must out in all directions, and so it forces itself through the pores of the iron and radiates heat through all the room. But are there not fire-proof materials ? No doubt there are ; and these materials may be so adjusted, as in a safe, as to keep fire out ; but no safe ever has been made, or could be made, that would keep fire in. Shut it in, give it no outlet, and presently there is none of it—as soon as you confine it, it dies. So is it with the fire of Heaven ; and it is greatly to be feared that many a soul, which has had its early fires of love and devotion repressed by conventional usages warranted fire-proof, has had the fire first burn low, and then lower and lower till it went quite out. It comes to this, then, that this quickening fire *will* find an outlet to warm and quicken others, or it will die. In dealing with the symbol of water, we found it quite possible for the Christian to drink himself, without being a fountain to quench the thirst of others. But this is not possible in the baptism of fire. The blessing comes first, like the other, as a personal blessing ; but it cannot stop there ; from the very nature of it, it is expansive, scattering light and heat, carrying life and blessing to all with whom the fire life is brought into contact.

Here, again, there is not only the irrepressibility of which we have been speaking, but there is far greater energy. Water flows down for the most part gently and quietly, but see how the light flashes and the fire spreads ! Water flows wherever there is a channel for it, but light and fire ask no prepared channels, no beaten track to travel on ; they make a track for themselves anywhere, everywhere, leap over obstacles, or clear them away, and make their power felt in all directions up and across and athwart, as well as down. Such was the power of the little church of one hundred and twenty members on the occasion of the first baptism by fire. Such has been the power of Christians and of churches whenever the promise has been welcomed and its fulfilment realised—a promise, be it remembered, which is as good now as it ever was: "The promise is to you and to your children, and to them that are afar off, even as many as the Lord our God shall call."

And yet it is greatly to be feared that only a very few look for the fulfilment of it, only a very few expect or receive the baptism of fire. It is to be thankfully acknowledged that the promise of the flowing waters is largely realised and fulfilled. It was not always so. A century ago, while there were not a few who quenched their own thirst at the fountain-head, there was very little accomplished in the way of sending streams out from the Church to fertilise the wastes around. But now it is generally understood that churches and congregations of Christians exist not only for their own salvation and edification, but for spreading the Gospel around them. There are channels of work carefully made, and in these channels the living streams do flow. We have our Sunday-school work, and our mission work, and our open-air preaching, and our tract-distributing, and so on, and along these and similar channels flow many life-giving streams. But it is greatly to be feared that we know almost nothing of the baptism of fire. Many Christians seem scarcely ever to think of such a thing, and some would shrink from it as almost a calamity. To have anything so startling would seem quite out of keeping with that quiet and even tenor of our way which seems so proper and becoming. We do not for a moment mean to say that there is no light and no warmth. God forbid! That would mean utter death. There is light and there is heat diffused all through the Church, as light and heat are diffused in the atmosphere on a bright summer day, and in fact even on a cloudy winter day; but what we do mean to say is, that there is very little of that powerful and concentrated light and heat which makes fire, which not only warms but *kindles.* Even the heat of August will not kindle the best set fire. It needs the touch of *flame* to set it going. Only fire can kindle fire in common coal or common clay.

Think for a moment how many fireplaces there are around us, and in the midst of us, too—in the midst of our Christian communities and congregations—how many fireplaces, with fires well laid, fuel all ready, plenty of Christian ideas and knowledge lying there in the minds of our young people and of many who are no longer young, but lying cold and dead, wanting the touch of fire—not the mere general warmth of a Christian atmosphere, but the hot touch of flame, which can come only from a heart baptized with the Holy Ghost and with fire! Now, even if we did not want the baptism of fire for ourselves, if we were content to float along in the accustomed channels of our life, without any sparkle or glow or flame of Christian joy to gladden our course, should we not earnestly desire that we had just a little fire to apply to these cold fireplaces? Do not we parents, who are mourning that our children are so cold in things spiritual, long for just a little of this baptism of fire on ourselves, that we might be able to touch their lives with the heavenly spark? Do not Sunday-school teachers long for it, or for more of it? Do we not all desire to have some share in this blessed work of kindling the flame of heavenly love in human hearts? If only we would all take to ourselves this promise and make it our own, waiting for its fulfilment as the one hundred and twenty did during those ten days, what a change there would be! What a blessed summer-time! What a glow of true devotion and warm brotherly love, and here and there and everywhere what flashes of light and gleamings of flame and kindlings of fuel! And presently our neighbours would feel it, our churches would feel it, other churches would feel it; and who can tell how far the warmth would spread and the light would shine? We were impressed as we thought of the grand possibilities there are for Christians and the Church, in view of the promise of the Spirit under the symbol of water; but they are grander still, especially as regards the prospect of speedy results as we think of the promise of the Spirit under the symbol of fire. It takes time, long time, for the tiny stream to grow into an Amazon; but " see how great a matter a little fire kindleth!" It takes very little time to produce great results with fire. We all know it as regards the destructive energy of earthly fire; it is equally true of the blessed energy of the fire that comes from Heaven. How important, then, that the Church should welcome the promise of the Spirit in all the fulness of life-giving power, which is within her reach in this "dispensation of the Spirit!"

Welcome, Blessed Spirit, in all the fulness of Thy grace, and love, and power; come as the wind to revive us—as water to cleanse and refresh us, and flow through us as channels of grace to others—as fire, to purify us in the inmost recesses of our souls, to quicken us to a warmer and brighter life, and to give us the blessed power of kindling life all round about us. "Come, Holy Spirit, come!"

XI.

THE DEMONSTRATION OF THE SPIRIT.

THERE are none of the heathen philosophers whose writings come nearer to the morality of the New Testament than those of Seneca. Seneca was a contemporary of the Apostle Paul. He must have been born about the same time, though we do not know the precise date in either case. While the youth Seneca was studying under Attalus, the Stoic, at Rome, the young Saul of Tarsus was "sitting at the feet of Gamaliel" at Jerusalem. At about the same time that Saul's conversion severed him from all his former associates, and ushered him into a life of hardship and vicissitude, the rising fame of Seneca for philosophic virtue alienated from him the corrupt Court at Rome, and led the way to many hardships and sufferings. During the quarter of a century which followed, the parallel sadly fails; for, while the path of the Apostle was like "the shining light that shineth more and more unto the perfect day," the path of the philosopher was tortuous and dark. His philosophy deserted him in the hour of need; he became wretched in banishment; and when restored again to Court favour on the accession of Nero, he disgraced himself by apologising for some of that monster's most atrocious crimes. And yet, at the close, the parallel almost reappears, for not only did both fall about the same time by the fury of the same tyrant, but there was a heroism about the death of Seneca, when the worst came to the worst, that, in the view of his admirers, atones to a considerable extent for the weakness and even wickedness of his life, and gives some ground for placing him, in his death as well as in much of his life and his writings, alongside of the great Apostle. It seems certain that St. Paul and Seneca never met, though both may have been at Rome in the year 61 or 62; but, though their paths did not cross, we have an interesting link of historical connection in the fact that on one occasion the Apostle was summarily dragged before the judgment-seat of Seneca's brother Gallio, the pro-consul of Achaia, an incident related in the 18th chapter of the Acts. It is just possible that Seneca may have heard St. Paul's name mentioned by his brother Gallio; but if he did, it is pretty certain that he would regard him with indifference or contempt, as Gallio himself evidently did. There seems, at all events, no reason whatever to imagine for a moment that the philosopher was indebted to the Apostle for the sound philosophy and lofty morality which have made his writings so deservedly famous.

We have had a historical parallel; let us now offer a historical problem founded upon it. The life of Seneca was strangely parallel with the life of St. Paul; the words of Seneca are strangely similar to the words of the Apostle. How comes it, then, that the words of Seneca fell powerless even on the Roman people, and are now read only by a very few scholars and antiquarians, while the words of St. Paul have stirred every community they have reached, have been translated into nearly all the languages of the earth, and have brought instruction, and comfort, and moral strength,—have brought light, and hope, and joy, —to millions of human lives? It is the fashion, in some quarters, to assert or insinuate that the morality of Seneca was little, if at all, inferior to the morality of St. Paul, or even of the Lord Jesus Himself; and this is triumphantly brought forward as telling against the divine claim of Christianity. There are Christians, too, who weakly tremble when such comparisons are made, and think it a serious thing for the Bible that heathen philosophy can be shown even to approach it. But look at it, —look at it,—and it will appear that in this very comparison lies a proof of the strongest kind that Christianity must be of God. If it could be shown that the morality of the New Testament was a thousand times better than that of the noblest and best of the heathen moralists, this difference would at once be seized upon as sufficiently accounting for the peculiar power of Christianity; and so there would be some colour for the cry, " What we want is a pure morality; give us morality, by all means, —more and more of it,—but away with your useless divinity; away with the superstition about the supernatural." But with the pages before us of such men as Socrates, and Plato, and Zeno, and Seneca, and Epictetus, and Marcus Aurelius, it cannot be said that the difference between the power of the moralists and the power of the Christians is accounted for simply by the superiority of the ethics of the latter. The reason must be sought elsewhere; and the question is, Where? Where else can it be found than in the claim of the Apostle himself· " My speech and my preaching was not with enticing words of man's wisdom, but in demonstration of the Spirit and of power; that your faith should not stand in the wisdom of men, but in the power of God"? In other words, the peculiar power on which the Apostle relied for the success of his words was not the morality of them, but the divinity of them. So far as " the wisdom of men" was concerned, there was little more reason why they should do great things for the world than there was that the words of Seneca should; but "*the power of God*,"—*there* was the hope, and *there* we find the only reasonable explanation of the wonderful historical phenomenon at which we have been looking.

In one of his Epistles St. Paul writes: "We have this treasure in earthen vessels, that the excellency of the power may be of God, and not of us." If "an angel from heaven" had been sent to preach the Gospel, the power of it might have been credited to the angel; but when a weak man does it, and results follow, as sometimes they do, which make even infidels amazed, then the obvious inadequacy of the instrument makes it manifest to those who have intelligence enough to appreciate the conclusion, that "the excellency of the power" must be "of God." There may be those of our readers who can remember the time when they were distressed that the Bible had not come to us in what seemed a state of ideal perfection, without anything in it, from beginning to end, that was not clear as a sunbeam, and as free from possible objections as it was conceivable that it should be; but who now perceive that they were entirely wrong. If this book had been any further set apart from other books than it is, men would have said, "The excellency is in the Book, and what wonderful geniuses these men that wrote it must have been;" and the names of Matthew, Mark, and the rest of them would have stood higher in the roll of the world's great ones than those of Plato, or Seneca, or Dante, or Shakspeare. It would have seemed that all the superiority lay in the words, and so the authors of the words would have been almost deified But coming to us as it has come, in such a way as to show that the words are not so much superior after all,— that, so far as "the wisdom of men" is concerned, it is not so very much loftier than the productions of earth's noblest, and wisest, and best; it becomes plain that the secret of its virtue and value is to be sought, not in the words, but in the wondrous power behind the words,—not in " the wisdom of men, but in the power of God."

Let us, by all means, hail the comparisons which are so frequently made between the morality of the Bible and that of the Rig-veda, or the Zend Avesta, or the Stoic philosophy, or the Eddas of our own forefathers. These comparisons are not always fairly made. A few brilliant specimens will be picked out of heaps of rubbish, and presented as a sample of the whole. After all the energy shown in collecting these pearls of heathen philosophy and morality, the Bible still towers manifestly above the highest and best of them, but yet not so much as to give colour to the idea that the superior wisdom of its words supplies the secret of its power. We may well be satisfied to find such possibility of comparison with the writings of moralists as to make it perfectly plain that the power of it cannot lie in its morality, but must be sought where Christ Himself, and His apostles, and all who have any experimental acquaintance with it, unanimously declare it to be found, namely, in its divinity.

A little reflection will show that it is not morality that men want, but divinity; by which is not meant theology, for theology, as it is commonly understood, is only a matter of words; and the whole drift of our reasoning is to show the comparative worthlessness of words in themselves. Not theology, then, but Divine Power is what men want. A distinguished opponent of Christianity is reported to have said, " If a man live only half as well as he knows how in this world, he will be all right in the next.' If this was intended for a sober assurance that when men give an account of themselves to God, on the great day of reckoning, the rate of ten shillings in the pound will be considered ample, we should be disposed to ask by what authority it is said, seeing that conscience and the Bible, the only witnesses of any respectability that even claim to speak authoritatively for God, agree in demanding that we live altogether up to the light we have, and not merely half way. But, taking it not as a sober assurance, but as a *jeu d'esprit*, attention may be called to the underlying fact, which gives it the little piquancy it has, that as a general thing men do not live even "half as well as they know how;" from which the inference is inevitable, that what men want to elevate and improve them is not more light, of which it would seem they have already twice as much as they use, but some power to enable them to do what they are not willing to do—some power to persuade them to live "as well as they know how." Just herein lies the essential weakness of moral lectures, or essays, or preachments; not that moralising is not a good thing,—it is a very good thing,—but it is not the thing men need. What a drunkard needs is, not a lecture on the evils of drunkenness, and the eternal fitness of sobriety, but some power to enable him to stop drinking. What a dishonest man needs is, not to be convinced that dishonesty is wicked, and that "an honest man is the noblest work of God;" that he knows as well as any one else; he needs something to prevail upon him to stop stealing and cheating. And so with all other crimes and sins There are cases, indeed, in which conscience needs to be enlightened; but for one case where enlightenment is required there are thousands where impelling or restraining power is the one thing needful. The difference between Seneca and St. Paul was just this, that one came with the wisdom of words, which men scarcely needed at all; the other came with " the power of God," which men needed above all.

Why do not the admirers of the Stoic philosophy scatter its noble monuments of lofty morality amongst the common people? Why have we not a million or two of Stoic tracts distributed among the criminal classes of our great city populations? Might not a little Stoic Bible be compiled, and a new Bible Society formed to scatter it abroad? We should have no reason to object. It would certainly do no harm. The question, of course, remains whether it would do any good. It may be here asked, however, quite appropriately, "Is not your Bible often just as innocent of results as a Stoic Bible could be? Are there not thousands of people who read it, and do not seem one whit the better for it?" Most true indeed; but in this way you only give a further illustration of our point. The words of the Bible are no better than other good words; and those who do not get beyond the words might almost as well be reading Seneca, or Epictetus, or any other good man. This is just what Christians always say, because it is what the Bible itself says. "It is the Spirit that quickeneth." He uses the Word as His instrument; but the instrument is powerless without the Agent. "My speech and my preaching," says our Apostle, "was in demonstration of the Spirit" To illustrate this point take the words, "Come unto Me, and I will give you rest;" or the words, "Thy sins be forgiven thee; go in peace;" or these, "Seek ye first the kingdom of God, and His righteousness; and all these things shall be added unto you." Whose words are they, and to whom are they spoken? For some people the answer would have to be, "They are the words of a man whom we never saw, and who cannot know us, inasmuch as He died centuries ago; and they were spoken to people we never saw, and of whom, therefore, we know nothing, and about whom we care little." In such a case it is unreasonable to expect that these words should have any power. But there are those who have a very different answer to give; for each of them would say, "These are the words of God, and they are spoken to *me:* I know it, because the Spirit of God has taken these things and shown them to *me:* I cannot explain how He did it; there are few things I can explain, and therefore it is not to be wondered at that I cannot explain this; but somehow or other He has done it; and now I know that these words are God's words to *me*, and the result of it is that I have found rest, and the joy of forgiveness; and whereas once the world was as much to me as it was to any one else, it is so no longer; I do 'seek first the kingdom of God, and His righteousness,' and I find that other things are added to me according to the promise."

The real difference between the Christian and the non-Christian is, not that some wise words have reached the one which have not reached the other, but that God has reached the one and not the other. God has been revealed to the conscience, so that it has become quick and sensitive to sins against God, as well as sins against men; and God has been revealed to the heart, in such a way that he has been constrained to say, "Whom have I in heaven but Thee, O Lord? And there is none in all the earth whom I desire beside Thee." It was not the *words* of the Bible that converted him, but the *God* of the Bible. And all those who will only allow the God of the Bible to do the same for *them*,—will only allow Him to have free access to their conscience and their heart,—will discover what it is to enjoy "the peace of God, that passeth all understanding," and to realise a moral and spiritual strength to which they were strangers before,—will know what it is to feel the constraining power of heavenly love, gradually separating them from worldliness and sin, and leading them up, step by step, into a higher and purer air, with a far wider horizon around them, and an infinitely grander prospect before them.

The power of God can reach no one without his consent; for personal freedom is, and ever must be, a sacred thing; hence one reason why faith is necessary. Faith is the free and willing surrender of the heart and conscience to God as He is made known in Jesus Christ; and, as soon as this surrender is made, there will be the consciousness of a mighty change. The conscience will be much more sensitive, the heart more tender, the will more commanding; the tastes will become purer, the aspirations loftier, the aims nobler, the hopes infinitely brighter; and so great will be the change, that the subjects of it will be fully convinced that no mere words could have brought it about,—that the words of St. Paul were as little adequate for the purpose as the words of Seneca could have been,—that, in fact, it was due to the "demonstration of the Spirit," to the power of God Himself.

The "demonstration of the Spirit;" that is the kind of demonstration that men need. Some people wonder that more is not made of the demonstration of the intellect. If the evidences of Christianity are so thoroughly satisfactory as they are said to be, why not keep at that? Why not bring forth arguments, and answer objections, until men are convinced? The answer is precisely the same as to those who object that the principal place is not given to morality. Morality is good, and evidences are good; and it is well that their place should be given them in public teaching; but neither the one nor the other is what men most need. It is not more light for the intellect that is wanted most; it is Divine power on the conscience and the heart; and this power is not to be had in "the wisdom of men," even when employed in making arguments and overthrowing objections. There is light in the evidences Let any one carefully and earnestly study them, and he will find that there is light. But, alone, it is like the sunlight in winter—beautiful, it may be, and clear, but fruitless, perhaps frosty. Such is the light of the intellect alone. The sun may shine as brightly in December as it did in June; but it has no longer the power it then had to put life into dead nature, to bring out the verdure of the leaf, the beauty of the flower, the richness of the fruit. Why the difference? Simply this, that the pole of our northern hemisphere is then turned away from the sun, and his rays, though bright as ever, fall so obliquely on the surface of the ground as scarcely to affect it; they do not go down into it to warm its bosom. And so, too, as long as the pole of the human conscience is turned away from God, even truth itself, shining ever so clearly, will fail to arrest the advance of approaching winter. If the man would only turn to the Lord, then the power of the truth would reach the conscience, the love of the truth would reach the heart, there would be warmth as well as light, spring would be around him, and summer at hand.

"In Him was life, and the life was the light of men." Observe the order: in Him, life; that life, the light. Those who believe in Him shall live, and in their new life will find a better and brighter light than all the powers of the intellect, or the resources of the evidences addressed to the intellect, can furnish. The "demonstration of the Spirit" is by far the best. It can stand all kinds of objections, as is most strikingly illustrated in the case of the man blind from his birth whom the Saviour cured, and who, to all questions and cavils had one unanswerable reply, "Whether the man be a sinner or no, I know not; one thing I know, that, whereas I was blind, now I see." Finally, this "demonstration" is within the reach of all It only requires hearty willingness, cordial consent, true and earnest desire. "For if ye, being evil, know how to give good gifts unto your children, how much more shall your Heavenly Father give the Holy Spirit to them that ask Him?"

XII.

THE VITALITY OF THE BIBLE.

(A Speech delivered at the Eightieth Anniversary of the Bible Society.)

I WAS reading a little while ago in one of our high-class reviews an article by an exceedingly able writer, in which he made a most important statement. He made it so confidently in the name of the thinking people of the present day that there surely must be something in it, and yet it has seemed to me to be quite irreconcilable, by any logical process I can think of, with the facts of this Report. The statement was to the effect that Bible Christianity was, at the time of writing, in the very article of death. That was a good many weeks ago, and so I suppose it must be quite dead by this time. Now, I am perfectly aware that this is not the first or the second or the hundredth time that wise and learned men have told us that the Bible was dying or dead, but this distinguished writer had actually seen the grave-clothes in which it was to be buried, so there could be no mistake about it this time. Many of you may not have heard of this before, but that is not to be wondered at, for the same distinguished writer speaks with great contempt of Exeter Hall and of all the people who go there! You will not wonder, then, that one who has read this able article should be in a difficulty, and expect to hear to-day of diminished sales and decreasing income, and the approaching collapse of the Bible Society, and to find one of the resolutions a motion to go into liquidation. But I have looked over the whole paper and can find no such motion. On the contrary, we are told of largely increased sales, finances advancing by leaps and bounds, and everything brisk and buoyant and hopeful. There must be some mistake somewhere. It surely cannot be with the distinguished and able writer, considering the constituency for which he spoke. It must, then, be with the stupid people of Exeter Hall. And yet the millions of copies and the hundreds of thousands of pounds! I cannot exactly make out how the stupidity of Exeter Hall can account for all that. And then all other business is so dull, exceedingly dull. I can speak feelingly on that subject, for I have been trying to raise a little money for a church-building fund, and I have been told, with what may be called a painful iteration, that business is very, very dull. I do not know much about business, but I know enough to know that when business generally is dull, business in books is especially dull, and that those who deal in old books have the dullest time of all. Now I am just coming to my difficulty. Here is a publishing Society that confines its operations to one book, and that book the oldest of all; a book with which the market is fairly glutted, hundreds of millions having been discharged into it; a book, moreover, which we learn, on excellent authority, is now quite dead; and yet the Society flourishes! It is not running down, it is running up, and if it were the fashion to quote this sort of stock in the newspapers, I fancy you would need a stronger term than "lively" to indicate the vitality of it.

You see the dilemma I am in. I am forced to one of two conclusions—either we have in all this a veritable miracle of the nineteenth century, to which I am afraid our learned friend would hardly give his assent, or—I shrink from stating the alternative, but I must do it—the statement cannot be quite correct. The Bible cannot be quite dead after all. There must be some life in the old book yet. Perhaps it is the same with the Bible as with some of those who wrote it, who spoke of themselves in a strange fashion, like this: "As dying, and behold we live;" "persecuted, but not forsaken; cast down, but not destroyed; always bearing about in our body the dying of the Lord Jesus, that the life also of Jesus might be made manifest in our mortal flesh." And it has occurred to me that possibly our learned friend may be somewhat like a certain rustic, whom the poet Horace, in a passage exceedingly well known and often quoted, speaks of as standing upon the bank of a river and waiting till it should have flowed past and disappeared; not considering that as the river had flowed on from age to age before he was there, so from age to age it still would flow on after he had vanished from the scene. The streams of the Water of Life are flowing still, and they still will flow; there is no sign of any slacking of the tide, for what is true of the little brook is no less true, but still more true, of this broad brimming river—

> "Men may come, and men may go,
> But I go on for ever."

The constant and ever-increasing demand for the Bible, which is reflected in the wonderful history of this noble Society, is well worthy of consideration, quite apart from a publishing point of view; for what does it mean? It means that this old Book, which it is the work of this Society to circulate, is as young as ever—that it is a Book for the times as much as it ever was. No publisher's device is needed to make it pass off as fresh. Sometimes a publishing firm will take care to put no date on the preface of a book, and no date on the title-page, and, perhaps, will put the word "new" into the title, and stereotype it there, calling it a "new" handbook or a "new" novel; or if they cannot get it into the title they will call it a new edition, in the hope that as years pass on the public will not too curiously inquire how new it is, and what was the date of publication. We need no such devices,—we do not fear the age of this Book. It is hoary with antiquity; and yet, strange to say, it has on it the dew of immortal youth. Our learned friend in the *Review*, and those who think like him, of course demur to this. In spite of the patent fact that its wonderful circulation is increasing every year, they tell us it is out of date. They tell us that, while it may take an honoured place in the literature of antiquity, which has served its time, its day is now past in the estimation of all people of sufficiently advanced thought. But if you were to press them very closely for the ground of their belief it would probably amount to this, that not one of all the sacred writers had ever read a line of Newton's "Principia," or of Darwin's "Origin of Species," or even of the "First Principles" of Mr. Herbert Spencer. But I submit that that has nothing to do with the question. There were, of course, certain notions about the heavens and the earth and the things that are in them, which were prevalent at the "sundry times" when the Scriptures were produced—notions which had no relation whatever—good, bad, or indifferent—to the object with which these Scriptures were written, and therefore those notions were very properly left alone Does any one suppose that Christ would have helped forward His mission if He had set Himself to correct the astronomy and the physics of the schools of Egypt and of Greece? Why, He did not even meddle with the politics of the Roman empire, which very much more nearly concerned His cause; and where would have been the sense of attempting to correct what was wrong in the science of the schools? The same consideration applies all through the Bible. The one subject throughout is God and His salvation; the one object, to save men from sin and bring them to God. When things in Nature are referred to, it is in language which the people of the time could understand. There was no attempt to speak over the little heads of the people of the time to the big folks that live in the nineteenth century, and represent its glorious culture. And accordingly, we even read such statements as these: "The sun ariseth, and the sun goeth down and hasteth to his place where he arose," though every schoolboy knows now that the sun does not arise and does not go down and does not haste to the place where he arose. But my difficulty is, that the almanacs are not corrected yet. If any of you could give me an almanac for 1884, according to modern science, I should be glad to have it. The Bible speaks about Nature in a natural way, in a way that would be natural to the people of the time: and that is what all sensible people do—except when they are weak enough to try to air their learning a little; and that is what all sensible people approve—except when they are very badly off for something to say against the Bible.

There is no pedantry in the Bible, no affectation of scientific accuracy. Great principles are laid down, such as the duty and the delight of searching out the works of God and learning what they tell us of Him—principles which in their application have greatly tended to promote scientific research and discovery. But there is no attempt made, as it is manifestly absurd that any attempt should have been made, to anticipate these discoveries. Remember that, if this work of setting science right had been begun at all, it must have been gone through with. Some people seem to suppose that, if the Bible had only been brought up to the standard of the ninth edition of the "Encyclopædia Britannica," all would have been well. But no, that would not meet the difficulty; because what should we do when the tenth edition came out? You remember what Newton said about gathering a few pebbles by the shore, while the great ocean of truth lay undiscovered beyond. There have been a good many more pebbles gathered since his time, but still there is the great ocean of truth undiscovered beyond; and so, you see, even the whole of the present edition of the "Encyclopædia Britannica" would not have been enough; and even that would have been a little cumbrous to carry about and take to Sunday-school. It is impossible to imagine what the Bible Society would have done if they had had the handling of that huge work; it would have been worse than a white elephant. Think of translating it into 250 languages! Oh, horror! I do not think my friend Dr. Wright would undertake the superintending of such a task. You know the story told by Macaulay about the Italian convict. When sentenced, the judge was kind enough to give him an alternative: he told him he might go to the galleys or read Guicciardini's history. The man very naturally chose to read the history; but after he had gone a certain distance, he changed his mind—it was too hard for him, and so he left the history and went to the galleys. We should have been somewhat in the same condition if we had had the Bible that a number of people think we ought to have had.

The fact is, all this talk about the Bible being out of date in matters of science is so much nonsense. Let us have done with it, and let us ask how the Bible stands on its own ground. How does it accomplish the object which it sets before it? Is it out of date as a book on sin, on righteousness, on salvation? All other books that have been attempted on these subjects, except those which have drawn their inspiration directly or indirectly from the Scriptures, were either out of date at the time they were first produced, or became so in a very few years. The ethical and religious productions of those who made their researches and recorded the results of them apart from the Scriptures,—where are they? Where, for example, are the moralists and philosophers of Greece and Rome? Their works, indeed, are on the shelves of every scholar in Christendom; but in what capacity? As authorities? Not at all, simply as monuments of genius and chapters of intellectual history. Who would ever think, when considering the question, "Wherewithal shall a young man cleanse his way?" of answering it by saying, "By taking heed thereto according to Aristotle's 'Nicomachian Ethics!'" And yet Aristotle's "Nicomachian Ethics" is the very best book ever produced on the subject without aid from revelation. Who would ever think of expecting a soul-satisfying solution to the problem, "If a man die, shall he live again?" in the "Phædo" of Plato, unrivalled as it is among the literature of antiquity on the subject of the soul's immortality? Is there a single Greek or Roman classic on the subject of man's condition and prospects that would be of the slightest use to a soul burdened with sin, or pressed with the weight of this most solemn of all questions: "How shall a man be just with God?" They are out of date— cold monuments of genius, dead relics of antiquity, almost forgotten attempts to sound the mysteries of life and death. And does any one suppose that the new "Data of Ethics," by Mr. Herbert Spencer, or the more recent "Science of Ethics," by Mr. Leslie Stephen, is likely to be the Sunday-school book of the next generation—say one hundred years hence—or to require some monster society to supply an exhaustless demand for it? And if those who are trying their hand in helping out the Bible, or in working along the same lines, get so soon out of date, what shall we say of those who write and fight against it? They go to still swifter and darker oblivion. Where are the authorities of our intelligent sceptical friends of the present day? All among writers of the last few years. And where are all the rest, from Celsus, Porphyry, and Julian downwards? They are all out of date. Most of them have disappeared entirely. They have perhaps gone to Milton's limbo, where all vanities are said to go. Where is the sceptical writer of two thousand years ago, or one thousand, or five hundred, or one hundred, or fifty,—I am almost tempted to come down, like Abraham, to ten, and to ask, Where is one of them that our sceptical friends will stand by, as we stand by Moses and David, by Matthew and Paul? They are all out of date, and their works are to be found, if found at all, amidst the dusty, decaying, moth-eaten relics of the past, in the British Museum, or on the antiquary's bookshelf. But who will venture to predict the time when you will have to ransack the antiquary's library to find a copy of the writings of Moses, David, Solomon, Isaiah, Daniel, Matthew, Paul, or John? These authors are all old, but they are always new. Old as they are, their words are as weighty, as powerful, and as confidently appealed to now as ever, and they are far more widely read to-day than at any previous time.

The path of the Bible is not like the path of the infidel production—a steep descent to dark oblivion—

but it is like the path of those who are justified by its faith, which is as "the shining light which shineth more and more unto the perfect day." In some old Bible of your grandfather, between the leaves which enclose some cherished passage that had often cheered the old man's heart, there is, perhaps, a little relic of the past—a rose leaf, a sprig of heliotrope, a forget-me-not. The colour is gone, the scent has evaporated, even the grace of form is crushed out of all recognition. You must touch it very tenderly, or it will crumble into dust, and be all gone. It abides, after a fashion, as human things abide; it does not live and abide as divine things live and abide. But the promise, over against which the little faded flower is lying, not only abides, but lives—lives! It lives in ten thousand hearts as well as in yours, as rich in colour, as fresh in fragrance, as delightful to the soul as ever it was. "All flesh is grass,"—and even our reviewers come under that head—"All flesh is grass, and all the goodliness thereof is as the flower of the field. The grass withereth, and the flower thereof falleth away; but the Word of the Lord endureth for ever." The Word of God is not like that of Demosthenes or of Cicero, whose speeches may still move to admiration, but can no longer lead men on to action as in the days when they were fresh and strong. The Word of God lives and breathes; lives with the life and breathes with the breath of the Spirit of the living God. This is the secret of its perennial freshness; this is the secret of its immortal youth. "It is the Spirit that quickeneth." "The words that I speak unto you, they are spirit and they are life." Of Homer, and Virgil, and Dante, and Milton; of Aristotle, and Seneca, and Descartes, and Bacon; of Demosthenes, and Cicero, and Burke—it may be said, "he being dead, yet speaketh;" but of the Author of the Bible, and of Him alone, it can be said, "He, being alive, yet speaketh." "The mighty God, even the Lord, hath spoken." And speaketh still: "I am He that doth speak; behold, it is I." The Spirit of God may use, often does use, other books; but He identifies Himself with the Bible. He makes it vocal with His loving voice, and vital with His living power. He breathes through it on the living soul, and thus communicates the life eternal. And so the work of this Society is not that of a mere publishing firm. It is a great missionary work. This Society is called of God to the grandest missionary work—called of God to send forth His light and His truth, His Word of ever-fresh and living power, to the ends of the earth.

XIII.

THE SPIRIT OF THE AGE.

IF we were asked for the thought which is most comprehensively characteristic of the intellectual development of the present generation, we should be inclined to give for answer, "The Reign of Law." On all sides the domain of Law has been extended until, in the minds of many, it bids fair to become universal and absolute. And this ever-widening reign of Law is not by any means confined to the domain of physics; mind as well as matter is now asked to bend beneath its yoke. Men's opinions are discovered to be not their own opinions at all, but simply the product of certain intellectual forces which were in operation before they were born. They think so and so, they believe so and so, just because they happen to have been born in such a country, at such a time, and in such circumstances. Alter a little the circumstances, or the place, or the date of their having come into the world, and their opinions and beliefs will be just so much, or so little, modified. Alter any of these things a great deal, and the difference will be vast. How vastly different would our ideas have been on almost all subjects if we had been born in Siam or in the interior of China; and how vastly different most of them would have been on many subjects if we had been born, even in any Christian land, two or three centuries earlier, or even fifty or twenty years earlier, than we have been!

It is not, indeed, denied that reason and argument enter into the case; but it has come to be noticed that they enter into it less than is generally supposed. The proportion of those who even attempt to make a thoroughly independent investigation into the grounds of their opinions is always small. It is much larger now, perhaps, than it has ever been before, but even yet it is small. And then even those who attempt to conduct a thoroughly independent examination never succeed in making it independent. There is always a bias on one side or another,—"on one side or another," we say; for it is a great mistake to imagine that the bias is always on the side of what one has been taught. When a person has entered, or supposes that he has entered, on an independent examination of the opinions he has learnt from others, he is very apt to come to the investigation with all sorts of prejudices against that which is old. The love of novelty may influence him; the love of singularity may influence him; the hankering after the merit of originality,—the ambition to be considered an independent thinker,—the notion that, in diverging from common ways of thinking, he is establishing a claim to intellectual superiority to other people,—motives of this sort are apt to have a very powerfully disturbing influence, adverse to the old, and favourable to all kinds of divergences from it.

Further, independent investigation now-a-days must largely follow the course of reading. It is obvious that that man's opinions would be worth least of all who would act the intellectual hermit, and resolve to form his opinions on all subjects without reading a word that had ever been written about them. No man has such a fount of wisdom in his own mind that he can afford to ignore all the wisdom of other people. He cannot even make himself master of the needful facts without availing himself of the labours of others; and he cannot read up even the facts without getting the philosophy of the men who recorded the facts inextricably mixed up with them. In this way a man cannot escape the influence of other minds; and in course of time it will be found that his opinions are traceable very much more to the course of his reading than to any independent thinking he has done.

Now this certainly does not look very encouraging. It is not a very attractive thing to be so necessarily and absolutely the creatures of circumstances; and our philosophic friends who insist so much upon it see that it is not at all pleasant. The attempt, accordingly, is sometimes made to get some relief; as an illustration of which we may quote a passage from the distinguished author of "The Rise and Influence of Rationalism in Europe":—" Those who have appreciated the extremely small influence of definite arguments in determining the opinions either of an individual or of a nation,—who have perceived how invariably an increase of civilisation implies a modification of belief, and how completely the controversialists of successive ages are the puppets and the unconscious exponents of the deep under-current of their time,—will feel an intense distrust of their unassisted reason, and will naturally look for some guide to direct their judgment I think it must be admitted that the general and increasing tendency in the present day is to seek such a guide in the collective wisdom of mankind as it is displayed in the developments of history.' This passage may be fairly accepted as expressing a sentiment widely entertained by thoughtful men in our time, most of whom, however, instead of speaking of "the collective wisdom of mankind," would prefer to use Goethe's personification of the *Zeit-Geist*, the Spirit of the Age, which may be considered its poetical equivalent.

But the painful question returns upon us, Does this make things any better? What is "the spirit of the age," or "the collective wisdom of mankind," but just the sum of the intellectual forces before which we seem compelled to drift so helplessly? And judging from the past, this same "spirit of the age" does not appear to be very worthy of confidence It is not very long since "the spirit of the age" was a decided and determined advocate of slavery. The spirit of the Bible was all the while against it. Nature was against it. Reason was against it. Some far-seeing individuals here and there were against it. But "the spirit of the age" was decidedly in its favour. Is this calculated to give us much confidence in "the collective wisdom of mankind?"

If we think of the cause of freedom in general, the case is no better. We can traverse century after century in which "the spirit of the age" has been entirely hostile to both civil and religious liberty. And it is a mistake to suppose that it was the spirit of the Church, as distinguished from "the spirit of the world," that was to blame. Even as late as the end of the seventeenth and the beginning of the eighteenth century, when freedom's victory was drawing near, the great freethinkers of the time, men like Hobbes and Bolingbroke and Hume, were, as a rule, thoroughly opposed to popular enfranchisement. The same is true of the early French freethinkers, Montaigne and others. These were the men who, as a matter of course, would have been the most pronounced advocates of freedom if they had lived a century later; but, living at the time they did, they were simply led astray, as generation after generation before them had been, by this same misleading "spirit of the age."

In that exceedingly brilliant age which followed the discovery of America, when so many fallacies were being dispelled, and so much substantial progress was being made on almost every line, we find the foremost nation of the time putting all its energies into the accumulation of the precious metals, with the idea that gold and silver constituted the real wealth of the world; and though Spain, on account of her advanced position at that time, took the lead in the great rush for gold and silver, and suffered most in consequence in after years, yet the rest of the civilised world was willing enough to follow her example as they could find opportunity. It all came from "the spirit of the age."

It was at the bidding of "the spirit of the age" that Western Europe was induced, in the twelfth and thirteenth centuries, to engage in the madness of the Crusades. Superficial or unjust writers or readers of history may credit this folly to Christianity, from the fact that it was done in the name of Christianity; but they would utterly fail to show anything in the Christianity of Christ or of His apostles which would give the slightest encouragement to it. It was all the doing of "the spirit of the age." It came from "the collective wisdom of mankind" at the time.

Illustrations of this kind might be multiplied indefinitely, but we presume it is not necessary. It is plain that no dependence can be placed on "the spirit of the age." We take for granted that no one would be guilty of the intolerable conceit of supposing that just because the number of this century happens to be nineteen, therefore it must necessarily be right, while all the rest were wrong. After all, as we have already hinted, it is just this very subserviency of all of us to "the spirit of the age" which is so humiliating and distressing. Our freethinkers are not freethinkers after all; they go with the multitude; they believe as they do because they happen to live in such a place, and at such a time; they go with the current. If it were an age of faith, they would believe. As it is an age of doubt, they doubt. Having read a certain set of books, they are Darwinians. Had it been as fashionable in their set to read German philosophy, they would for the same reason have been Hegelians, or something else. It is a simple matter, first of the currents which are flowing at the time, and secondly of the particular current which they happen to get into. A chance acquaintance, a stray book, may be the means of their getting into the current. Alas! alas! for boasted independence of thought; alas! for delusive originality; alas! for the miserable subjection of men to "the spirit of the age."

But are we, after all, in such a wretched plight? Must we necessarily drift with the current? Is there no criterion of truth, even with regard to matters which are of the utmost importance? Is there nothing but currents beneath us? Are there no gales from heaven by the use of which, while not escaping the force of the currents altogether, we shall nevertheless be able to steer our course across them, or even against them if need be?

Most undoubtedly there are. The Apostle Paul knew well enough about "the spirit of the age;" he had gauged well "the collective wisdom of mankind" as a safe guide, though he did labour under the misfortune of living at so great a distance from the glorious nineteenth century; and this is what he says:—"Now we have received, not the spirit of the world"—that is precisely the same thing as "the spirit of the age"—"but the Spirit which is of God; that we might know the things that are freely given to us of God." Here, surely, is something to

THE SPIRIT OF THE AGE. 181

anchor by, if it be as he says; and it *is* as he says. In saying this we do not dogmatise; "we speak what we do know."

There was One who came into our world at a period which is known in the Bible as "the fulness of the time," who put forth this unique and extraordinary claim, "I am the Light of the world; he that followeth Me shall not walk in darkness, but shall have the light of life." Did He live in a great country? No. In a great age? No. In circumstances fitted to induce a marvellous development of intellect and spirit? No. Then the claim must have been ridiculous? No. On the contrary, it stands out clearer than ever to-day, though eighteen centuries have rolled away since it was made. He expressed Himself on all the topics that are of chief importance to mankind. His words have stood the test of time. The world has made amazing progress since that time, but His words are still in advance, shining before us of the nineteenth century as a light to beckon us on, still on, and up to heaven and to God. It was no fantastic claim that He announced when He said, "I am the Light of the world."

He lived only a short time in the world; but, before He left it, He made this promise, "I will pray the Father, and He shall give you another Comforter, that He may abide with you for ever; even the Spirit of truth;" and "when He, the Spirit of truth, is come, He will guide you into all truth." This promise He fulfilled a few days after He left the world; and those to whom it was fulfilled give us abundant evidence of its fulfilment, not only in their lives, but in the writings which they have left us, which are as different from anything which the spirit of that age could have produced, as light is from darkness. Men have interpreted these writings of the New Testament very differently from age to age, because in their interpretations they have allowed themselves to drift with the currents of the times; but much as the Sacred Scriptures have been perverted in the interest of persecution, in the interest of tyranny, in the interest of slavery, in the interest of all kinds of iniquity, it has always been found that only by perversion could they be made to point in any but the one direction, and that, as soon as the unhallowed spirit of the age was removed from the scene, the light shone, full and clear and bright as of old, and still far, far in advance of the times.

Now this same "Spirit which is of God," who guided these early disciples of Christ so marvellously, is with us still. This is our safeguard, and our only sure safeguard, against the treacherous currents of the times. By faith in the Lord Jesus Christ we draw near to God; and, as soon as we take this attitude, the Spirit of God comes to the soul, and "in His light we see light" clearly on those great matters which are the subject of revelation. And so long as we keep near to Him, though, of course, we cannot but be influenced by the currents which are flowing under and around us, yet we are secured against wandering away from the course which leads to the haven of rest and harbour of truth.

The main current of the age in which we live is like the Gulf Stream. It is flowing steadily, apparently resistlessly, north, north, north, to the cold, and the rain, and the fogs, and the ice,—to the dreary land where the blessed sun, when it sets, seems to set for evermore. The "advanced thinkers,"—who are they? They are those who are farther north than the others, nearer the ice, nearer the pole, nearer the unbroken darkness. Oh! terrible, terrible current, if indeed we must all follow it!

But listen: hear you not that sound as of the wind? It *is* the wind. It is a steady wind. It is the Trade Wind, blowing gently down towards the region of the cedar and the palm, the orange and the myrtle, and all the glory of the sunny South. You need not fear the current after all. You need not travel to the pole. Spread your sails. Invite the blessed gale. Catch the heavenly inspiration; it will carry you safely, happily home to "the better land," in spite of all the currents that are flowing north.

Does this influence of the Spirit of God interfere with our freedom? Not at all; no more than reading a book does it. When we read a book, we give our minds up for the time, so far as the train of our thoughts is concerned, to the author of the book, allowing him to present what he thinks proper for our consideration. And this is just what we do with God's Spirit; we give Him our attention; we allow Him to present His truth to us. We are, of course, powerfully influenced thereby, but not against our will. As soon as a man's will is set against the Spirit, He leaves. All He does is in accordance with our nature. He never forces anything upon us; He simply shows us things that we should not have seen without Him. He opens His celestial hand, and sets the heavenly treasure before us. He takes of the things of Christ and shows them unto us.

In all this He undoubtedly obtains a powerful influence over our minds, but no more than He is entitled to. We still remain susceptible of other and lower influences. We still feel the power over us of the society in which we live, and especially of the men of genius whose books we read. We feel as keenly as ever the force of those difficulties which the many able opponents of Christianity have to present. We cannot read their books without feeling the spell of their power over us; but we are not quite at their mercy, as many are. We can look at all they show us, for our minds reason in the same way, and the mysteries of life are around us as they are around them. But then we have things before our minds which they have not. "We have received the Spirit which is of God, that we might know the things that are freely given to us of God." And powerful as is the influence which these great men have over us, and legitimate as it is that they should have it, on account of their genius, there is a still more powerful influence over us, that of God, to whom it is surely as reasonable and proper to listen as to the most gifted of men. This influence which is over us from above is a steadying influence amid the currents and eddies, not to speak of the shallows and breakers, of life. While men of genius are ever making new departures, and ever contradicting one another, and even themselves, the testimony of the Heavenly Spirit is the same from age to age. Cannot we sing the Psalms of David, and Asaph, and the sons of Korah, as if they were written yesterday? We can read the prophets of old, and find them in no wise behind the prophets of the day. We can take the words of the Lord Jesus Christ, and of His apostles, as texts to preach on from year to year, from generation to generation, from century to century, and find that they are no nearer being worn out than when they were first uttered or written. We find that while science and philosophy have been continually changing,—while theology,* psychology, and ontology, and all the "ologies," (all, that is, which comes under the

---

* Theology, however, does not alter nearly so much as other sciences. It never shifts its centre, as astronomy has had to do. The Sun of Righteousness has been its centre from the beginning, and will be without end. See Rev. i. 8.

domain of the human λογος or reason), have been flowing here and eddying there, and changing so much from age to age, that their very identity seems almost lost at times, —man's spiritual experience has been always the same. May we not appeal to our hymnology as a proof? There are hymns in our possession from all the centuries, and the same spirit breathes through them all. Take, for instance, a hymn of the eleventh century, the very darkest that we know; we despise the philosophy of that century, we look with pity upon its science, we cannot sympathise even with its theology, but we can sing its hymns. Here is one of them:—

> " Come, Holy Ghost, in love;
> Shed on us, from above,
>   Thine own bright ray,
> Divinely good Thou art;
> Thy sacred gifts impart,
> To gladden each sad heart;
>   Oh, come to day!
>
> Come, tenderest Friend, and best,
> Our most delightful Guest,
>   With soothing power;
> Rest which the weary know,
> Shade 'mid the noontide glow,
> Peace when deep griefs o'erflow;
>   Cheer us this hour.
>
> Exalt our low desires;
> Extinguish passion's fires;
>   Heal every wound;
> Our stubborn spirits bend;
> Our icy coldness end;
> Our devious steps attend,
>   While heavenward bound.
>
> Come, Light serene and still,
> Our inmost bosoms fill,
>   Dwell in each breast.

> We know no dawn but Thine ;
> Send forth Thy beams divine,
> On our dark souls to shine,
>   And make us blest.
>
> Come, all the faithful bless ;
> Let all who Christ confess
>   His praise employ :
> Give virtue's rich reward ;
> Victorious death accord,
> And, with our glorious Lord,
>   Eternal joy."

And not only have we such utterances, expressive of the heart's devotion, from all the centuries, but throughout them all, wherever the Gospel has been preached, the experience of those who have received it has been substantially the same.

The history of Christianity affords abundant evidence that the Saviour's promise has been fulfilled, that there has been, and still is, among us a Heavenly Guide, not misleading and changeful like the spirit of the age, representing "the collective wisdom (or folly ?) of mankind," but trustworthy and changeless, leading those who trust Him into all truth, which it is necessary for them to know in order to life, and peace, and deathless hope.

XIV.

THE SOUL OF BUSINESS; OR, THE LAW OF CHRIST AS APPLIED TO TRADE AND COMMERCE.

IS it possible to be at once a thorough business man and a thorough Christian? Is it possible in these times to live a business life that shall be Christian in its spirit as well as in its conduct? Can the law of Christ be written in the heart of it, as an inspiration within, according to the New Testament idea? Or must it suffice to hedge it in from without by the restraints of a law, which takes the form, "Thou shalt *not ?*" Is it enough never to deviate by a hair's-breadth from the path of rectitude, or is something more required than this mere negative virtue?

The writer of these pages believes that questions of this kind present real difficulty to many earnest men of business; and it is in the hope of contributing in some small measure to their solution that he ventures respectfully to ask the attention of Christians engaged in business to the considerations which follow, bearing on the ethics of commerce, from what seems to him the Christian point of view.

The law of Christ is more than mere morality. A law of righteousness it is; and so far it is coincident with the universally accepted code of morals. But over and above the law of righteousness there rises another law, which is distinctively *the* law of Christ. This is the law of love, in two great branches: "Thou shalt love the Lord thy God with all thy heart, and with all thy soul, and with all thy mind;" and, "Thou shalt love thy neighbour as thyself." No one doubts that common morality should rule the Christian and everybody else in the ordinary business of life; and therefore we need not spend any time in insisting on the claims of the law of Christ so far as it coincides with the other: it is with the higher law of love that we must deal.

It will be at once seen, then, that our subject is not what is generally understood as "commercial morality." I firmly believe that we shall never have the right kind of commercial morality till men take the higher standard of thoroughgoing Christian principle, and insist not only on that righteousness which no one disputes, but also on that love which very few acknowledge as binding in the ordinary business of life.

It is true, indeed, that while men in general are sound enough in theory as to commercial morality, they are very far from being as universally sound in practice; and therefore there is abundant scope for the most strenuous enforcement of common honesty and integrity; occasion enough, and quite too much, for urging, and urging again, the duty of fair and square dealing as between man and man; and such appeals can be properly enough made, and ought to be made, in the name of Christ and of Christianity, but the question comes whether, while not neglecting this, there may not be something better for us to do.

It may have been observed how little, comparatively, Christ has to say about common honesty. It might be said, indeed, that trade and commerce did not bulk at all so largely in Palestine life as they do in ours; and yet they did constitute so large a part of it that it would have been unpardonable to omit them or pass them lightly by. Besides, Christ was legislating, not for Palestine alone, but for the world; and not for that century alone, but for all the coming centuries; and therefore we must seek some other explanation of what to some might appear a strange omission or neglect. We cannot do better, probably, than examine, with this view, the Sermon on the Mount. That sermon may be fairly considered a summary of the law of Christ. It has been aptly called by Dr. Dykes "The Manifesto of the King;" and while it is by no means a legislative code, in the proper sense of the term, it is a summary of principles of wide enough range to cover all the common relations of life. Now, if we were to ask what place commercial morality has in that code, what would be the answer? Those who take low ground on the subject would probably say, "No place at all." The main substance of it is an exposition of the righteousness of the kingdom, and yet the one commandment which directly covers the ground of commercial morality is deliberately passed by: the eighth commandment is not even mentioned. The great Lawgiver of the new Covenant deals with all the rest of the second table of the Law, but omits all reference to the one commandment which some people now-a-days seem to consider "the be-all and the end-all" of morality. What is the reason?

A careful reading of what follows will suggest that it is because He has something better to say. He has something more efficient in reserve. He sees that the tenth commandment gives a far stronger leverage than the eighth; and so He urges and presses it, not only in its own light, but in the light of the "first and great commandment," warning us against "laying up treasures on the earth;" warning us against attempting to "serve God and mammon;" warning us against too much anxiety as to the supply of our bodily wants; and closing a long and sustained appeal by the positive rule, "Seek ye first the kingdom of God and His righteousness, and all these things shall be added unto you." It is in this large and wise way that He deals with the business of ordinary life; lifting it out of the region of mere morality, and setting it in the full light of "the first and great commandment" of the law of love; and then, further on, He urges a similarly high standard in the light of "the second, which is like unto it," when He lays down the golden rule, "Therefore, whatsoever ye would that men should do to you, do ye even so to them; for this is the law and the prophets." Thus we see that He does not omit or neglect the ordinary business of life, but reaches and deals with it in a way of His own.

This method is consistently kept up throughout all His teaching. Instead of treating of business relations on the lower ground of fair and honest dealing, He always tries to lift men up to the higher ground. When a certain man comes to Him with the appeal, "Master, speak to my brother, that he divide the inheritance with me," He not only will not interfere, but He uses the opportunity, not, as might have been expected, for the enforcement of honesty, but for an earnest warning against covetousness; "He said unto them, Take heed, and beware of covetousness, for a man's life consisteth not in the abundance of the things which he possesseth." So it is all the way through. He by no means undervalues honesty, but He lays far greater stress on having a heart set on higher things than money or any earthly possession. He lays the axe at the root of the upas tree. He plants His danger-signal not at the spot where the ice ends and the water

begins, but at the place where the ice begins to get thin
He treats not the mere symptoms, but the deep-seated
disease within.

And His example is faithfully followed by His apostles.
Their warnings against covetousness are far more frequent than against dishonesty. And even when honesty is
urged, it is a larger and loftier honesty than is involved
in mere fair dealing. It has in it the idea of nobility
and honour, as well as of mere justice. They did not
make it a mere matter of the *exchange* of money, or of
that which money represents, as our modern moralists are
so apt to do, but of "the *love* of money." It was the
root they were aiming at. And even when they do look
at the matter from the lower point of view, how naturally
they rise to the higher; as when the Apostle, writing to
the Roman Christians, says, "Owe no man anything,
but to love one another; for he that loveth another hath
fulfilled the law. . . . Love worketh no ill to his neighbour; therefore love is the fulfilling of the law."

We find, then, that the method of Christ and His
apostles was one which, while assuming and requiring
the broad basis of righteousness in all things, specially
urged the law of love in both its branches, as the true
means by which even the commonest morality in the
business of life could be most effectively secured

Was the method a sound one, then? If so, is it
applicable still, and likely to be effective, in all the complexity of the business life of the nineteenth century?
This is our main question, and a very important one it is.

There are those who emphatically say, No; and we
must listen to what they have to urge. There is, first, what
may be called the objection of the average business man.
It may be thus expressed: " Business is business, and must
be conducted on strictly business principles, according to

the law of demand and supply, and the common-sense rule of buying in the cheapest and selling in the dearest market. This talk about the law of love is all very well for 'pulpit eloquence,' or pulpit twaddle, as the case may be; on 'Change it must be, 'Every man for himself, and ———'" well, instead of finishing the adage in the rather rough way which shows what is the fate of "the hindmost," we shall give the modern equivalent, and call it "the survival of the fittest." And the use of this scientific phrase reminds us that, besides the objection of the average business man, there is that of the sociologist, which, however, is just the old popular objection put into scientific form. It is fully and ably set forth by Mr. Herbert Spencer, especially in his "Data of Ethics," where, according to himself, he shows to a demonstration that the Christian law is not only inapplicable to the ordinary business of life, but would be positively ruinous to society if it were actually carried out. It may be well to quote some of his own words, premising that by "egoism" he means the doctrine, "Every man for himself," and by "altruism" the doctrine, "Every man for his neighbour," which, according to him, is the Christian doctrine. He says:—

"It does not seem to be suspected that pure altruism is actually wrong. Brought up, as each is, in the nominal acceptance of a creed which wholly subordinates egoism to altruism, and gives sundry precepts that are absolutely altruistic, each citizen, while ignoring these in his business, and tacitly denying them in various opinions he utters, daily gives to them lip-homage, and supposes that acceptance of them is required of him, though he finds it impossible. Feeling that he cannot call them in question without calling in question his religion as a whole, he pretends to others and to himself that he believes them—believes things which in his innermost consciousness he knows he does not believe. He professes to think that entire self-sacrifice must be right, though dimly conscious that it would be fatal."*

The enormous mistake on which this criticism is based is due to a confusion of ideas between what is required of a Christian as towards God, and what is required as towards his fellow-man. It is true that we are asked to surrender ourselves implicitly and entirely to God. " Thou shalt love the Lord thy God with all thy heart, and with all thy soul, and with all thy mind." If this is " pure altruism," it is an altruism which can never do any harm in the most complex state of society, but will always, and in all circumstances, secure the highest possible welfare, both of the individual and of society. Let a man implicitly and fully surrender himself to God—to obey His commandments, to do His will, to live for His glory— and it will be the best for the man himself, the best for his family, the best for his friends, the best for his enemies, the best for the society in which he lives, the best for the world at large. Would that all mankind were only altruistic after this fashion, and the great problem of sociology and of Christianity would be finally and fully solved. There would be a heaven upon earth!

But the scientific critic of the law of Christ seems to know nothing of this kind of altruism. The altruism he is thinking of is the surrender of everybody to his neighbour; and no intelligent Christian needs to be told that there is no such surrender asked of us by the law of

* " Study of Sociology," International Series, p 184 It need scarcely be remarked that the opinions of Mr Spencer are important, not only on account of his personal ability and eminence, but because he is the chief exponent of ethical views which are widely prevalent amongst the most cultured people of the day.

Christ. "Thou shalt love thy neighbour." How? With the whole heart? No; "Thou shalt love thy neighbour *as thyself.*" This, as we are taught, is the sum of the second table of the Law, which has to do with our duty to our neighbour. And what a grievous misrepresentation of it are the words above quoted! And still more so, when our critic goes on to say that it calls us to the "continual giving up of pleasures, and continual submission to pains," "so that its final outcome is debility, disease, and abridgment of life." There are, indeed, some exhortations here and there in the New Testament which seem open to this kind of criticism, if literally pressed; but the difficulty entirely disappears if we look at the evident spirit of them; and this is what both Christ and His apostles remind us we must do. For instance, "Look not every man on his own things, but every man also on the things of others." Here the first part seems to forbid attention to our own interests, while the second summons us to attend to the interests of others. But does not the word "also" show clearly that a proper attention to our own interests is taken for granted as a thing of course? "Look not every man on his own things, but every man *also* on the things of others." It is abundantly clear that the spirit of this is to caution us against seeking after our own interests to the disregard of the interests of our neighbours. And surely this is good enough social doctrine. It is not at all at variance with the strictest social science. And then, lest any should be disposed to run into the altruistic extreme of which the critic is afraid, have we not such reminders as this, "If any provide not for his own, and specially for those of his own house, he hath denied the faith, and is worse than an infidel"? Thus we find that the scientific objection to the Christian law of love does not deal fairly with the second commandment of the Law, and, what is still worse, leaves out of sight the first commandment, which takes precedence of the second, and therefore, of course, modifies its application. Such objections are valid against certain systems of modern humanitarianism, but they have no force whatever against the Christian law of love.

So much for the scientific objection. But a little more may be said on the practical difficulties of the average business man. There are, undoubtedly, quite conscientious and excellent business men who do not see how the law of love can be carried into ordinary business. Let us, then, investigate a little as to whether it is practicable to carry on business without interfering with either of the two great branches of the law of love—either with the supreme devotion of the heart to God, or with that love to our neighbour which the law of Christ requires.

As to the former, the noble inscription on the Royal Exchange in the city of London is quite sufficient to settle the matter. We have only to remember that "THE EARTH IS THE LORD'S, AND THE FULNESS THEREOF; the world, and they that dwell therein," to see that if a man is engaged in any sort of occupation which tends, in however humble a manner, to replenish the earth and bring out its fulness, to benefit the world or any of its inhabitants, he is engaged in the Lord's service, and may do, and ought to do, what he is doing "as unto the Lord." No matter what kind of service he is rendering, whether he is ministering to bodily or intellectual or spiritual wants, whether he is making shoes or sermons—and it is far better work for God to make a good shoe than a poor sermon—pictures or pins, provided only he is doing some good in God's world, he may and ought to look upon his work as service rendered to the great Ruler of the world and King of men,* and therefore may do it not only without interfering with, but in fulfilment of, the claim which God makes on the supreme devotion of the heart and life. And as to the lower motives which do and must come in, there is not one of them belonging to human nature, apart from sin, that is incompatible with supreme devotion to God. All that is necessary is, that they be kept in due subordination. For example, is it not God's intention that we should make a living, and support our families, by our business? Clearly, then, it may also be ours, without interfering with the supremacy of our devotion to Him. Or take the desire to achieve success—is not that a part of the nature which God has given us? And does not common-sense tell us that a man without ambition to succeed and to excel is anything but a lofty specimen of humanity? It is only necessary to take care that the ambition to excel be not the highest ambition of our life. Or take the widespread and well-nigh universal desire to make money. This is more difficult to deal with, inasmuch as there is such a fearful tendency to excess in this direction. But even here it is very evident that the same position may be taken, namely, that in its proper place of subordination it is right enough. Acccording to the laws which God has appointed to regulate society, it is necessary not only that each man should earn his living by his industry, but that some men should earn more than their living. This is necessary, not only that there may be a surplus for those that cannot earn their living, but also for the creation of capital. All who have given any thought to the subject are aware that there could be no progress in civilisation without capital. Just as separate capital is needed for a separate business, so for the general business

* " He did God's will ; to him all one
  If on the earth or in the sun."
  —ROBERT BROWNING.

of society the accumulation of capital is absolutely necessary. It is therefore manifest that it is God's will that some men at least should make more than they need for their personal and family expenses, and accordingly He has implanted in us the desire corresponding to that necessity—a desire, therefore, which may be gratified in moderation without interfering with the supreme devotion of the heart to God.

As to the second table of the Law, we have already seen, in dealing with the scientific objection, that self is not excluded—"Thou shalt love thy neighbour as thyself;" and, further, that this, being the second commandment, must not be dealt with as if it stood alone, but must be looked on as modified by the first. But a few words may be necessary to illustrate the practical effect of this. Take the familiar case of giving alms to a lusty beggar. If we had only the second part of the law of love to guide us, we might feel constrained to reason after the manner of Mr Spencer:[*] "If I love this beggar as myself, how can I refuse him at least half of the money in my pocket?" But immediately the higher duty comes in, and with it the thought, "If I were to do this I should be disregarding my duty to God; I should be going contrary to what I know to be His will, who says that 'If any man will not work, neither shall he eat;' and not only so, but I should be violating the spirit of the second commandment itself; for I should be doing, not a benefit, but a wrong to my lazy neighbour." God is Light as well as Love; there is "lucidity" as well as "sweetness" in His law; and we must respect those ordinances of His, which are written on society and enforced in His providence. The application of the principle is specially obvious in the sphere of charity; but it is quite as applicable to business relations. Does any one say, "Because I must

[*] See "Data of Ethics," p. 199.

love my neighbour as myself, I must therefore supply him with goods at half their value; or, after he has got them, let him off with paying half the price?" My reply is, that this would be entirely inconsistent with my duty to God, and even to my neighbour, as set forth in the law of love. It would, indeed, be a treble wrong, or rather a wrong in every conceivable direction. It would not only be bad for myself (and the law forbids me to wrong myself, if it forbids me to wrong my neighbour; for it is as myself that I am required to love him), but it would be bad for the man with whom I was doing business, and bad for society, and manifestly against the will of Him who "rules among the inhabitants of the earth," and is "not the Author of confusion," but of order. As we remarked at the beginning, righteousness is the broad and deep foundation of the law of Christ; and the law of love comes in to reinforce it and to supplement it, to animate it with life, to fill it with soul; but never in any degree to abrogate, annul, or supersede it.

Or we may put it in another way, which may be still more obvious. When rightly looked at, all legitimate business, honestly done, is done on the principle of loving one's neighbour as one's self. Take the familiar case of buying at a certain cost, and selling at an advanced price Why is the buyer willing to pay a higher price than the seller has paid? Because of the benefit the seller does him in the shape of saving him the trouble of going a distance to get what he wants, or the waste of buying a larger quantity than he needs, or some such convenience. It is far better, manifestly, for a resident of London to buy a small piece of Manchester goods at a small advance in price than it would be to go himself to the manufacturer in Manchester, and then find that to get any he must take ten or a hundred times what he wants. It would, in fact, be better for him to pay a very much larger advance than he does pay rather than to be left to his own resources in the matter. But here the laws which regulate trade come in to cut down the advance to the lowest point, so that he pays very little indeed for a great service. And it may be remarked, in passing, that few of us realise at how little cost we obtain the very needful and valuable services which are done us on all hands by our neighbours. According to the working of the laws just referred to, it comes to pass that the services rendered by the different persons engaged in business are set off against each other in very fair equivalents; so that, if only strict honesty be observed, each man gets, in the main, just what his services are worth —no more, no less. And, therefore, in demanding and accepting the fair market value of what he has to offer, he is literally acting upon the principle of loving his neighbour as himself. If he were dishonestly to ask more, he would be sinfully turning the balance on his own side; if he were foolishly to take less, he would be unwisely turning the balance on his neighbour's side. And this shows, by the way (it is well to note it as we pass), that it is just as contrary to the law of Christ for the buyer to endeavour by undue means to beat down the seller as it is for the seller to try to get more than its worth for what he sells. But the point we are making now is this, that in fair buying and selling a man is carrying out as nearly as possible the Divine law, "Thou shalt love thy neighbour as thyself." And the same principle applies to all kinds of business where services are rendered and equivalents accepted either as wages or as profit.

But it manifestly does not apply to what is familiarly known as "speculative" business. I know that it is very difficult to draw the line between legitimate and speculative business, and that one who is not thoroughly acquainted with what he is talking about must be very chary of condemning this or that way of making money, which may seem to him to partake of the nature of speculation. But there can be no mistake in standing by the manifest application, in all cases, of "the royal law according to the Scripture." This law, as we have seen, does not forbid us to enrich ourselves in the ordinary transactions of exchange; for in these the gain of A is not the loss of B, but the price which B willingly pays for the benefit A does him. But it does forbid our enriching ourselves at the expense of others; as, for example, is manifestly done when an "operator" in grain makes an artificial scarcity in the market for the purpose of raising the price. In the legitimate transaction the profit of the grain merchant is the equivalent he receives for the benefit of bringing the grain to those who need it; in the other case, his profit arises from the loss inflicted on the community by his holding it back from them. In all ordinary business transactions a man simply gets a fair equivalent for certain services he renders to his neighbour; and in rendering the service, and accepting the equivalent, he is, as we have seen, manifestly keeping the law which tells him to love his neighbour as himself; but when his gain, instead of being a reward for services rendered, is a penalty paid by his neighbour for a disservice which he has done him, it is seen to be a serious violation of the law of love.

Thus we find that the law of Christ, while it would undoubtedly put an end to some ways of making money, which public opinion only too feebly censures, is the very life and soul of all legitimate business.

Now that objections to the law of Christ have been

dealt with, and its practicability maintained, it remains to show the immense advantage of laying stress upon the higher rather than on the lower law. We have already indicated in a general way the advantage of the method of Christ as one that, instead of merely lopping off the branches, cuts away the roots of the tree of evil—one that prefers to deal with the deep-seated disease rather than to confine attention to the treatment of its outward symptoms; but we may now look at it somewhat more closely.

The causes which lead to commercial immorality are mainly these two—covetousness and extravagance: too great eagerness to get, and too great eagerness to spend. Each of them is a spring of action, which is apt to grow into a habit, urging on, with ever-increasing force, him who indulges it. Each of them is "a stream of tendency," which not only readily becomes an idolatry, but which, when it has engrossed the life, is very apt to sweep away the barriers in its path. Conscience is a strong barrier to resist the outbreak of the evil waters; but when the whole force of a man's life presses in one direction, the barrier needs to be very strong indeed—far stronger than it is, or can be expected to be, in the average man —not to give way at some point; not to admit of little leakages here and there, which speedily prepare the way for something more serious. Now what does the law of Christ do? It does not simply fortify the barrier: it does that, but it does a great deal more; it diverts the stream of evil tendency, or rather so changes it that it becomes a stream of most blessed tendency. It insists on a man's pouring his life into another channel altogether. It calls upon him to "seek first the kingdom of God, and His righteousness." Thus it not only keeps him from directing his life in such a way as to press and surge against the barrier which conscience erects against evil, but it aims to make conscience itself a master passion of the soul by insisting that he shall "seek first the kingdom of God, and His righteousness;" and if he do this, if he even honestly try it, it is impossible for his eagerness to get rich to gain dangerous headway. He is not only fortified against temptation, but kept out of temptation's way—kept in a region of life where the temptation to anything like deceit or dishonesty cannot reach him.

It is much the same with the other great source of temptation, namely, extravagance. The law of Christ, indeed, allows in moderation the desire to enjoy the good things of this life; but it not only forbids a man to live beyond his income, which the lowest code of honesty forbids him to do, but it keeps him far away from the vulgar motives to extravagance. The commonest of these, namely, ostentation, it utterly condemns, making it a first duty to be "meek and lowly in heart." It renders a life of mere self-indulgence impossible to all who will, with any honesty, try to keep either its first or its second commandment; to say nothing of the attempt to keep them both, without which, indeed, no one can fairly consider himself a Christian at all.

The attempt, we say; for it is very important to notice that the mere attempt, if only it be an honest and earnest one, to keep the law of love will be almost an absolute safeguard against any form of dishonesty. For the objection might be urged, "It is all very well to say that if a man only loved God supremely, and his neighbour as himself, dishonesty would be impossible; but, seeing that no man can do either the one or the other perfectly, what does it all amount to?" But what we say is, not that the perfect keeping of the law of love, which no one can do, but the honest attempt to keep it, which any one can make, will be as near a safeguard as it is possible to come to with human nature as it is. The same could not be said of honesty. If a man's honesty, indeed, be absolute, perfect, immovable, his conscience above the reach of all blinding, or blunting, or befogging influences, then it is quite certain that such an one will not fall into any doubtful practices. But of what man living can this be said? Or if it can be said of any, of how very few!

In order to see this more clearly, let us distinguish between a principle and a passion. Principle has the strength of an embankment, or a rock, as the case may be: passion has the force of a stream, or a torrent, as the case may be. Principle belongs to the statics, passion to the dynamics of character. Now common morality looks to principle, and in this it does wisely; but it neglects passion, and in this it falls fatally short. It is quite sound on the statics of virtue, but its dynamics it almost utterly ignores; and just as running water, if only the current be strong enough, will wear away a strong embankment, or even the hardest rock, so, if the passions be allowed to get force sufficient, they will carry away any mere principles that may stand in their way. Now the law of Christ does not neglect the statics of character; but it gives special attention to its dynamics · it makes much of principle, quite as much as any moralist can; but it makes still more of the passions of the heart. It does not at all attempt to suppress the enthusiasm and energy of human nature, but it turns it in a direction in which it can safely flow in all its strength—turns it in a direction in which the more energy, and ardour, and enthusiasm, the better for the man himself, and for all interests concerned. It forbids the disastrous passion for money; it forbids the similarly disastrous passion for display; it calls out a passion for God and His righteousness.

We have already seen how our Saviour deals with the ordinary business of life in the Sermon on the Mount; but before He comes to it, He says, "After this manner pray ye," and then furnishes a prayer, and *such* a prayer! The first petition, " Hallowed be Thy name; " the second petition, " Thy kingdom come; " the third petition, " Thy will be done in earth, as it is in heaven; " and then, and not till then, the petition for daily bread, expressed not only in such a way as to suggest studied moderation, but in such a way as to keep in view the claim of our neighbour—" Give *us* this day our daily bread: " a prayer, therefore, which no one can possibly offer in sincerity without at least trying to make the glory of God his chief ambition, and to keep all selfish desire in strict subordination, and in such moderation as the golden rule requires. Now, may it not be asserted, without the slightest fear of contradiction, that where a man only *tried* to live a life the desires of which are represented in the Lord's Prayer, it would be simply impossible to issue a lying advertisement; simply impossible to make or encourage the making of a false invoice; simply impossible to represent goods as better than they really are, or as having cost more than they actually did cost? Would it be possible, think you, for such a man to have anything to do with the getting up of a bubble company, or to encourage in any way the risking of people's money by holding out hopes of dividend which he, as projector, knows to be absurdly extravagant? Would it be possible for such an one to trade on other people's capital, or to expose the property of another to a risk to which that other had not consented? Would it be possible for such an one to tempt his neighbour to sin, as is done by those who offer to young men in their employ commissions on amounts realised from the sale of otherwise unsaleable stock, without any inquiry as to the means by which the said stock has been got rid of? Would it be possible for such an one in any way to take advantage of the ignorance or weakness of any with whom his business led him to deal, in order to gain an unrighteous end? All such things would manifestly be out of the range of possibility for any man who put even the smallest degree of real earnestness, day by day, into that prayer which teaches us what the deepest desires of our hearts should be.

It is sadly to be confessed that there are Christian people—so called at least—among the number of those who are guilty of mean and dishonest practices. But among these there is not a single case of a Christian who has honestly tried to make it the habit of his life to " seek first the kingdom of God, and His righteousness." Many of them may be in the daily or weekly habit of *saying* the Lord's Prayer, but not one of them is in the habit of *praying* it. Without the slightest fear of contradiction, I assert, that wherever a so-called Christian man is guilty of anything approaching to dishonesty, he is not one of those who try to regulate their conduct by the law of love, but one who, contenting himself with the ordinary code of morals, has allowed his passion for money, or some other ungodly lust, to master him, and to scatter his feeble morality to the winds. If all this be true, it is manifest that the method of Christ is the method which this age still needs, and sorely needs; that what is wanted is not so much more homilies on honesty as more earnest warnings against covetousness and extravagance, and a more earnest presentation of that Gospel of divine love which will touch men's hearts, and lead them so to set their affections on higher and better things as that they will count no sacrifice in the lower sphere too great to make for the sake of maintaining "a conscience void of offence toward God and toward men."

I do not believe that things are so bad in the world of business as many pessimists imagine. I do not believe that a man cannot be strictly honest without suffering loss. I believe that our best men are, in the main, our most successful men. I cannot believe that cheating and lying are so common in any kind of respectable business as those say who wish to justify their part in such practices; and I do not believe, nor do I think that any thoroughly honest man believes, that deceit and falsehood are necessary in any shape, however veiled and disguised, for success in any legitimate business. Yet the state of things is such that there is a grand field for witnessing for Christ in the world of business. The ranks of "the noble army of the martyrs" are not yet full. The demand to "take up the cross" for Christ's sake has not yet been withdrawn. And though, in the eyes of men, there is not the same show of heroism when a young man gives up a good situation, without any prospect of another, for the sake of truth, as if he had gone cheerfully to the stake in the same noble cause, there may be quite as much of the reality of it, quite as much that is noble, and admirable, and heroic in the sight of God. Christ needs many witnesses in the wide field of business; men that will witness to Him in the heights of success; men also that will witness for Him not only in the depths of failure, but by their willingness to fail for His sake; men that are willing to "suffer the loss of all things;" men who are willing to go through life as poor as Christ Himself, rather than do any single, smallest act at variance with "that good, and acceptable, and perfect will of God" which finds expression in the law of Christ.

Our chief object has been to show that the inspiration of Christian principle is far more effective than the restraints of moral law in securing commercial morality; that to give business a new heart and soul is better than to attempt, without such regeneration, merely to repress its disorders; and having, as we hope, done something to make this evident, we shall not pursue the subject further than to suggest this additional thought, which might be readily developed: that not only is the method of Christ much more effective in securing commercial morality, but it elevates the life of business to a far higher plane, and gives it a nobility and grandeur that seldom enter into the thoughts of those who look at it from the worldly point of view; and that instead of its being a hindrance, as it so often is, to the development of the Christian life, it might be, as it is so often proved to be, as fine a field as any other for its manifestation and growth up to "the measure of the stature of the fulness of Christ." And so it might be shown that if only the law of Christ were faithfully and fully carried into the ordinary business of life, we should see on every hand a new fulfilment of an old prophecy: "The parched ground shall become a pool, and the thirsty land springs of water: in the habitation of dragons, where each lay, shall be grass, with reeds and rushes. And an highway shall be there, and a way, and it shall be called The way of holiness; the unclean shall not pass over it; but it shall be for those: the wayfaring men, though fools, shall not err therein. No lion shall be there, nor any ravenous beast shall go up thereon; it shall not be found there; but the redeemed shall walk there."

XV.

THE PROPHET HOSEA ON THE CAUSE AND CURE OF SOCIAL EVILS.

THE study of a book like the Prophecy of Hosea is mainly an historical study, and as such it is exceedingly interesting; and those who read it with any exercise of the historical imagination must be impressed with the grandeur of this great-souled man, so stern in his denunciations of the sins and follies of the times, and withal so tender in his human sympathies. Though for the most part his prophecy is a trumpet-blast against the iniquities of the time, yet throughout it there is a thrill of mother-love which is ever and again melting his message into tones of deepest pathos, as in that wonderful passage in the eleventh chapter in which he expresses the yearning of the Heavenly Father's heart over His wandering one. Listen to some of the strains of it: " When Israel was a child, then I loved him, and brought my son out of Egypt . . . I taught Ephraim also to walk, taking them by the arms; and yet they knew not it was I that tended them. I gently led them on with human cords, with bands of love; I was to them as one that from the tired ox takes off the yoke and offers it its food. . . . And yet my people are bent on backsliding from me. . . . How shall I give thee up, Ephraim? How shall I let thee perish, Israel? How shall I make thee as Admah? How shall I set thee as Zeboim? My heart is melted within me, my compassions are kindled together." And yet it is this loving, tender-hearted man, who sets the trumpet to his mouth, and regardless of the storm he is raising all around him, delivers his soul on this wise (chap. v.): "Hear ye this, O priests: and hearken, ye house of Israel, and give ye ear, O house of the King; for judgment is against you, because ye have been a snare upon Mizpah and a net spread upon Tabor." Verily it does one's soul good to enter into sympathy with a noble hero like this great prophet of Israel.

We have said that the study of the book is in the first place an historical study, and its immediate interest is in giving us a picture of the times. But, like all other Scripture given by inspiration of God, it "is profitable for doctrine and for reproof, and for correction and for instruction in righteousness." And this general use of it seems to be especially indicated in the closing verses: "Who is wise, and he shall understand these things? prudent, and he shall know them? for the ways of the Lord are right, and the just shall walk in them; but transgressors shall fall therein."

There are some very obvious applications of the prophecy which every one must make, because they are written so large that they cannot be missed. There is, perhaps, no part of the whole Bible where there is such boundless encouragement to each and every sinner that repenteth, to each and every backslider that desires to return to the Lord his God. It is difficult to imagine a worse case than that of Israel. Read their history during the half-century which preceded their final overthrow by the Assyrian armies; or read such an indictment as that in the beginning of the fourth chapter of this prophecy: "Hear the word of the Lord, ye children of Israel; for the Lord hath a controversy with the inhabitants of the land, because there is no truth, nor mercy, nor knowledge of God in the land. By swearing, and lying, and killing, and stealing, and committing adultery, they break out; and blood toucheth blood." And yet, in dealing with this people—*this people*, remember—while there is no paltering with their sin or weak overlooking of it, but the most scathing exposure and denunciation of it, with darkest threats of vengeance unless they will repent, yet there is an outpouring of heart which exhausts the highest forms of human affection—the husband yearning over his wife, the mother weeping for her child. What do we learn from all this?—that there is no love on earth, not the highest and purest and most self-forgetful and most unconquerable, that is sufficient to give us an idea how our Father in heaven loves even the greatest sinners, and longs for their return from the storm and darkness of their wandering in the far country to the shelter and comfort and wealth of His home. Are there those who think God does not care to have them now, because they have so long neglected Him and rebelled against Him? Let them listen to these tender pleadings of the prophet, and be assured that He yearns over them. Are there backsliders who have wearied the Lord as much as Israel did?—they cannot have done it more—let them listen to that other word of tender pleading and gracious promise: " O Israel, return to the Lord thy God; for thou hast fallen by thine iniquity. Take with you words and turn to the Lord; say unto Him, Take away all iniquity, and receive us graciously. . . . I will heal their backsliding, I will love them freely, for mine anger is turned away from him. I will be as the dew unto Israel; he shall grow as the lily, and cast forth his roots as Lebanon. His branches shall spread, and his beauty shall be as the olive-tree, and his smell as Lebanon.

They that dwell under His shadow shall return; they shall revive as the corn, and grow as the vine; the scent thereof shall be as the wine of Lebanon."

How delightful it is to rest in these last words! Reading the prophecy of Hosea is like passing through a stormy day—great storms of thunder, lightning, rain, and hail, with glints of sunlight in between, all the more beautiful by contrast; for never does sunshine seem so glorious as when it breaks out between storms—but when the day of storm is over, at evening-time it is light; the clouds are cleared away; and in the night which follows (for night did follow, Israel did not return; the Assyrian came, and Israel was carried away into captivity), in the night which sets in, the stars of promise are left shining in the sky. And the morning broke again, when a Greater than Hosea came, repeating in tones still more tender the old invitation, the old promise: "O Israel, return!" "*I* will heal thy backsliding, I will love thee freely, for mine anger is turned away."

These are some of the very obvious applications of the book. But it may be well to refer to some others that perhaps need a little more thought. Of this kind are the applications of the prophecy to the social difficulties and evils of the day. It cannot be said, indeed, that our position as a nation is like that of Israel in those days when she was tottering to her fall. The evils among them had reached such a height that they were threatening her very existence, to which indeed they did soon after put an end. We certainly are not of those who think that we have come to a pass like that. And yet the same, or very similar, evils to those which proved the ruin of Israel exist among us to a deplorable degree—not yet, as we believe, threatening our very existence, but certainly weakening us, and a constant source of danger and continual disgrace. Those who are familiar with the prophecy will know what we mean when we say that evil with us is at the moth stage, not yet at the lion stage. It will be remembered how in the fifth chapter these two stages are spoken of. The moth stage is when evil keeps eating like a canker into the vitals of a people, but where there is nothing or very little to attract attention; no noise, nothing to alarm, the mischief done in secret and on a much more serious scale than is apt to be supposed, as every one knows to be the case with the ravages of the moth But let the moth stage go on, let corruption increase among a people, and presently the roar of the lion will be heard, there will be tumult and commotion, there will be the outbreak of open rebellion against the powers that be, on earth and in heaven too. Wherever there are the ravages of the moth in society there is danger of the breaking forth of the beast of prey, of which we have, indeed, some indications in our own times; not, indeed, of the very serious nature that some timid people suppose, for these outbreaks* in Trafalgar Square and Hyde Park are mere surface explosions, blazings of light chips and straws, and not volcanic fires, as some foreign newspapers represent —still, they do give some idea of the danger which threatens. And, by the bye, it is interesting to notice that in Hosea's time there evidently had been Trafalgar Square meetings, only less moderate in tone; for it was not work those people were demanding, but wages without work, as would appear from a passage in the seventh chapter, where it is said, "They assemble themselves for corn and wine; they rebel against Me."

Now the prophet Hosea has it for his great object throughout to show the cause and the cure of all these evils, which began by eating like a moth and ended by

* In the spring of 1888.

tearing like a lion. The cause is unfaithfulness to God, and the cure is returning to Him with the whole heart. He is continually showing them that what they have put in place of the God whom they have cast off proves, not their safety, as they supposed, but their destruction. There, for instance, was the great stroke of policy by which Jeroboam the son of Nebat sought to strengthen the Northern kingdom—the setting up of the calves at Bethel and at Dan, to keep the people from being attracted to Jerusalem, and the rival kingdom of the South of which it was the capital. Thus Samaria sought to make herself strong against Jerusalem by casting off the God of their fathers, and making sanctuaries of their own; and this sin of Jeroboam the son of Nebat was never given up all through the history of Israel. What has Hosea to say about this foundation-stone of the national policy? Does he keep quiet about it, as too dangerous a subject to touch? He has a great deal to say about it again and again throughout the prophecy; but nowhere is there more vigour in his tone than when he puts it thus: "Thy calf, O Samaria, hath cast thee off!"

Has modern society no calf? Aaron, we remember, set the example of calf-worship; and we cannot forget how Moses spoke of it when he came down from the mountain: "Oh, this people have committed a great sin; they have made them a god—of gold." Does not modern society make a god of gold? Is not that "covetousness which is idolatry" a national vice? And when social discontent manifests itself, when pauperism threatens to increase, with its attendant evils, there are many who can think of no other way of meeting it than by appealing to the god of gold: if only the money of the rich could be got hold of and distributed among the poor! And yet there is nothing so demoralising as the mere distribution of money, especially if it have in the least degree the appearance of blackmail. Even when it is given in genuine charity, if nothing else is done than the mere distribution of money, it is apt to do far more harm than good. It is greatly to be feared that even "The Mansion-House Fund," excellent as was its intention, did more harm than good on the whole. No, no; money alone is of no use, mostly worse than useless; money, of course, is needful for all good works that are done, or can be set on foot for the elevation and improvement of the people; but to make it a mere matter of getting or taking money from one class and giving it over to another is a delusion, and if carried out by force would be ruin to society. Gold in itself works no cure. Its uselessness seems even to mock those who in their hearts have regarded it as almighty. "Thy calf, O Samaria, hath cast thee off!"

Israel had a calf at Dan as well as at Bethel. The calf at Bethel was in the extreme south, as near to Jerusalem as possible. The calf at Dan was in the far north, as far from the temple of God as possible. Has modern society a calf at Dan as well? The giving of money is something which lies very near to the sacred territory of true Christianity; for it has the appearance of charity, though genuine charity it is not, unless it be accompanied by that thoughtful love which is quite wanting in the indiscriminate giving of which we have been speaking. Still, it lies near enough to it to be often confounded with it, often seen in the same line as looked at from the hill of Samaria. But suppose we travel away in the other direction, away from all connection with Christianity, away to the north; we find the people there gathered round another idol, which has the name of Natural Law. Their trust is in the laws of Evolution, working through the struggle for existence to the survival of the fittest. And the great effort of these people is to bring man and all that concerns him under the stern operation of that law. They may not, indeed, trouble themselves much about social questions, but the whole drift of their teaching is to consign everything to the interaction of great forces which work out their own ends without any help or comfort from above. And, as a matter of fact, is not business carried on very much according to the idea of these people? We ask business men, Is not business becoming more and more a struggle for existence with the survival of the strongest—competition so keen everywhere that the weak must go to the wall? And how does it work? Its working can be best seen where it has had a fair field with no favour of vested rights or great landed proprietaries. How, then, has it been working in America? It has tended to the building up, at the one end of the social scale, of a few colossal fortunes, perhaps larger accumulations of wealth in the hands of single individuals than has ever been reached even under laws of entail; at the other end degradation (in the slums of New York, for example), quite as bad as the worst in London; and between the two extremes the great middle class, throughout which there is ever closer and closer competition, involving harder and harder work with smaller and smaller returns. Is not that the way in which the principle of every man for himself in the struggle for existence, with the survival of the strongest and the pushing of the weak to the wall—is not that the way in which it is working itself out everywhere? The Northern calf is no better than the Southern one.

Well, what shall we do? A question much more easily asked than answered. But there is some help towards an answer in this prophecy. Let us endeavour to follow its hints a little further. In chapter v. 13 we read that " when Ephraim saw his sickness, and Judah saw his wound, then went Ephraim to the Assyrian, and sent to King Jareb: yet could he not heal you, nor cure you of your wound." King Jareb means, as is seen in the margin, one who will contend, who will use the rough-and-ready remedy of force. And we have those among us who think that King Jareb is the very man. They believe in doing it all by Act of Parliament, registering the decrees of King Demos, who will in that way entitle himself to the name Jareb. Now legislation can do a great deal, and there is much to be hoped for from it in the way of amelioration, and of redress of injustice and of grievances; but it cannot cure society, or heal it of its deadly wounds. There are many things needful to be done that cannot be done by force.

There are many reforms, and these by far the most needful and far-reaching in their result, which can only be accomplished by the diffusion of a spirit of love; and this is only possible by a general return of the people to the Lord their God. The humanitarian spirit which is shown by not a few of those who make no profession of faith in God is much to be commended; but it never can by its inherent force make way in society. To flow as a fertilising stream through the waste places of society, it must take its rise in the high mountains of divine faith and hope and love; the nether springs of human generosity must be fed by the upper springs of divine grace. And this is the reason why the prophet Hosea so continually reminds the people that the only hope for better days is to return to the Lord their God, and the prophet Joel sets before the society of his day as its great hope, "I will pour out my Spirit upon all flesh." That is what we need to-day.

Let us try to indicate how it would work in a particular case. Our hearts have been harrowed lately by hearing of the sufferings of the matchmakers, who have to work so terribly hard for such a wretched pittance. Who is to blame? "The firms employing them," you say. Well, go to one of the firms and remonstrate, and what answer do you get? Something like this perhaps: "My good friend, there is no one who would be more willing to halve the labour and double the pay of these poor creatures; but if we did it we could not sell our matches. You Christian people are bound always to have things at the very lowest rate at which it is possible to produce them, and this is the result" Thus you are thrown back on the universal demand for excessive cheapness; and you see at once that it is wrong. Are you not ashamed to buy a box of matches, or a dozen boxes rather, at the miserable rate you pay for them? But what can you do? If you could deal directly with the poor girls who make them, you would most gladly pay all that they are worth, and more too; but you cannot; you cannot get at them in the way of business—by paying two or three prices to the shopkeeper you would not do the poor matchmakers a fraction of service. And that is not saying anything against the shopkeeper; for he could not, however willing he might be, send the excess that you had paid him to the poor girl at the cost of whose life-blood they had been made.

Perhaps some one says, "Why not have a grand association banded together to pay a sufficient price for matches?" But then it is not only matches that are too cheap. There are a thousand things for which we pay less than we should; and what can be done? It is evident that to meet the case we are thrown back on the necessity of some force that will operate all through society, and it cannot be external force; it is no use sending to King Jareb; we cannot ask Parliament to fix a minimum for prices—the veriest tyro in social science knows that is out of the question; we must have a force acting on society through its heart, a force which will counteract the miserable selfishness that always keeps beating prices down. We need a force operating on society in such a way that a match manufacturer (to keep to our original illustration) might pay his *employés* a fair remuneration for their work, charge a corresponding price for his goods, and feel sure that there would be no less demand for the dear matches that were innocent of blood than for the cheap ones that were not. Now, where can we get such a force? Only from above; only from God, the Father of us all, through the Lord Jesus Christ, who alone teaches effectually the true brotherhood of man; not, of course, by the mere formal assent to His teaching which is given by all those who call themselves Christians, but by the genuine, living, loving Christianity which would be the result of the outpouring of the Spirit of Christ. The enthusiasm of humanity will never do it alone; especially in these days, when the social system is so complicated that we never look into the face of one in a thousand of those who are working for us. Nothing else will do it than the love of God shed abroad in the hearts of men by the Holy Spirit given to them. If this Divine love were diffused all through society, there would be no need of appealing to King Jareb, or any king but the King of Love Himself. The calf of gold would be destroyed; the miserable law of natural selection based on the struggle for existence and survival of the fittest would be dominated by another law, even the law of God, as summed up in these two golden precepts: "Thou shalt love the Lord thy God with all thy heart, and with all thy soul, and with all thy strength, and with all thy mind—and thy neighbour as thyself."

Then would the moth perish, then would the canker disappear from our civilisation; there would be no colossal fortunes, beyond all reasonable demand of capital to carry on works of usefulness; and at the other end of the scale there would be no more destitution than could be dealt with by the natural outflow of private beneficence. And there would be an end of that rigid system of close competition, which, as things now are, is forced even upon those to whom it is most uncongenial by the imperious demand for cheapness, and the determination of some to take advantage of this demand to possess themselves of the business which belonged to their neighbours. Then we should begin to see around us the meaning of these old words of promise: " They that dwell under His shadow shall revive as the corn and grow as the vine."

Well, what can we do to hasten on that happy day? (1) We can work and pray for the spread of the Gospel, and the establishment upon the earth of the kingdom of "righteousness, and peace and joy in the Holy Ghost." This is the one hope of society as of the individual. (2.) We can in all possible ways show the spirit of the Gospel in all our dealings with our neighbours, making it evident that love, not selfishness, is the mainspring of our life. So shall we best help to hasten on the day when society as a whole shall return to the Lord our God, and men shall find that "His going forth is prepared as the morning"—the morning dawn of a brighter, better day.

XVI.

LAY HELP IN CHURCH WORK.

(*A Paper read at the Presbyterian General Council, held in Belfast in* 1884.)

THE subject is not a new one, and therefore it is not necessary to begin at the beginning of it. There are certain positions that may be fairly assumed. One is, that the great work of the Church is to win the world for Christ—a vast aggressive enterprise. It is true that there is much to be done by the Church, important, necessary work, connected with its support and the administration of its affairs; but all that should be mere "office expenses" in proportion to the whole. A man is not idle when he is eating or dressing, but he does not count these exertions into the business of the day. The work of the Church is not to maintain herself and administer her own affairs, but to "preach the Gospel to every creature."

We may further assume that the responsibility of this great enterprise rests, not on certain individuals in the Church, but on the Church as a whole, and that therefore each individual member should have a share in it. It is admitted, of course, that this is not the only field of Christian service "Whatever we do, in word or in deed," should be done "in the name of the Lord Jesus;" and, accordingly, the Christian mother in the home, the Christian man of business in the city, all Christians in whatever capacity they serve, have the right to be considered Christian workers. That it is the duty of all Christian people to be engaged in Christian work, in this wide sense of the word, has always been admitted; but it is now also acknowledged to be the duty and privilege of all to do what they can in the specific work of the Church, the work of carrying the Gospel to all who need it. We may, therefore, assume this point also.

But while these general principles may be fairly enough assumed, there are certain applications of them which need consideration, some of which it may be well to state. It is very often taken for granted that until a congregation is self-supporting it need have little, if anything, to do with what may be called the out-door work of the church. It is supposed to be necessary for a time to husband its resources. This may seem a common-sense policy, but it is not a Christian one. Let us not forget what the Master says, and repeats so often and so earnestly, anent husbanding resources: "He that will save his life shall lose it, and he that will lose his life for my sake shall find it." This is the foundation-principle of Christian life. And can it be that the Church, as a Church, has nothing to do with it? Where are we to seek the guiding principles of the New Testament Church if not in the Sermon on the Mount? Have, then, weak congregations "neither part nor lot" in a certain magnificent passage of that sermon, of which the following are the salient points: "Be not anxious for your life, what ye shall eat, or what ye shall drink; nor yet for your body, what ye shall put on. Is not the life more than the food, and the body than the raiment? . . . But seek ye first the kingdom of God, . . . and all these things shall be added unto you."

Is not the word "self-sustaining" too large a word

in our ecclesiastical vocabulary? Are not many congregations, strong as well as weak, weak as well as strong, ready to die of saving their own lives? Think of the amount of energy, of real life and work as well as money, absorbed by hundreds of our congregations in the mere struggle to house themselves And the question is suggested, whether all that is really needed in the way of church building and the maintaining of ordinances would not be more easily reached if it were put in the second place instead of the first, if the order of the Lord's Prayer were made the order of Church anxiety—first, the hallowing of the Divine name, the coming of the Divine kingdom, the doing of the Divine will upon the earth; and then, secondary and subordinate to these, the securing of daily bread.

This reminds us, that even the spiritual welfare of the Church, represented as it is by the two last petitions of the Lord's Prayer, should be subordinate to the general interests of the kingdom, represented by the first three. Not that spiritual welfare can be overestimated, but it is subject to the same law as to losing and saving. In the higher sphere, as well as in the lower, in our Church relations too, as well as in our private life, we should think more of giving than of getting, more of work than of food, more of edification in its active than in its passive sense. The true way to be healthy in spiritual as well as in temporal things is, to give ourselves so heartily to our work that both the food itself and the appetite for it come to us without special thought or care. And so, again, it is in Church life. "Satan finds some mischief still for idle hands to do;" and he does not confine his operations to the outside of the Church. It is written that "Jeshurun" (*even* Jeshurun, the righteous one) "waxed fat and kicked;" from which the lesson plainly is,

Give Jeshurun more work to do of a legitimate kind; give him more work to do with "feet shod," as they ought to be, "with the preparation of the gospel of peace," and there will be less abnormal use of his heels. Overfeeding and underworking is unquestionably an evil to be dreaded in Church life. Has not Presbyterianism in the past suffered oftentimes and in many ways from a plethora of doctrine in proportion to practice, of sermons in proportion to service? And by "service" here we do not mean "divine service" in the popular English sense—a very misleading expression, from the New Testament point of view at all events. In the House of God it is not we that serve Him; it is He that serves us, in order that we may be strengthened and prepared to work for Him in the world without—our proper sphere of service. The Scotch expression, "diet of worship," is a much happier one. But it is doubtful if even Scotch Presbyterians have borne sufficiently in mind that "where much is given" in the way of diet, "much is required" in the way of exercise. Think how many unprofitable speculations on matters too high for us, and distracting controversies consequent thereon, might have been spared if there had been more work doing, more of the real hard work of winning souls to Christ. How much of mere ballooning has there been in the history of theological thought, how many battles fought in the upper air, with no other result to the weary and heavy-laden multitudes below than the dropping on their heads of some of the fragments from the fray? If only the Apostle's practice could have been kept up, of closing every doctrinal discussion with a "Therefore, my beloved brethren," a new trumpet-call to be "always abounding in the work of the Lord"! It is true that the same Apostle was once caught up to "the third heavens;" but, when he came down again to common earth, he was wise enough not to try to give the world the benefit of his discoveries. He simply tells us that he "heard words unspeakable, which it is not lawful for a man to utter,"—a most wise reticence, and much to be imitated. He, no doubt, could have said much, but he probably could not have ended with "Therefore, my beloved brethren." He was too much in earnest in saving men to think it worth his while to satisfy the curiosity of speculative minds. And if even such "visions and revelations of the Lord" as the Apostle might have given were out of place when so much work was to be done, what is to be said of the endless hair-splitting which has so often taken the place of heart-winning in the energies of Christian people? But this is happily an age of work, and we have probably learnt at last that it is of immeasurably less consequence to discuss Supralapsarian and Sublapsarian theories than to restore lapsed Presbyterians and bear our share in rescuing lapsed masses.

Still another important application of the axioms of our subject bears on the relative importance of Church order and Church work. It is said that "order is Heaven's first law." But Heaven's order is the order in which things are *done*. It is not capable of being used, like Parliamentary order, and Church order too, we fear, for hindering anything being done. In a certain convenient and oft-quoted text there has been too much emphasis on the adverb and too little on the verb: "Let all things be done decently and in order." Yes, "decently and in order," by all means, that is the adverb; but do not forget the verb, which, as every Latin scholar knows, is *the* word in the sentence. "Let all things be *done*." Some of our authorities on Church order are sometimes apt to forget that there are many things which, though best done in order, are better done even out of order than not done at all. I had a letter recently from a friend in reference to some work which the churches in the neighbourhood had been slow to take up, because it took them so very long to find out the best and most orderly way of doing it. He writes:—" Our Society plunges into it, and does not pause to work it up to principle, or to state the case." Now, it is good, and it may be necessary, to lay down principles and state the case before a new departure is made, and a pause for so good a purpose is a good thing. But church pauses are apt to be too closely up to the definition of the old παυω, from which the word comes—" I cause to cease "—they are apt to be of the kind too fitly described in the language of the poet—

" An awful pause, prophetic of the end "

In regard to new departures, especially in Presbyterian Church Courts, it may be sometimes expedient to press the exhortation, " Stand not upon the order of your going, but go at once."

To sum up these general considerations, it is evident that in order to approach the ideal of the Church the word " WORK " must be written in much larger letters in our assemblies, synods, presbyteries, sessions, congregations, hearts, and lives. There is, thank God, a spirit of work abroad among Christian people. Already it has been too much constrained to seek channels for its activity outside the Church; it is high time we were giving it fullest scope within. And if " work " were written larger, " money " might be written smaller, which would be a great blessing. But though the type would be smaller, the figures would be larger; for when men first give *themselves*, there is no withholding of their means. " Not yours, but you," should be our motto everywhere, with the richest as well as with the poorest.

There is plenty of money in the great Presbyterian Church; and wherever it is manifest that an earnest work is going on, not the mere erection of a church building or providing for a minister's stipend or a missionary's salary, but the gathering in of souls, the manifest extension of the gospel of Christ, there money will flow in quite sufficient abundance. And then, apart from the money power of the Presbyterian or any other Church, we have the old promise, given, let it be remembered, in connection with the very difficulties as to self-support which so often paralyse the enterprise of Christian congregations, "God is able to make all grace abound unto you, that ye, having always all sufficiency in everything, may abound unto every good work: . . . and He that supplieth seed to the sower and bread for food" ("seed to the sower" first, "bread for food" next) "shall supply and multiply your seed for sowing, and increase the fruits of your righteousness' (here, again, the "seed for sowing" comes even before the "fruits of righteousness"); "ye being enriched in everything unto all liberality."

It will be evident from the foregoing that it is more than help that is expected from the laity, that is, from the people. Or, if we keep the word, it is help in the American, and not the English sense. In America a maid-of-all-work is sometimes called a "help," to save her feelings, but she has the work to do nevertheless. The mistress does the directing. So in a Presbyterian congregation there ought to be so much work going on that minister and elders have all they can do in originating, inspiring, directing the abundant labours of the people, and setting the new-comers to work. Properly speaking, the people are the doers, and the minister and the elders the helpers. We have had far too much in the past of what may be called the General-without-Army policy, which will not work though you have generals like the great Napoleon or the magnificent Gordon. One of the best generals I know in mission work in London is one who was almost given up as a failure, and, what is worse, almost gave himself up as a failure, because he set to work at first with no army at his back. Since he has had a band of workers round him from a Christian congregation, the only limit to his success has been the straitness of his barns to hold his fruits and his goods. An enlargement made a year ago leaves him to-day as hard pressed for room as he was before.

If the officers of the Church were set more free from the actual doing of the work, to keep an eye over the whole field, so as to be well acquainted with its different departments, and to be ready to find the right place for all right men and women who joined the establishment (I use the word in its business, not in its ecclesiastical sense, the idea being that every Christian congregation is as definitely an establishment for winning hearts and lives to Christ as a mercantile establishment is for doing its particular business)—if the officers of the Church were thus set free to survey the whole field of battle, might there not be a much better disposition of the forces, as well as a much larger force to make disposition of? Then it would not be necessary, as it would not be possible, to turn the whole force into the Sabbath-school, offering to almost everybody the same work —a very poor way of striving after the ideal of the Christian household which our Lord Himself has left us: authority given to the servants, "and to every man his work." "Necessity is the mother of invention;" and if it were laid upon the conscience of the officers of the Church to find useful and suitable employment as soul-winners for every member of the Church, our Christian wits would be much sharpened, and our Christian activity much enlarged and diversified, and the wants of individual cases would not receive so little special attention as they do now. There is too much disposition to restrict Church work to that which is done in meetings and classes, to the neglect of that individual dealing which is likely to be the most effective of all. We take the promise, " Where two or three are gathered together in my name, there am I in the midst of them," as an encouragement when a meeting is small which ought to be large; but is there any reason why it should not be applied to the smallest possible meeting, when it is neither expected nor desired to have more present than the two who claim the first share in the promise? The minister is supposed to endeavour to reach his people individually; but this is possible only to a most limited extent when the congregation is a large one. The Sabbath-school teacher also is supposed to deal with individual members of his class as well as with the class as a whole. But beyond this, there is little done in the way of individual dealing under the auspices of the Church. Now, why should not the ministry to individuals be divided among Christian people? Consider how much more a minister has accomplished by setting others to this work than by merely doing it himself. Suppose he has, as every minister ought to have, a number of inquirers, who are anxious for spiritual guidance, and that instead of taking the cases one after another himself, and hurrying through them, as he must needs do, he distributes them, not hastily, but with much thought and care, among several earnest and prudent members of his flock, laying upon them the responsibility of dealing with them in detail, and only keeping the general direction and guidance in his own hands, what may be expected as the result? First, there will be brought to bear far more force of thought and sympathy and prayer, as well as of personal attention and effort; and these, be it remembered, are the great forces on which we have to rely. The minister does not relinquish his own responsibility, and probably gives as much thought and prayer to the whole number as if he had kept them in his own hand. And then each one of those who work under his directions gives his own thought and prayer to it, and will probably write letters and watch for opportunities of doing good which would be impossible for the minister under the pressure of other claims. Whatever value there is in official authority is retained; for those who do the work do it, not in their own name, but in the name of the minister or elder, and thus are free from the imputation of intrusion; and, on the other hand, the work is secured from the disadvantage of officialism; for it cannot be set down to the mere discharge of duty, but must be accepted as evidence of real, warm, human interest. It avoids the Scylla of the officious on the one hand, and the Charybdis of the official on the other. And then, to crown all, not only is the work done, and done in the best way, but it brings rich blessings to those through whom it is done, giving them the very exercise they need for their spiritual growth. The same principle manifestly applies to the visitation of the sick, and to all cases requiring individual attention.

But the subject widens out, so that the limits imposed demand the most rigid compression; and, therefore, we shall content ourselves with giving specimens of questions that would come up for consideration and decision in all our congregations if only it were distinctly understood and acknowledged that there ought to be work found for everybody in the congregation to do. Ought not the ministry of the Word to be as varied as it evidently was in apostolic times, so that not only ministers and elders, but deacons and private members, should all share in "holding forth the word of life?" Should not much more use be made of the musical talent in our congregations, not only *inside*, in leading the praise, but *outside*, in commending the Gospel? And in outside employment of our musical talent, would not "teaching and admonishing in psalms and hymns and spiritual songs" be a much more noble and dignified service than that of giving concerts to raise money? In view of the importance of winning men to church as a means of winning them to Christ, is it really the best thing to leave to official doorkeepers and pew-openers the duty and privilege of acting as hosts in the Lord's House? Would it not be better if some of our best men had the pleasant duty assigned them of giving a hearty welcome to those who come as strangers to dine with us at our diet of worship on the Lord's Day or to lunch with us in the middle of the week? Ought not medical mission work to be a distinct branch in the congregation, superintended and guided by the medical men who are members of the congregation, and calling out in the most sympathetic way the loving helpfulness of those who are willing to watch by the bed of the sick for Jesus' sake? Ought not training-classes for the different departments of Christian work to be instituted and kept up; and ought not teachers in the Sabbath-school, and visitors, to be drawn as much as possible from those who have been so trained? And ought there not to be an evangelistic department in connection with our colleges for training students for the ministry? Ought not the office of the deacons, and the work of those who have to do with money matters, to be specially guarded from the secular spirit, as in the days of the apostles, not only by insisting on high spiritual qualifications on the part of all who are selected for the purpose, but also by associating with it some such share in the ministry of the Word as the primitive deacons manifestly had? And ought not the office of the deaconess to be revived, without any further separation from the duties of ordinary life than in the case of the elder, but with the right and privilege and duty of attending to that large portion of the ordinary district visitation which neither minister nor elder can well overtake?

As I have been led into a series of questions, I shall put in the same form all that I have left myself time to say on that part of the subject of woman's work which gives rise to the keenest discussion, namely, her sphere in the ministry of the Word. Since woman has an acknowledged sphere in teaching children and youth, at what age must the scholars have arrived when it shall cease to be proper that she should continue to instruct and guide them? And since she has an acknowledged liberty to speak about Christ and His love in the presence of two three, four, or more, so long as the company is a small one, at what particular point does the company cease to be small enough? And seeing that there is evidently some little difficulty in settling definitely these simple questions, the further question is suggested—What other line can be drawn than that which the Providence of God without, and the Spirit of God within, seem to indicate in each particular case?

XVII.

THE MISSIONARY OUTLOOK.

(A Sermon preached on behalf of the Baptist Missionary Society, April 25, 1888.)

"The Lord hath made bare His holy arm in the eyes of all the nations: and all the ends of the earth shall see the salvation of our God."—ISA. lii. 10.

WHAT a marvel are these missionary chapters of Isaiah! Almost every sentence is a wonder. To us it is no longer so, because it is so old a story *now*, and so much has happened since it was first told. But think of words like these being spoken *then*. If the traditional date is correct, it was the time when Israel had just been overthrown, and Judah was hastening to its fall. And yet this prophet of Judah declares, with absolute assurance, and in the most majestic language, that the God of Israel and His salvation shall be known to the uttermost parts of the earth; and time has proved that what he said was true. This is miracle enough. But the wonder is greater still if those modern critics be correct who bring down the date of these chapters to the days of the exile; for in that case the voice comes to us, not from the sunset of the nation, but from its midnight; it is a shout of victory out of Judah's grave.

What utter nonsense these glowing periods must have seemed to the politicians of the day—to all the people, indeed, except those of "like precious faith" with the prophet himself! Will any one dare to speak of them as nonsense *now?* Take the sentence before us as a sample. It consists of two parts, holding forth prospects both equally out of sight at the time, the one as purely visionary as the other when the words were spoken. More than twenty centuries have rolled away; the first is now literal fact, the second is plainly drawing nigh. The Lord God of Israel "*hath* made bare His holy arm in the eyes of all the nations:" the Bible in two hundred and fifty languages; the heralds of the Cross in every part of the world; all tongues and all lands open to Isaiah's gospel of salvation; converts multiplying, not, indeed, as we could wish, but enough, at least, to verify the prophet's words: "Lo, these shall come from far: and, lo, these from the north and from the west; and these from the land of Sinim." Most unquestionably "the Lord hath made bare His holy arm in the eyes of all the nations;" and this being so, it ought not to be so very difficult, in looking forward to the future, to read the second member of the sentence with as unfaltering tones: "All the ends of the earth shall see the salvation of our God."

The first thought suggested to our minds by considerations like these is the exceeding hopefulness of our present position as compared with times that are past. We have seen how dark was the outlook in the days of the prophet Isaiah; and yet even he felt that there was encouragement to be had by looking back. See how he avails himself of this in the chapter immediately before: "Look unto Abraham your father; . . . for when he was but one I called him, and I blessed him, and made him many" (Rev. Ver.) "When he was but one;" and to this one man was given the missionary promise in its largest scope: "In thy seed shall all the nations of the earth be blessed."

And this one man believed it, too—believed it no doubt as firmly as our most successful missionaries do to-day. Well indeed might he be called "the father of the faithful"

Have you not observed that it has been in the days of deepest discouragement that the great missionary promise has rung out in fullest and clearest tones? Recall, for example, that time in the history of God's people when they had reached the borders of their promised land, and the scouts had been sent forward to prepare the way for an advance in force. Back came the scouts with this report: "The people be strong that dwell in the land, and the cities are walled, and very great: and moreover we saw the children of Anak there." "And all the congregation lifted up their voice and cried, and the people wept," and clamoured for a captain to lead them back to Egypt. What an army! Oh miserable failure! After all the patriarchal training, after all the discipline in Egypt, after all the wonders of the Exodus, after all the inspiration of Sinai, after all that "glorious marching" through the wilderness, the hosts of the Lord, instead of going forward to set up His kingdom in the appointed place, are about to beat an inglorious retreat back to Egypt and slavery again. But all is not yet lost. There remain still on the Lord's side the prayers of one old man, and the faith and courage of two young men; and in answer to that old man's prayer, and to fortify these young men's courage, while the decree is passed that not one of all this faithless multitude shall ever set foot in the land, there is given this grand assurance, "As truly as I live, all the earth shall be filled with the glory of the Lord" (Num. xiv. 21).

Recall another time later on. The land has been won and occupied for centuries, but the nation has not fulfilled its lofty destiny; it has not been the blessing to the world it was meant to be; the people have failed of their high vocation to be "kings and priests to God," and now the days of the nation are nearly run, and a prophet is charged with the heavy burden of having to announce the coming of the Chaldeans to put an end to its career. The prophet ventures to plead with the Lord, like Moses of old; and having urged his plea, he says, "I will stand upon my watch, and set me upon the tower, and will look forth to see what He will speak with me . . . concerning my complaint." So he betakes himself to his lonely watch-tower, and the answer comes—confirming, indeed, the sentence of judgment, but giving the assurance at the same time that this crowning disaster will not interfere with the fulfilment of the great missionary promise, for on the thick thundercloud of judgment there is spread once again the bright bow of promise: "The earth shall be filled with the knowledge of the glory of the Lord, as the waters cover the sea" (Hab. ii. 14).

We are sometimes discouraged when we see those missionary diagrams, with their little spots of light and their great masses of darkness. What sort of a missionary diagram should we have to draw for the days of Abraham, or of Caleb, or of Habakkuk? A pin-point of light on a page of darkness would be too much. And yet it was at these times that the faith of God's people took firmest hold of the great missionary promise, that "the earth" should one day "be filled with the glory of the Lord, as the waters cover the sea." Surely this is a rebuke to little faith in days like ours, when, however far we may be yet from the grand consummation, it is at least plain that "the Lord hath made bare His holy arm in the eyes of all the nations."

We might refer to other epochs in the history of the

missionary enterprise. We might speak, with reverence, of "the Holy One of Israel" Himself, who, when Israel as a nation had finally failed to be the "light to the Gentiles" she ought to have been, came forward Himself to fulfil the ancient covenant. You remember that when the shadow of the Cross was darkest, and to all earthly appearance failure seemed about to be stamped upon His mission too, a few Greeks came to one of the disciples with the request, "Sir, we would see Jesus." To Philip it no doubt seemed a very slight occurrence, not so to the Master. In these few Greeks He recognises the first-fruits of the Gentiles; and the shame and pain of the Cross being lost in the thought of "the glory that shall follow," He exclaims, "The hour is come, that the Son of Man should be glorified;" and after struggling with the dark forebodings which fill His human soul with dismay at the thought of the awful darkness immediately before Him, He closes with this note of triumph, "I, if I be lifted up from the earth, will draw all men unto Myself."

We might speak of the last of the apostles in lonely Patmos, his fellow-labourers all gone, himself silenced—sadly aware that error and corruption are eating out the life of the churches he and his fellow-apostles have planted, while persecuting Rome seems everywhere triumphant—not a gleam of light, one would say, in all the dark horizon; and yet out of that darkness comes the great Apocalypse,—a vision of storm indeed; but beyond all storms there is peace and final victory, again the great missionary promise rings out, strong and clear as ever: "The seventh angel sounded; and there followed great voices in heaven, and they said, The kingdom of the world is become the kingdom of our Lord, and of His Christ; and He shall reign for ever and ever."

Even since the canon of special inspiration closed, there

have never been wanting men, in days of deepest discouragement, to hold high above all the changes of the passing time the hope of a regenerated world. We might speak of Augustine of Hippo, in those days so dark and dreadful to the Christians of the time, when the heathen barbarians were pouring in on all sides, and threatening to sweep away that empire of Rome on which, since the days of Constantine, had been fixed the hopes of the faithful for the final conquest of the world for Christ. To the Christians of the West the fortunes of the kingdom of Christ seem absolutely bound up with the fortunes of Rome, and there is Alaric the Goth thundering at its gates; he has broken in, and Rome is at his mercy; the churches are burning; the worshippers are scattered; their blood is flowing fast; again the hopeless cry goes up to Heaven, "O God, the heathen are come into Thine inheritance . . . The dead bodies of Thy servants have they given to be meat unto the fowls of the heaven. . . . We are become a reproach to our neighbours, a scorn and derision to them that are round about us." Across the sea, in little Hippo, the great Augustine answers the taunts of the mockers of the time by that monumental work, so influential from that day to this, in which he summons the people of God to look above and beyond the falling cities of men to the great City of God, the only eternal city, which must rise, though all Babylons and Romes should perish, "in the light of which all the nations yet shall walk." And just as the Master, when the Cross was near, cried, "The hour is come, that the Son of Man should be glorified," so did the disciple, when Christian Rome was tottering to its fall, rally the faith and courage of a well-nigh despairing age with the old assurance, "Glorious things are spoken of thee, O city of God."

Or we might refer to Carey, only a century ago, when the Church of Christ was as oblivious of her high calling as ancient Israel ever was—the old missionary covenant made with Abraham treated as so much waste paper—the idea of the Church of God "awaking and putting on her strength," in order that all the nations of the earth should see the salvation of God, as much despised and ridiculed as it could have been in the days of Isaiah himself—and there that noble hero stood, braving all ridicule and scorn, another Caleb, stemming almost alone the tide of unbelief and cowardly retreat; encouraging the people, as he did, with the words, " Let us go up at once and possess the land; for, with God on our side, we shall be well able to do it;" another Abraham, leaving his country and his kindred, and going out to a strange land, feeling well assured, though he sees not how, that the Lord will, in His own time and way, fulfil His ancient covenant that in His Christ all nations shall be blessed, and the whole earth "filled with the knowledge of the glory of the Lord, as the waters cover the sea" Are we not ashamed that our faith should waver or our courage fail, when we think of these men? These men "against hope believed in hope;" they "staggered not at the promise of God through unbelief," but were "strong in faith, giving glory to God, and being fully persuaded that what He had promised He was able also to perform." And shall we stagger at the promise of God through unbelief, now that " the Lord hath made bare His holy arm in the eyes of all the nations," now that " the little one has become a thousand, and the small one a strong nation," now that we have a thousand times as much to encourage us to believe in the future of the Divine Kingdom as had Abraham, or Caleb, or Habakkuk, or John, or Augustine, or Carey? Let us be done, then, with unbelief and cowardice, and let our faith and courage be at least as strong in days when the world is open before us, and light is spreading fast, and the morning star of hope has risen on the darkness of heathenism, as it was in the hearts of these faithful ones when hope seemed dead and light was quenched in night.

So far we have only been looking at one side of the great question. It is indeed true that never before has there been nearly so much to encourage us in looking forward to the future of the kingdom of God. But it is equally true that never have the discouragements been so prominent and conspicuous as they are to-day. The combat thickens as the Church of Christ advances. The faithlessness of friends and the fury of foes may be no greater in the thick of battle than when the opposing forces eye each other from a greater distance; but they are more alarming. Unbelief and apathy on the part of Christian people were so far excusable a century ago; it needed such strong faith in these days to believe in God's ability and willingness to " make bare His holy arm in the eyes of all the nations " that it was little to be wondered at that so many, even of those who might fairly be called good Christian people, showed themselves quite incapable of it. But similar apathy and unbelief now are much more discouraging, just because they are so utterly inexcusable and unaccountable. We have our heroes of faith and devotion—men who, no doubt, could stand alone if it were necessary, like Caleb, or like Carey. And besides these, we have tens of thousands in fullest sympathy with them. But, on the other hand, the great majority of those who call themselves Christians are so faithless, so selfish, so apathetic, so indifferent to the progress of the Gospel of Christ among the nations, that it would seem as if this generation, taken as a whole, were as unfit to set foot in the promised land as were the contemporaries of Caleb and of Joshua. And when we look back a hundred years, to the time when all that the Church of Christ could raise for missions in a year was not one-tenth part of what is sometimes given by single individuals now in a day, instead of boasting of our progress, we are inclined rather, as we think of what the Lord has wrought since then to encourage our faith and call out our devotion, to say that if the mighty works which have been done in sight of this generation had been done in the days of Sydney Smith and the other critics of the "consecrated cobbler," they would have repented long ago in sackcloth and ashes. When looked at in this light, the apathy of the majority in our day is as deeply discouraging as the apathy and unbelief of all a century ago.

And then there is the enemy sowing tares, with far busier hands than ever, with powers at his disposal such as were not dreamed of a century ago. As before, he has the world at his back, and the world is a far mightier force than it ever has been. As long as he can have selfishness for his prime minister, the world is his, and its forces are on his side. It costs money to send missionaries and Bibles, but it makes money to send drink and sell opium. So drink is sent in cargoes, cargoes of death passing continually from Christendom to heathendom, over those seas of which our country boasts herself the mistress; and the trade in opium is sacred, because, though it is ravaging with ruin the most populous country on the face of the earth, it pays. What hope for the world's redemption can there be, so long as selfishness can deal out death with far more lavish hand than love can scatter words of life?

Another discouragement is, that after all the progress which has been made, the field is larger and the work vaster than ever before. It is true that on our side "the little one has become a thousand;" but then, on the other side, the millions have increased. It is true that the proportionate increase of Christian converts in heathen lands is most encouraging, much greater than even of Mohammedans, of whose multiplication we have lately heard so much. But then in these Eastern lands the figures on our side are so very small, and on the other so enormously large, that though our *rate* of increase is much higher, yet the numerical increase on the side of Mohammedanism and heathenism is much greater than ours can be. So, though we are certainly gaining in a mathematical sense, we can scarcely be said to be gaining practically, for it is at so slow a pace that there seems no reasonable prospect, at the present rate, of even getting within sight of our goal.

From all this it follows that while, if we simply look at the progress which has been made in the last hundred years, from the days of Carey until now, we might conclude that we were already within measurable distance of our glorious goal; yet, when we look at the other side, and think of the magnitude of the work still to be done, the terrible might of the forces arrayed against us, and the sad lack of faith and hope, and love and devotion, on the part of very many whom we reckon on our side, it becomes evident that, though victory is certain, it is certain simply because "the mouth of the Lord hath spoken it," and before it can be reached there must be a change, a mighty change; the Church of Christ must "awake and put on her strength" as she has never yet done. While we have a thousand times as much to encourage us as there was at any of those past times of which we have been speaking, we have as much need as ever for faith in God, and for that devotion without which "faith is dead, being alone."

It is true that the work is God's, and He alone can do it; but it has been His purpose from the beginning that it shall be done through human agency. When Israel refuses to go up against the children of Anak, the Lord's purpose is not frustrated, but its execution is delayed. It would have been easy for God to drive out the Canaanite, and leave the land open for His people to enter without opposition; but it is His will that Israel shall do the work, and so nothing is done till Israel is ready. So was it, again, when Israel finally failed of her high vocation. The purpose of God, that in the seed of Abraham all nations should be blessed, could never fail; but the chosen nation lost the privilege of being the arm of the Lord to carry it out. The Holy One of Israel was compelled in sorrow to pronounce the sentence: "The kingdom of God shall be taken from you, and given to a nation bringing forth the fruits thereof." Now it is our time. Even if we were as foolish and selfish as Israel of old, the purpose of God, that all the ends of the earth should see His salvation, would not fail; but then it would fail of accomplishment by us. By other instruments the great work would be done. God could do it by miracle, of course. As at the first He said, "Let there be light, and there was light," so over the darkness of heathenism the same *fiat* might go forth to-day, and in a moment the earth would be filled with the glory of the Lord. But that would not be the accomplishment of the Divine will. That would not be the salvation of the world: it would be the annihilation of the world that now is, and the creation of another. It is the purpose of God that His people shall carry the light, that His Church shall stretch forth her hand to save the world. "The Lord shall make bare His arm." What is the arm of the Lord? Is not the Church His body; and if the Church is suffering from atrophy of the heart or palsy of the arm, how can the work be done? The old watchword is as true as ever, "Not by might, nor by power, but by My Spirit, saith the Lord." But the Spirit must animate the body, the vital current of force must flow from Him, "who is the head of the body, the Church," into the heart, and out to the arm, which then, and not till then, will be "the arm of the Lord," and, therefore, mighty to carry His salvation to the ends of the earth.

First of all, then, the heart must be right. There must be more life and warmth and power at home. This has always been the first necessity. Caleb recognised this when he said, "If the Lord delight in us, then He will bring us into this land." In the same way, when Habakkuk received the answer to his "complaint," he at once poured out his heart in the prayer, "O Lord, revive Thy work in the midst of the years." The Apocalypse begins with an earnest appeal to the seven churches to come back to their first love. And the old missionary psalm, which mingles prayer and prophecy in such a wondrous way, enshrines the same thought: "God be merciful to us and bless us, and cause Thy face to shine upon us, that Thy way may be known upon earth, Thy saving health among all nations." Nor can we forget how our Blessed Lord Himself connects in the closest way His own personal devotion, His being "obedient unto death, even the death of the Cross," with the ultimate triumph of His cause. "I, if I be lifted up from the earth, will draw all men unto Me." "This He said, signifying by what manner of death He should die." In every way is borne in upon us the great law of the kingdom, that if we would have more power in the arm, we must have more love in the heart; if we would win those that are without, we must have more of the spirit of self-sacrificing devotion within. "Ye shall receive power, after that the Holy Ghost is come upon you." The first and great thing, then, is more life and love and power at home.

Does this mean the slackening of effort abroad? That would be the last thing that would help the cause at home. Some people foolishly imagine that the fewer men and less money we send to foreign lands the more we can accomplish at our own doors. Experience proves that it is rather the exact contrary. It is not men, it is not money, we lack at home. There is abundance of both. What is wanted is an outpouring of the Spirit of God to consecrate the men, to consecrate the money we have. If only the Church would awake and put on her strength, she might quadruple her foreign force and her foreign contributions, and at the same time increase tenfold her power at home. Is not one man endued with power from on high far more influential than a thousand commonplace Christians content with the saving of their own little souls? Suppose we could halve the number of Christian workers at home by sending the other half away to far more needy fields abroad, and at the same time double the faith and love of all, does any one imagine that the work at home would suffer any loss? It would be an incalculable gain; for the doubled zeal of those that remained would not only accomplish more, but it would enkindle others, and, before many months were gone, the army of workers at home would be more numerous than ever. Devotion is like steam; it must be concentrated, or it cannot accomplish anything. Suppose the faith of Paul had been divided among a hundred men, would the whole hundred have accomplished as much as the one? Distribute the steam of one engine among a hundred, and see how much driving-power you can get. If we could reduce the Church of Christ in the world to-day to one-hundredth its present size, and let that part have as much faith and devotion as there is in the whole of it now, it would be like Gideon's three hundred, a power that nothing could resist. We need not be afraid, then, of diminishing our outward bulk, so long as that diminution is the result of increased energy in our proper work. Though exercise diminishes bulk, it increases strength and promotes health. Let us by all means, then, have, not less, but more exercise, especially at the extremities, where there is most need and greatest scope for it, but as to the vitals, what is above all necessary is purer blood. What is wanted is far more devotion, more of the Spirit of the Master, more of the blood of the Cross in the veins of the Church.

Almost every one has heard of the beautiful device, adopted by some American missionaries, of an ox standing between an altar and a plough, and, engraved beneath it, the motto, "Ready for either"—to do or to die for Jesus' sake. That spirit is wanted all through the Church, and it is a great thing that, even in these self-indulgent times, we have so many stirring examples of it in the foreign field, and notably in Africa, of which no better illustration could be given than the history of the Congo Mission. The heroism of General Gordon is known to all the world, because his name was connected with great national enterprises, and for this reason it has been of priceless value; but the records of purely missionary enterprise in the Dark Continent can show many Gordons —men by the score as brave, as devoted, as self-sacrificing to the uttermost; whose heroism would stir men's blood all over Christendom, if only the history of missions received half the attention it deserves; and no mission has been more highly honoured in this respect, perhaps none has furnished a larger contingent to "the noble army of the martyrs," than the Congo Mission of the Baptist Missionary Society.

Were such faith and devotion to become general, all men would see and recognise the unity of Christians. Who thinks of Hannington as an Episcopalian, or Comber as a Baptist? We only think of them as servants of Christ, and missionaries of His glorious Gospel. So ought it to be everywhere; and when it is so, the Church may lift up her head, for the day of the world's redemption will then be drawing nigh. We learn from our Lord's intercessory prayer that, as soon as the Church is seen to be one in Him, the world will believe; and our prophet gives a hint of it, too, for he has just been saying (verse 8), "Thy watchmen shall lift up the voice; with the voice together shall they sing; for they shall see eye to eye, when the Lord shall bring again Zion." And throughout all these missionary chapters the summons is addressed, not to individual believers, but to the Church as a whole. But the unity the prophet has in view does not preclude diversity; it is the unity of an army, which may be made up of different regiments and of various services, all united, however, under one banner. What this banner is he makes very plain. It is what all the ends of the earth are yet to see, the salvation of our God.

"The salvation of our God"—this is the keynote all through the great missionary epic. Not ritual, not philosophy, not theology, but *salvation* is the word. And the nature of the salvation is set forth with wonderful distinctness. Centuries must yet elapse before the Christ of God can come; but already the prophet of the Lord sees Him afar. "Behold, my servant!" he cries, and then describes the suffering Saviour, in that wonderful fifty-third chapter, as if the Gospel story had been already told. Later on he sees the Saviour-King at the head of His forces: "Behold, I have given Him for a Witness to the peoples, a Leader and Commander to the peoples" (lv. 4).

The salvation of our God through a crucified and exalted Christ, this was the banner of "the Evangelical Prophet;" and surely it should suffice for us, as it sufficed for the great Apostle who wrote: "I determined to know nothing among you, save Jesus Christ, and Him crucified" Here, then, is our rallying-point. It need not mar our unity that we differ on those matters of the circumference of truth in which true Christians of all ages have differed, so long as we are one in Christ Jesus, glorying in His Cross, accepting for ourselves and proclaiming to the world the salvation of our God. Why, then, should not the people of Christ, of every name, on whose banner is inscribed, "The Salvation of our God," advance together now as a mighty army, responding to the summons—

> "Onward, Christian soldiers,
> Marching as to war;
> With the Cross of Jesus
> Going on before"?

Then should we march to victory. It was a true instinct that led Constantine to put the cross on his banner, and set round it the device, "*In hoc signo vinces.*" Had not the Lord Himself said, "I, if I be lifted up from the earth, will draw all men unto Me"? See, too, how our prophet, immediately on concluding his great prophecy of Christ crucified, breaks forth in these inspiring strains: "Sing, O barren, thou that didst not bear; break forth into singing, and cry aloud, thou that didst not travail with child: for more are the children of the desolate than the children of the married wife, saith the Lord.

Enlarge the place of thy tent, and let them stretch forth the curtains of thine habitations: spare not, lengthen thy cords, and strengthen thy stakes; for thou shalt break forth on the right hand and on the left; and thy seed shall inherit the Gentiles, and make the desolate cities to be inhabited. Fear not; for thou shalt not be ashamed: neither be thou confounded; for thou shalt not be put to shame: for thou shalt forget the shame of thy youth, and shalt not remember the reproach of thy widowhood any more. For thy Maker is thine husband: The Lord of Hosts is His name; and thy Redeemer the Holy One of Israel; The God of the whole earth shall He be called." We can readily see how all this would come about, if only Christian people of every name made it evident—as evident as those African missionaries have made it—that they were followers of the crucified Saviour. If the Christians of every denomination were only thoroughly consecrated—living in the world as Christ was in the world, loving one another as He loved us—entitled, every one, to say, "To me to live is Christ"—would the world ever think of raising the question whether we agreed as to methods of government or form of worship? or even whether we were all at one as to the philosophy of that salvation by the atoning death of Christ, on which we rest as the only sure foundation for the hopes of lost sinners of mankind? No; they would see Christ in all, and that would be enough to make it plain that all were one in Him. Against such united testimony unbelief could not hold out for a single generation. Then would the Church grow as she did in the glow of her first love and devotion; the nation would speedily become Christian, not in name, but in very deed; our commerce would be converted; our ships would no longer carry drink and death, but life and light everywhere. Then the work would not be too great for us. We could do it very speedily. Even if we stood alone, we could do it; and of course we should not stand alone. Closely linked as are now all the nations of the civilised world, there could not be such a revival in Britain without similar movements in the United States and throughout all Christendom. But even if we stood alone, the one Christian nation on the face of the earth—but Christian to the very core—Christian through and through—Christ lifted up everywhere, His Gospel everywhere believed, His will everywhere done—the nation, as a nation, seeking first the kingdom of God and His righteousness—we could bring the heathen world to the feet of Christ in a very short time. The whole world is open to us in such a way that, with our great resources consecrated, as they would in that case be, to the cause of Christ—delivered from apathy at home and antagonism abroad—our politics, our trade and commerce, our literature, all the forces of the nation, on our side—we should soon see the most glowing prophecies of these missionary chapters fully realised. Even the sixtieth chapter would cease to be prophecy and become plain history—the history of our own times.

But, alas! to talk in this way seems almost as utopian as it must have seemed in the days of the prophet. We are so far from it, so sadly far from it. It is true that, if the Church were thoroughly roused, she could gain the nation; and if the nation were saved and sanctified, she could gain the world; but who or what will rouse the Church, who or what will unite all her forces, and so prepare the way of the Lord? Will not you rouse us all a second time? You did it a century ago. From you sounded out the Word of the Lord to a slumbering Church, to awake and put on her strength. Now that a century has gone, can you not give us all another impulse that will make the coming years as much greater and more fruitful than the present, as these are better than the old days, when the claims of the heathen were utterly neglected and forgotten?

We can all at least fall back on faithful Habakkuk's prayer; and we can look to ourselves and see to it that we, as individuals, are thoroughly devoted to our Master's service, and never cease from our endeavours to maintain and promote the unity of the Spirit, on which so much depends; that we do what we can, and give what we can, for the sending of the Gospel of salvation to the ends of the earth; and then, even though this generation too should pass away before the great promise is fulfilled, ours will be the honour of Caleb and of Carey, of having done what we could; and it will not be our fault that, though, at the time we lived upon the earth, the Lord did make bare His arm in the sight of all the nations, there had to be a further postponement of the day when all the ends of the earth should see the salvation of our God.

XVIII.

THE GOSPEL ACCORDING TO CHRIST.

THE differences which distinguish from each other the various branches into which the Church of Christ in the world, in its true Scriptural sense, is divided, are not of the essentials of the faith, and therefore do not affect its real unity and catholicity any more than the branching off of a tree interferes with its oneness as an organism. It is the sharing of the life of the tree, and not inclusion within the trunk, or even similarity of form and structure to other parts of the tree, which marks the vital connection of the branch with the root; and experience has proved that none of the truly evangelical denominations, as they are called, is excluded from the life which flows from Christ to all who are united to Him by a living faith. It has been made abundantly evident in the history of the Church that the Spirit of God will visit His people and dwell in their hearts, and make manifest the power of His grace among them, whatever mode of church government they may have thought it best to adopt. His presence and power are not made to depend on the monarchical and oligarchical institutions of Episcopacy, or on the republicanism of Presbyterians, or on the democracy of Congregationalists, but on a state of mind and heart which is to be found among them all quite irrespectively of these differences. It is no less certain that the Spirit of Christ is neither secured on the one hand, nor grieved away on the other, by any mode of administering the rite of baptism, or by any conviction that may be held as to the relation of infant children to that ordinance. Even the doctrinal differences which, in our time at least, distinguish Calvinists from Arminians, turn much more on deep questions of metaphysics than on the fundamentals of the faith. The modern Calvinist does not deny the freedom of the human will, nor does the modern Arminian deny the sovereignty of the Divine will; each may lay stress on certain doctrines which, when looked at alone, seem to involve the denial of the one or the other, and may do it in such a way as to betray a deficiency in the logical power which would lead an acuter mind to perceive the necessary consequence; but the Spirit of God can neither be won by good reasoning nor lost by bad logic; it is the trustful mind, the loving heart, the obedient will, which He demands; and wherever these are found, whether or not there be the power to argue wisely "of fix'd fate, freewill, foreknowledge absolute," *there* will be revealed the glory of His presence and the power of His grace.

It is otherwise, however, with certain far more serious differences which cross the lines of the different denominations; we refer especially to the Ritualism, which on the right runs out into superstition, and the Rationalism, which on the left passes into sheer infidelity.

These were the two great dangers of the apostolic times; and they are no less to be dreaded in our time. It was against these, and not against any of the positions which have been taken up by those who are commonly called Evangelical Christians in our day, that the apostolic warnings and anathemas were directed. Wise cautions were given against errors even in minor matters; but these were denounced most unsparingly, because they were regarded as entirely subversive of the Gospel; and sad experience has only too plainly proved that the apostles were altogether right.

It is true that the substance of the Gospel may be held in combination with many of the superstitions of Ritualism; and where this has been the case, God, in His abounding mercy, has not withheld His Spirit from those who have accepted His Son, even though in ignorance they have adopted views or followed practices which His Word discourages or condemns. So long as they have held faith and a good conscience—genuine faith in Christ, together with an honest following of Him according to the light that was in them—God has accepted them, and blessed them, and even in a marvellous way, considering their grievous errors, owned and honoured their efforts for His cause. This, too, is abundantly evident to all candid students of the history of the Christian Church. But none the less is it true that Ritualism, as such, is in direct antagonism to the Gospel. Those who have held the two together have done so by a happy inconsistency which has saved them from what would otherwise have been the fatal consequences of an essentially anti-evangelical belief. That it is no exaggeration to speak of ritualistic error in these terms is sufficiently evident from the solemn warning which the Apostle Paul addressed to the Galatian Church against this same heresy of Ritualism into which some of them had fallen: "I marvel that ye are so soon removed from Him that called you into the grace of Christ, unto another gospel, *which is not another.*" The Ritualism of our day, however, scarcely ventures to call itself the Gospel of Christ; rather does it claim to be something superadded to it on the authority of the Church. The Ritualist of our day, accordingly, is to be met, not by a discussion of what the Gospel is, but rather by enlightenment as to the Scriptural idea of the Church, and the nature and limits of its authority.

The Rationalism * to which we refer, on the other hand, not only claims to represent the Gospel of Christ, but to set it forth in its original simplicity and purity, free from those accretions which encumbered and disfigured it, after it had passed from the hands of the Founder of Christianity into those of His disciples. Its representatives make no attempt to harmonise their presentation of the Gospel with that of St. Paul or St. John; rather do they appeal from them to the higher authority of their Master, and profess to give to the world the original Gospel of Jesus Himself. On the strength of this appeal they deny all that is distinctive in the Gospel, as the announcement of a divine interposition for man's salvation, and reduce it to the mere setting forth of duties which we are counselled or enjoined to perform, and commendation of dispositions, which we are exhorted to cultivate. Thus Christianity is merged in moral culture; and in place of the old Gospel of the grace of God, there is offered a new gospel of the goodness of man, founded on those moral precepts which are more or less common to all religions.

The position thus taken is still more fatally antago-

---

* It may be well that something should be said here as to the sense in which this term is employed, inasmuch as there is exceeding vagueness in its current use. It is sometimes applied, on the one hand, to those who are thoroughly loyal to Christ, and to His truth so far as they are able to ascertain it, but who, in some of the ways in which they set it forth or illustrate it, exhibit, or are regarded by their critics as exhibiting, rationalising tendencies; and, on the other, to those who reject Christ altogether, and avowedly substitute philosophy or science for His Gospel. To neither of these classes do we refer in this paper, but to those who, while they claim to be considered disciples of Christ, and seek for their doctrines the shelter and sanction of His great name, reject the supernatural in every form as unworthy of belief, and try to rear upon the authority of Christ as a teacher a system of mere natural development and education.

nistic to the Gospel of the New Testament than that of the Ritualist; for, while the latter endangers the Gospel by adding to it so much of man's device that it is often entirely lost in that which envelops it, the former destroys it by taking from it all that gives it life and power. The essence of the Gospel, as it is set forth at large in the New Testament, is the good tidings that our Father God, through His Son Jesus Christ, whom He has sent into the world to take away its sin, saves from sin and death all who yield themselves to the control of His Holy Spirit, whose work in the world it is to convince men of sin and lead them to accept Christ as their Saviour and Lord, that they may be made like Him, and prepared for a life of perfect purity and blessedness with Him in the world to come. There is in this a very large divine element, while the human element in it is comparatively small. The divine element is nothing less than "the grace of the Lord Jesus Christ, and the love of God, and the communion of the Holy Ghost." The human element is faith, understood of course in the large Scriptural sense, as not the mere assent of the mind, but also the consent of the heart and the surrender of the will. Both of these essential elements are lost in the Rationalistic gospel. There is no place for direct divine agency in a system of mere ethical instruction, and there is as little room for faith, in the Scriptural sense of the word; nothing is left but law and duty, law without a sanction, and duty without any help to do it.

Now, if those who hold and teach this barren doctrine would give it forth in their own names, or in the name of pagan philosophy, little harm would be done; but when they connect it with the great and holy name of Christ, and represent it as His Gospel, they do a most grievous wrong. The injury is all the greater because of the plausibility of the position they take. There is the proverbial half-truth in the comparison they make between the teaching of Christ in the days of His flesh and that of His apostles afterwards. It is true that there is a difference, and that the earlier is simpler than the later; it is true that the ethical element preponderates more in the teaching of the Master, and the doctrinal in that of the apostles; but these differences, as we shall afterwards see, are only what are to be expected from the nature of the doctrine of Christ, and its progressiveness from the simple elements to the fully developed truth. But our main object in this paper will be to show that, after all has been conceded, the teaching of Christ Himself concerning His own Gospel is in fullest harmony with that of the apostles; including, if not in full development, certainly in germ and essence, all that is distinctive of the apostles' "gospel of the grace of God."

In following out our inquiry into this matter we shall not select any single discourse, as is too often done by those who wish to limit the range of the teaching of Jesus, but shall endeavour to get an idea of its general scope, and of those features on which Christ Himself laid special stress. To this end let us inquire:—

I. WHAT CHRIST HIMSELF TAUGHT AS TO THE NATURE OF HIS GOSPEL.

The great question here is, Did He represent His Gospel as a system of ethical instruction, or as a way of salvation? Did it amount to certain directions how man might save himself, or was it a revelation of how God would save him? This is the fundamental question. On it depend all the other great questions as to the doctrines of our faith which the Rationalist especially dislikes and denounces. We refer particularly to the Divinity of Christ, the necessity and central importance of the Atonement, and the personality and work of the Holy Spirit. Is the Gospel a system of instruction? Then there must be at the head of it—a Teacher. But a man may be a teacher. We do not need even angels from heaven to be at the head of our colleges. Of course any man will not do. He must be of exceptional character and ability. But to suppose that God Himself should think it necessary to come down to earth in order to found a school of morals seems quite irrational. Thus the Deity of Christ is rendered incredible. In the same way, if all that men need is good teaching, where is the necessity for atonement? True, Christ died; and a great deal is made of His death in the Scriptures. But Socrates died also by his enemies' hands, and a great deal has been made, and much more might be made, of his tranquil and cheerful demise, without any suggestion of its having atoning value. If we settle first in our minds that instruction is all that is needed, then the death of Christ may be adequately represented as the crown of His teaching. It is sufficient in that case to regard it as a glorious example of faithfulness to the last extremity, so that thereby He enforced, in the most impressive way that could be conceived, one of the great lessons which in His life He taught, the duty and the beauty of self-sacrifice. Thus the doctrine of the Atonement is set aside. Further, if Christ be only a teacher, who ended His lectures, as all earthly teachers do, when He died, what becomes of the truth concerning the Spirit of Christ? It necessarily disappears, for there remains only the spirit of a man, and there is no other possible way in which to explain or explain away the innumerable passages referring to the subject in the

Scriptures than by representing it as an impersonal influence, just as we may say that the spirit of Shakespeare lives in the influence of his dramas, and the spirit of Rowland Hill in the power of the penny postage. And the story of Pentecost becomes only a poetical way of saying that, after ten days' meditation, the early disciples entered more fully than they had ever done before into the spirit of the teaching of their Master. Thus we find that the denial of the leading doctrines of the Gospel is the logical outcome of a partial, and therefore erroneous, view of what the Gospel is.

It is, then, of great importance to settle first what Christ taught as to the nature of His Gospel. As soon as this inquiry is proposed, we naturally think of the Saviour's first formal announcement of His mission in the synagogue at Nazareth, as recorded by St. Luke: "The Spirit of the Lord is upon Me, because He hath anointed Me to preach the gospel to the poor; He hath sent Me to heal the broken-hearted, to preach deliverance to the captives, and recovering of sight to the blind, to set at liberty them that are bruised, to preach the acceptable year of the Lord."

Dr. Channing has a sermon[*] on this passage, or rather on the first clause of it, to which he confines himself. He had, of course, a perfect right so to limit his range; but in doing so he gives a meaning to the central word of his text which he could not have given it if he had remembered what immediately followed. Throughout the entire sermon he translates the old word gospel by what he evidently considers the modern equivalent, viz., "moral and religious culture." Now moral and religious culture is good, very good. The more the poor can have of it, and the more we all can have of it, the better. But

[*] Complete Works, p. 60. Williams & Norgate. 1880.

that moral and religious culture is not the equivalent of the Gospel of Jesus is made abundantly evident before the sentence is finished. We do not deny that, in a certain sense, the word gospel might have been applied to a system of instruction. We speak of the school of Plato and the school of Zeno in Greece; and it certainly was a good thing that these philosophers did establish their schools in that centre of the old world's culture. We speak also of the school of Christ; and if it was a good thing that the great philosophers of Greece set up their schools in Athens, it may fairly be considered as a still better thing that Jesus of Nazareth set up what is acknowledged to be a better school than any other in Galilee. In a certain sense, then, we might say that the information that such a school had been established, and that its teachings had been given to the world, was a gospel, or good news; but to say that it is the Gospel of Christ is quite another thing. Moral and religious culture represents the best that man can do for himself. But all experience proves that the best man can do for himself is not enough. He must have something done for him, which only God can do; and the Gospel of Christ is the good tidings that God has done, is doing, and will do for him all he needs, if he will only allow Him; and we have only to study this weighty announcement of the Master Himself in order to see that the Gospel which He announced is such a Gospel of divine salvation.

We might at the outset summon to our aid the Old Testament prophecies concerning the Great Deliverer Who was to come; for Jesus here expressly claims these as His own. He quotes from the prophet Isaiah one of the most striking of the Messianic prophecies, and then, by way of introducing Himself and His work, makes this momentous declaration: "This day is this scripture fulfilled in your ears." There is no passage in the entire Old Testament which could have been more fitly selected for the purpose of advancing His claim to be the Messiah. The very word is in it, though it is veiled from the ears of foreigners like ourselves. To the Hebrew ear the passage in Isaiah would read, "The Spirit of the Lord is upon Me, because He hath made Me His Messiah to preach the gospel to the poor;" and to a Greek ear the passage in St. Luke would read, "He hath made me His Christ." Now, was it only, or was it mainly, as a teacher that the Jews were taught in Old Testament times to look forward to the Messiah that was to come? Was it not chiefly as a Great Deliverer, an Almighty Saviour, that He was set forth in the long line of prophecy and promise, from that early declaration that the coming seed of the woman should bruise the serpent's head, to the closing assurance of the last of the prophets, "The Lord whom ye seek shall suddenly come to His temple." True, He is set forth as a prophet, and no one denies that He did come as a prophet, and that His prophetical office, including, of course, all His ethical teaching, was an important part of His work; but that He came only as a prophet, or even mainly as a prophet, is sufficiently disproved by the fact that, for one of the Messianic prophecies which so present Him, there are twenty and more which set Him forth as One who is coming to do a great and royal work of salvation.

The same view of the nature of the Gospel is fully borne out by a detailed examination of the text of our Lord's discourse. We might refer first to the very way in which the Gospel is referred to as especially for the poor. Schools of philosophy have not as a rule been for the poor. A college is for the more cultured and better class of the community. Moral and spiritual culture is, of course, good for the poor, if it could be brought to bear upon them; but they are just the people whom it is hardest to reach by such educational influences. A gospel of this kind would be best adapted to men who have little temptation, very few burdens, abundance of learned leisure And it is well known, as a matter of fact, that it is among the rich and the learned and the leisurely that Rationalism finds its chief adherents, amongst people who have never had it suggested to them by the hard pressure of outward circumstances that they have wants deeper than can be met by mere words, however wise. It will be seen, then, that some light is thrown upon the question before us as to the nature of the Gospel of Christ from the very first clause of the series, in which our Saviour speaks of it as characteristically a Gospel for the poor.

But we need not delay on mere inferences; for we have express statements in the succeeding clauses. Let us look at them and see if instruction for the ignorant, or higher teaching for the wise, be a fair representation of their scope. "*He hath sent Me to heal the broken-hearted.*" Will an essay heal a broken heart? Did a course of lectures ever do it? Did the most brilliant professor that ever filled a chair of moral philosophy ever heal one broken heart? He might most skilfully and most brilliantly analyse the different feelings that entered into its woe; but to take away the woe—that he could no more do than he could raise the dead.

> "Canst thou minister to a mind diseased ?
> Pluck from the memory a rooted sorrow,
> Raze out the written troubles of the brain,
> And with some sweet oblivious antidote
> Cleanse the stuffed bosom of that perilous stuff
> Which weighs upon the heart ?"

To ask such a question of man at all is to call forth a hopeless No. And if the Lord Jesus had been only a very learned Rabbi, a very wise and great and good man, could He have done it? No: it is not human learning but divine power that is needed for the healing of the broken-hearted. "*To preach deliverance to the captives.*" What is suggested here as to the work of Christ? Going into a prison cell and reading in richly modulated tones an eloquent discourse upon freedom, coupled with a solemn reminder that eternal vigilance is the price of it? Or is it rather the overthrow of the tyrant, the breaking open of his prison, the striking off of his captive's fetters and setting him free? Is it not much more than education? Is it anything less than salvation? "*And recovering of sight to the blind.*" Are there any directions which can be given to a blind man by which he can get his sight back again by any exertions of his own? Would a course of lectures by the most eminent oculist that ever lived be of any avail? Is it human wisdom or is it divine power that is wanted here? "*To set at liberty them that are bruised.*" There is a lower deep here than even the depths of the dungeon. Mark the progression in the series of terms which describe that lost condition from which the Saviour comes to rescue men. The poor, the broken-hearted, the captive in the dungeon, blind and bruised,—could any language more powerfully depict man's lost condition as a sinner? Ah! these are deeper needs than can be met by moral and religious culture. The one thing needful for the poor, broken-hearted captive, blind and bruised, is not instruction; it is help and healing, light and liberty. And must not all this come from One who is mightier than all the powers that can be arrayed against Him, Master of all that makes for human weal or woe?

It may be good news indeed, and therefore something of a gospel, to a man of learned leisure sitting in his study with his books around him, to know that many hundred years ago there lived a great philosopher whose instructions on the highest subjects were more valuable than those of all other instructors put together; but let even such an one once realise that he is a sinner; that his heart is at enmity against God; that, however correct his outward life may have been, his inner life cannot bear the scrutinising eye of the Judge in the Great Day of final reckoning—let him realise all this, and he will find that even he needs not only a wise instructor, but a compassionate Saviour, a Divine Helper, Healer, and Comforter, such as Jesus of Nazareth here represents Himself to be.

It is true that our Lord does not at this early stage bring prominently into view the great doctrines of which we have been speaking—His own Divinity, the need of atonement in order to open a way of salvation, and the necessity of the Holy Spirit's work in the hearts of men. There are very good reasons for this reticence, as we shall afterwards see when we shall have before us what Christ taught on these subjects, as soon as, in His wisdom, He recognised that the time to unfold them had come. But meanwhile who can fail to notice how thoroughly everything in this preliminary announcement of the Gospel is in harmony with these afterwards developed truths? In the opening sentence the work is recognised as that which God alone can do. "*The Spirit of the Lord is upon Me*, because He hath anointed Me to preach the gospel to the poor." The same thought is left on the minds of the listeners by the concluding words: "To proclaim the acceptable year *of the Lord.*" And this very expression, "the acceptable year of the Lord"—*i.e.*, the year of acceptance, or grace, or favour of the Lord—of which the Jubilee was a type, is fully understood only in the light of the great propitiation which was to be offered up on Calvary; for if the proclamation of the acceptable year of the Lord was simply, as the Rationalists would tell us, the informing men that God was ready to pardon their sins and receive them into His favour,—if it was simply this announcement, this piece of information or instruction, without any special work by which the favour was to be secured, what title had our Lord's mission to this distinction above the mission of the prophet Isaiah, for instance, or of any of the prophets? For do not the writings of all of them abound with offers of forgiveness? This expression, then, "to proclaim the acceptable year of the Lord," which Christ claims to be fulfilled in His mission, prepares the mind for some special work which He is anointed to accomplish, and in the accomplishment of which He shall usher in the dispensation of divine grace; and what work can this be, if not the great Atonement by which He broke down the prison walls in which we are confined, and opened up the way of access to the light and liberty of the children of God?

The prominence which our Saviour gives to His own personality is another feature well worthy of note. He makes comparatively little reference, we may say He makes no reference at all, to the truths He is about to teach. He directs the attention of the people to Himself at the outset, and keeps their thoughts there throughout, as is manifest from the emphatic and repeated "Me." The apostles thus were only following their Master when they made Christ Himself, "Christ, and Him crucified," the centre of all their teaching.

It is unnecessary, however, to dwell on these points now; they will appear much more clearly as we proceed.

Meantime it is made at all events abundantly evident, from this preliminary announcement alone, that the Gospel of Jesus Christ is not represented by Him as a mere system of instruction, by following which a man may learn how to save himself, but as, above all, the offer of a Saviour, with all human sympathy indeed, but at the same time with all divine power to meet the deepest needs of the worst of men.

Let us now inquire—

II. WHAT CHRIST HIMSELF TAUGHT AS TO THE CENTRE AND PIVOT OF HIS GOSPEL.

It is universally acknowledged by students of the Gospels that our Lord's conversation with His disciples in the neighbourhood of Cesarea Philippi marks a great crisis in His history, and a definite and important stage in His teaching. It is recorded by all the three Synoptists, and with great fulness and emphasis by St. Matthew especially, from whose account it is evident that it was intended to be the summing up of one great lesson and the beginning of another. The finished lesson is the truth concerning His own Person; the lesson just beginning is the truth concerning the necessity of His being offered up as an atoning sacrifice: "from that time forth *began* Jesus to show unto His disciples how that He must go unto Jerusalem, and suffer many things of the elders, and chief priests, and scribes, and be killed, and be raised again the third day." We shall at present restrict our attention to the finished lesson, that which regarded the Person of Christ, which is, as we shall see, set forth in this remarkable conversation as the very centre and pivot of the Gospel. The lesson just commencing will be better dealt with at a later stage, after the disciples have had time to learn it.

We have already remarked the prominence given by our Lord to His own personality, even in His first announcement of His Gospel. This feature of His teaching is manifest throughout His ministry. Even the Sermon on the Mount, so confidently appealed to by Rationalists as free from any such dogma as the Divinity of Christ, is no exception; proof of which may be found in the solemn declaration at its close: " Many shall say unto Me in that day, Lord, Lord, have we not prophesied in Thy Name? and in Thy Name have cast out devils? and in Thy Name done many wonderful works? And then will I profess unto them, I never knew you: depart from Me, ye that work iniquity."

But while, throughout all His teaching, divine prerogative and power are invariably assumed, there is no definite dogmatic instruction on the subject. It was evident that He intended not so much to *tell* His disciples as to *show* them Who He was. It was in His deeds rather than in His words that He expected them to read the great lessons of the Incarnation. As an illustration of this method of Jesus we may point to His answer to the question of John the Baptist, " Art Thou He that should come, or look we for another?" Instead of telling him in set terms that He was indeed the Christ, the Son of the living God, He gives this reply: " Go and show John again those things which ye do hear and see: the blind receive their sight, and the lame walk, the lepers are cleansed, and the deaf hear, the dead are raised up, and the poor have the gospel preached to them." In conformity with this method, He does not hastily put His disciples to the test on this great theme. He gives them time to see, and think, and form their own conclusions. But now, as we have seen, He has reached a great crisis in His history. Henceforward His path will be one less of manifested glory than of deepening shame. Dr. Edersheim, in his "Life and Times of the Messiah," divides the ministry of Jesus into two parts, with the scenes in the region around Cesarea Philippi as the turning-point. The former he speaks of as "the Ascent, from the River Jordan to the Mount of Transfiguration;" the latter, as "the Descent, from the Mount of Transfiguration into the Valley of Humiliation and Death." The former of these periods was the fit one for manifesting His Divine Glory, the latter for teaching the lesson of His Atoning Sacrifice Accordingly, before He enters on the darker experiences of His life and work, ere yet the sorrowful journey to the place of sacrifice is begun, He must make sure that His followers have learned the great lesson which belongs to the period of His ministry just closing, and so we read that when Jesus came into the coasts of Cesarea Philippi He asked certain questions, the manifest object of which was to ascertain whether His disciples had attained to clear and decided convictions as to His personality; and when it was evident that they had, He marked the occasion as one of the very greatest importance. How plain is it from all this, that though our Lord Himself, for strong and sufficient reasons, did not as a rule urge His claim to be the Son of God, often, in fact, forbade that anything should be said about it, yet when the fitting opportunity came, He not only made it, but insisted upon it; and, far from treating it as a matter of indifference, whether it was allowed or not, made it manifest that He regarded its full acknowledgment as absolutely essential and fundamental.

It may serve to set all this in a still stronger light if we compare in this respect, or rather contrast, the position taken by Christ with that taken by His forerunner, who, be it remembered, was no ordinary man, but one of whom Christ Himself said, "Among men that are born of women there hath not risen a greater than John the Baptist," and who therefore takes rank as the very greatest of all the Old Testament prophets. It is true that Jesus began His work with the same message as John: "Repent ye; for the kingdom of heaven is at hand;" but it is as plain as it can possibly be that He claimed an entirely different relation to the Kingdom. John resolutely kept himself in the background, retreating as it were behind his great message, as every ordinary ambassador of God should do, and then suddenly disappeared from view. He was "a voice," no more—himself personally, nothing. But Jesus identifies Himself with His message. In preaching the Kingdom He preaches Himself. He, in fact, took just as much pains to make Himself the great object of His disciples' regard as John the Baptist had taken to keep his disciples from a similar homage to their master. What was the reason of this wonderful difference? Was it that John the Baptist was the humbler man of the two, the less selfish, the less disposed to self-assertion? Was it not this, that while John the Baptist proclaimed the coming of the Kingdom of Another, even of One before Whom he bowed low in humble adoration, One the latchet of Whose shoes he was unworthy to stoop down and unloose, Jesus proclaimed His own Kingdom. The salvation it brought to men was His own salvation. The faith it exacted from men was faith, not in another, but in Himself. Hence it is that in summoning the subjects of the Kingdom the call is, "Follow Me." In laying down the law of the Kingdom, it is not, "Thus saith the Lord," according to the time-honoured formula of the prophets of Israel; it is, "Verily, verily, *I* say unto you." In healing the leper, it is, "I will; be thou clean." In answering the application of the blind men of Jericho, He inquires, "Believe ye that I am able to do this?" In making the great offer of the blessings of the Kingdom it is, "Come unto Me, . . and I will give you rest." And, in pressing the claims of the Kingdom, it is in this astounding language—astounding, that is, on any other supposition than that of His true and proper Divinity—" He that loveth father or mother more than Me is not worthy of Me; and he that loveth son or daughter more than Me is not worthy of Me. And he that taketh not his cross, and followeth after Me, is not worthy of Me.' From all this (and every intelligent reader of the Gospels knows that this is a specimen of the whole style and strain of our Saviour's teaching) it is evident that, while John the Baptist kept himself quite in the background, Jesus brought Himself ever into the foreground. And, in this particular, Jesus was distinguished, not only from John the Baptist, who came substantially with the same message, but from all who have ever come with any message from God. The messenger is always hid, as it were, behind his message. This is just what we expect of every true messenger, if he be only a messenger. An ambassador may indeed magnify his office; but if he magnify himself, and speak as if he himself were the potentate he represents, he only makes himself ludicrous and contemptible. And if Jesus had been only a messenger from God, only an ambassador, how could we explain, in consistency with His acknowledged humility and self-forgetfulness, the way in which He uniformly speaks of Himself? But if we bear in mind Who He was, if we keep before us the fact that He was not an ambassador merely, but Himself the King, not a messenger of God, but God Himself in human form, then these strong personal claims are seen to be thoroughly natural, and perfectly consistent with that self-abnegation and deep humility which are so conspicuous in His entire life and character.

We see, then, that there is nothing unnatural, or out of keeping with the attitude He has taken from the beginning, in the questions which our Saviour puts so pointedly to His disciples in the neighbourhood of Cesarea Philippi: "Who do men say that I am?" "Who do ye say that I am?" Such questions would have been most extraordinary, if He had been only a teacher come from God. What should we think of any teacher on any subject whatever, who would say more about himself than about anything else? There are such teachers and preachers. There are those who, professing to deliver a message, are really exhibiting themselves. There are those who are much less careful about delivering their message rightly, or teaching their subject well, than they are about getting an answer to the questions, "What do men think of me?" "What do you think of me?" We say there are such teachers and preachers; but they are always despised; and most justly. Suppose a minister of the Gospel were to preach even a single sermon about himself—his country, his parentage, his powers, his dignity, his prospects, and so forth—what would men think of him? It may often be of great importance to society what a man is—it is of very little consequence who he is. It may be interesting to know the name of St. Matthew's father and mother; but it is of no consequence. The Apostle Paul was one of the greatest men that ever lived, one whose life has been most fruitful of great results, and yet even he would have made himself ridiculous by asking such a question as Jesus here asks of His disciples For you will observe the question is not, What am I? but Who am I? Whose Son am I?

It will be observed that the first answer our Saviour

THE GOSPEL ACCORDING TO CHRIST. 271

gets is the rationalistic one. The ordinary people of the time class Him amongst great men indeed, amongst the greatest men that ever lived—still only among men: "Some say that Thou art John the Baptist; some, Elias; and others, Jeremias, or one of the prophets." Is the answer satisfactory? Does Jesus accept the verdict of these Unitarians? Nay; He turns from them to His true disciples, and He asks them, "Who do ye say that I am?" and He gets for answer, "Thou art the Christ, the Son of the living God." This answer He accepts, and attaches so much importance to it as to pronounce a most special benediction on him who has first given it, and at the same time marks the height and depth and reach of it by the solemn declaration, "Flesh and blood hath not revealed it unto thee, but My Father Who is in heaven."

It seems incredible that there should be those who explain away this second answer so as to make it mean no more than the first; yet so it is. Any candid person can see in a moment that this is mere trifling with a great subject. Surely it is as evident as human language can possibly make it, that when St. Peter calls Jesus "the Son of the living God," he indicates a sense quite different from that in which a man can be called the son of God, a relation so distinct and proper and peculiar, that it is shared, and can be shared, with no other.

It is time now that we should give careful consideration to a point which has been touched before, but demands separate and distinct treatment; we refer to our Lord's delay in bringing out a truth so very important. Why is He so long in putting this question? Why did He not make all as clear at the beginning as He makes it now? We have already indicated a reason for this in the method of self-revelation adopted by our Lord. But there are other reasons which are sufficiently obvious on reflection. There were reasons for His reticence, both as regarded His enemies and as regarded His friends. As to the former, we have only to call attention to the fact that, again and again, as, for example, on this very occasion (Matt. xvi. 20), He cautions His disciples and others not to make Him known, and gives as reason that His hour has not yet come. It will be remembered that it was this claim of Divinity that more than aught else stirred up His enemies against Him. Once and again, when He claimed equality with God, "the Jews took up stones to stone Him." It will be remembered, too, that it was when He was asked directly whether He were the Son of God, and answered in the affirmative, that the High Priest rent his clothes and said that no further witness was necessary, inasmuch as He thereby stood convicted of blasphemy. If, then, He had publicly advanced His claim to be the Son of God at the first, it would have led to His apprehension and death long before the fulness of the time. The reason, therefore, is obvious, so far as His enemies were concerned. But there is just as plain a reason, when we think of His relation to His friends. What would have been the consequence if He had told His disciples at the first that He was indeed the Son of the living God? Would it not have been to overwhelm them with dismay? When the Apostle Peter witnessed one of the early exhibitions of the power of Christ, he was so oppressed with a sense of the Presence in which he was, that he was constrained to say, "Depart from me, for I am a sinful man, O Lord." And if this was the effect of an isolated miracle upon the bravest of the apostles, what would have been the consequence of a full revelation of

His Divine Glory to His disciples, ere yet they had learned to know, and love, and trust Him as a man and a brother? It would, indeed, have frustrated the very end and purpose of His Incarnation, which was that He might come near to man, that He might hold loving, friendly, unembarrassed intercourse with him, and thus lead him up gently from knowledge to knowledge, from strength to strength, from grace to grace, from glory to glory, until at last, fully prepared for appearing before God, he should see Him as He is. To illustrate this point, let us think of our Queen's first visit to the cottages of the poor in the North of Scotland. She began by going quite *incognito*, or, where that was impracticable, with as little of the queenly and as much of the womanly as possible. Her simple unassuming manners won the hearts of the poor; and there was kindly, familiar, pleasant intercourse. Would the intercourse have been of the same kind if she had gone in her royal robes, entered in stately magnificence, and announced herself as Queen of England? Clearly, in this case, all would have been stiffness and formality, and the most pleasant part of it would have been the going away. This is, of course, a very humble and inadequate illustration, but, as an illustration, it may help us a little. We can see in a moment how much kinder it was; we can see, in fact, how necessary it was for the success of His mission of love, that the Lord Jesus should conceal at first His true Divinity even from His most trusted disciples, that He should only gradually reveal Himself to them as they were able to bear it. They have now, however, been about two years with Him ; and the truth has been gradually dawning on their minds. He sees that it is time that their convictions should begin to take form ; and hence the putting of the great question at this particular time.

We are not to suppose, indeed, that the full truth is even yet steadily and constantly realised by the disciples. They have obtained a glimpse of it, such a glimpse as enables them to put the thought into language; but it is evident from the whole subsequent history that they did not fully take it in until after their Lord's resurrection and the descent of the Spirit. The great truth has been floating before their minds up till this time in vague, indefinite forms, in broken glimpses and gleams; it now assumes a definite form and finds expression for itself; but not till long after does it take full possession of their souls. Hence it is that we have to wait for the utterance of those who were filled with the Spirit, before we have the full development of the doctrine. It *is* true that Jesus never develops the doctrine of His own Divinity in the clear and full way that St. John does in the beginning of his Gospel, or St. Paul, as, *e g.*, in the Epistle to the Colossians (chap. i. 15–17), or the author of the Epistle to the Hebrews in his first chapter. But we see clearly the reason—it is because His disciples are not able to bear it yet. Still, though He does not expressly announce Himself as the Creator of all worlds, and the Upholder of the universe, He speaks of Himself in such a way as to make it perfectly evident that He claimed Divinity in its fullest, largest sense, in all the plenitude of its prerogative and power. Who but the Most High could without arrogance have made such demands on all mankind as those which are made by Jesus of Nazareth, claiming as He does the homage of every heart, the service of every life, nay, the absolute sacrifice of everything for His sake? Who but the Infinite and Eternal could without audacity have undertaken to control the minds and hearts and lives of men that should live on earth centuries after He had passed away from it, or promised to be present wherever two or three of His people were gathered together in all the world to the end of time? Who but the great God could without blasphemy have represented Himself as sitting on the Throne of Glory, and all the holy angels with Him, welcoming the righteous to the Kingdom above, and sending the wicked to the regions of woe, on the sole ground of the way in which they had treated Himself? Clearly, most clearly, does the Saviour make Himself the great centre, the great subject of His own preaching. He makes the question, "Who am I?" the great question of theology. He makes His own Divine Sonship the great foundation on which His Church is built. The true and proper Divinity of the Lord Jesus Christ is, according to Himself, the very centre and pivot of His Gospel.

Our third inquiry shall be—

III. WHAT CHRIST HIMSELF TAUGHT AS TO THE SUM AND SUBSTANCE OF HIS GOSPEL.

To discover this we naturally look for some passage at the very close of the Saviour's ministry; just as, in our inquiry as to what He taught in regard to the nature of His Gospel, we looked for a passage at its opening. And what we are in search of again we find in the pages of St. Luke, who, it will be remembered, especially undertook "to set forth in order" (chap. 1. 1–3) what he knew of Christ and His words, and is therefore the most likely of all the Evangelists to preserve and record at the beginning and at the close the most comprehensive utterances of the Master. The following, then, are the last words of Christ which St. Luke records: "And He said unto them, These are the words which I spake unto you, while I was yet with you, that all things must be fulfilled which were written in the Law of Moses, and in the

Prophets, and in the Psalms, concerning Me. Then opened He their understanding, that they might understand the scriptures, and said unto them, Thus it is written, and thus it behoved Christ to suffer, and to rise from the dead the third day: and that repentance and remission of sins should be preached in His name among all nations, beginning at Jerusalem. And ye are witnesses of these things. And, behold, I send the promise of My Father upon you; but tarry ye in the city of Jerusalem, until ye be endued-with power from on high."

It will be at once seen that this concluding summary bears fully out what we have already discovered as to the nature of the Gospel, and as to the central importance of the personality of Christ Himself. As to the former point, who dares say that these most weighty last words of Christ convey the impression that He came as a mere Teacher of morals, giving us good advice as to how we ought to live, and leaving us to do the best we can to follow it? Who can deny that they plainly intimate that the great object of His coming was, not merely to show us what we ought to do, but to do for us what we could not, and cannot by any means, do for ourselves? As to the other point, the central importance of the Person of Christ, we find it no less marked in this concluding summary than it has been throughout, and especially in the epoch-making conversation at Cesarea Philippi. The entire Old Testament Scriptures are here dealt with as a testimony to the coming Christ. From the ethics of the law, from the rites of the Jewish Church, the thought of the apostles is at once carried forward to Him to Whom the Law and the Prophets and the Psalmists all bear witness. The focal point of all the light that has been shining in the Scriptures of the Old Testament from the beginning could not be more strikingly marked than in these words, "concerning Me." And that the Person of Christ is to have the same central position in the New Covenant is marked by the emphatic words, "in His name," connected with repentance and remission of sins to be preached among all nations. We thus find, in this concluding summary, abundant confirmation of the main points already reached.

But what is most remarkable in this summing up of the Gospel is the outstanding prominence given to the new doctrine which Christ only began to teach His disciples on the occasion of the conversation at Cesarea Philippi. As we follow the history from that point onwards we find the subject again and again referred to in such a way as to make it plain that it was the subject above all others to which the Master wished, in that second and most important stage of His ministry, to turn His disciples' thoughts; and now here, when all has been accomplished, we find it set forth as the very sum and substance of the Gospel. It is not the coming into the world, it is not the pure and spotless life, it is not the marvellous teaching, it is not even the healing; it is the suffering, it is the dying and the rising again, which is given as the ground on which repentance and remission of sins are to be preached in the name of Jesus. We thus find that the atoning sacrifice of Christ, sealed by His resurrection from the dead, is the substance of the Gospel according to Christ.

It is a favourite assertion with those who wish to get rid of all that is especially distinctive in the Gospel, to say that the doctrine of the Atonement was an invention of the Apostle Paul and other philosophising disciples of Christ; that He Himself says nothing about it; that instead of talking about atonement and justification, and such matters of theology, He simply tells us to love our neighbour as ourselves, to speak the truth, to pay our debts, and work our passage to heaven like honest men. They point to the Sermon on the Mount, and ask, Where is your doctrine of Atonement? Not a word about it. They take up the parable of the Prodigal Son, and say, Where is your doctrine of Atonement? The prodigal offers no sacrifice, gets no one to offer a sacrifice for him; he simply comes back, and is welcome. All which sounds very plausible, and is very apt to mislead those who have not looked carefully into the matter, or who do not take time to reflect how unfair it is to say that Christ did not teach such-and-such a doctrine, because He did not teach it in such-and-such discourses. It is to no purpose to show that there is no mention of the Atonement in the Sermon on the Mount, or in most of the Parables, if in the first place we can give the reason why it is not mentioned there, and in the second place can show that it is very strongly insisted on elsewhere; both of which can very easily be done.

As to the reasons for reticence on the subject of the Atonement, there is first the general fact of the progressiveness of the teaching of Christ. He began with that which was simpler, and led His disciples on step by step to that which was more difficult. He knew what was in man as well as what was of God, and accordingly He had wisdom and skill enough to adapt His revelation of truth to the stage of His disciples' advancement. He was a true philosopher who said, "If I had all truth in my hand, I should let forth only a ray at a time, lest I should blind the world." It was on this wise principle that Christ acted in His teaching and training of His disciples. It will be remembered that even when He was about to part with them, when His heart was full, and He longed to pour forth its still pent-up treasures, He put severe constraint upon His feelings, and only suffered Himself to say, "I have yet many things to say unto you, but ye cannot bear them now." Now this doctrine of the Atonement was evidently one of the very hardest things for them to bear, connected as it was with the sufferings and death of Him Whom they loved so much, and on Whom they were so utterly dependent. This appears very plainly from the conduct of St. Peter when the subject first was broached, and from the strong language of more than deprecation which he used: "This be far from Thee, Lord; this shall not be unto Thee." We need not wonder, then, that a Teacher so wise, and kind, and sympathetic should keep back as long as possible a subject so painful and unwelcome. This is set in a strong light by the fact already mentioned, that in so many as three of the Gospels the exact time and circumstances are specified in which Jesus began to give instruction on this subject, especially when it is observed how appropriate the occasion was, inasmuch as the disciples had for the first time reached those convictions in relation to His Person as Son of God as well as Son of Man, without which there could be no conception at all of the true meaning and value of the Atonement. It is plain, moreover, from what has been said as to the crisis in His history our Lord had reached, that the subject could no longer be deferred. Not only, then, is the absence of this doctrine from the earlier teaching of our Lord, and its cautious introduction even in the closing months of His earthly ministry, accounted for by the general fact of the progressiveness of His teaching, but we can see that it is introduced as early as possible, and at such a time and under such circumstances as to give it its due significance and weight.

Then there is this further consideration, that it would

have been manifestly premature to have said much about the doctrine before the fact. It was time enough, surely, to give full explanations about the Atonement after it had been made. We must always remember that there is this difference between Christ as a teacher and other teachers, that He Himself was the subject of His own teaching. Other teachers have their facts ready to hand, or at all events ready made, and they have only to find them. He had His to make. He was Himself the centre of the truth He taught. All its developments were connected most closely with facts in His own history; and, inasmuch as facts must precede their explanation, the doctrine could not be completed till after the facts had been accomplished Before His death He could only speak prophetically, and prepare them for that which was to come by impressing on their minds its absolute necessity: "From that time forth began Jesus to show unto His disciples how He *must*" suffer and die; only after it was over could He begin to give those fuller explanations which St. Luke summarises in these words: "Beginning at Moses and all the Prophets, He expounded unto them in all the Scriptures the things concerning Himself" (Luke xxiv. 27)—an exposition which plainly had the Atonement for its centre, as is evident from the way in which it is introduced (see vers. 25, 26.)

When we think of all these reasons why there should be but little reference to the Atonement in our Saviour's teaching, we may perhaps be inclined to wonder rather that there is so much. There are, in the first place, the numerous references to the subject in language more or less veiled and enigmatical: the taking up of the cross, the destroying and rebuilding of "this temple," the sign of the prophet Jonas, with an occasional statement more direct, as this: "The Son of Man is come, not to be ministered unto, but to minister, and to give His life a ransom for many." The conversation with Nicodemus, as recorded by St. John in his third chapter, seems at first so 'distinct and emphatic as to be at variance with what has been said as regards the progressiveness of the teaching of Christ. The exposition of the brazen serpent, followed by the full declaration of the Gospel in the oft-quoted words of the sixteenth verse, seems more than could be expected at so early a period of the Saviour's ministry. But the special circumstances of the case must be borne in mind. It was a private interview by night; and Nicodemus was a learned Rabbi, far better prepared for entering into the deeper things of the Kingdom than the fishermen of Galilee could be at first; while, on the other hand, he was not so bound by personal ties to Jesus as to make such references so delicate and difficult as they would have been to Peter, James, and John. It is, in fact, one of those exceptions which, according to the proverb, "prove the rule." We see in it the evidence that while, as a rule, Christ felt it necessary to use great reticence concerning this doctrine in the earlier part of His ministry, yet, when the circumstances did admit of it, He availed Himself of the opportunity of setting it forth as clearly and strongly as possible.

There are other passages in St. John's Gospel which ought to be studied, in order to do justice to the amount of our Saviour's teaching on this cardinal doctrine. But we prefer to rest our case on the abundantly sufficient testimony of the other three Evangelists; inasmuch as it is on them that our Rationalist friends rely, while they regard the fourth Gospel with much suspicion, as if it had in it more of the mysticism of John than of the simple ethics of Jesus. While, then, our case would be greatly strengthened by the use of the fourth Gospel, it is so strong otherwise that we can quite well afford to dispense with it; and accordingly our great passages have been from the Synoptists, the conversation with Nicodemus having been referred to because it seemed at first sight inconsistent with one of the positions we had laid down.

Still further, we have been restricting ourselves to the words of Christ; but the case would be much strengthened if we took into consideration His whole bearing throughout these last months of His ministry, and especially during the days of the Passion Week. Truly that death, which occupies so very large a space in each one of the four Gospels, which even the Evangelist Mark, with all his turn for condensation, does not venture to shorten, is no ordinary death, is something more than even a martyr's last testimony. Hear Him in the garden · "O my Father, if it be possible, let this cup pass from Me." The event proved it was not possible; and why was it not? Because it was necessary that atonement should be made for sin, even as the Lord Himself explained it after the agony was over: "Thus it behoved Christ to suffer, . . . that repentance and remission of sins should be preached in His name." Again, hear Him on the cross: "My God, my God, why hast Thou forsaken Me?" Why this sense of forsakenness? Had He not been the holiest of men? Had He not been a better, was He not a braver man than Stephen—

> "Who heeded not reviling tones,
> Nor sold his heart to idle moans,
> Though cursed, and scorned, and bruised with stones;
>
> But, looking upward, full of grace,
> He prayed, and from a happy place,
> God's glory smote him on the face.'

Why, then, the difference? Why had the Master this

agonising sense of forsakenness, when the disciple enjoyed in his last hours such a raptured sense of acceptance? It cannot be otherwise explained than as the apostles explained it, and all Evangelical Christians understand it, that Christ was bearing the sins of the world, while Stephen had no such burden to bear.

There is, however, one of the incidents of the Passion Week which comes strictly within the scope of our subject, inasmuch as it may fairly be included as part of the teaching of Christ, while yet He remained on earth; we refer to the testimony He bears to the importance of the great subject before us by the institution of the Supper. Of all the great events in His history, the one of which alone He established a memorial was His death. He made no provision whatever for the commemoration of His birth. The very day on which He was born is unknown; and Christmas, as every one knows, is not at all of His appointing. He has left no memorial of His baptism, when the heavens were opened above Him, and the voice from the excellent glory proclaimed His Divine Sonship. He has left no memorial of His transfiguration, when Moses and Elias came from the other world to do Him homage. He has left no memorial of His ascension, when a cloud of glory received Him out of His disciples' sight. We have, indeed, a memorial of His resurrection in the Lord's Day, the first day of the week, observed thereafter as the Christian Sabbath, or Rest Day; but for this change of the day of the Christian's worship there is no recorded command of the Master. But of His ignominious death He has left us a most enduring memorial in the ordinance of the Supper, instituted in close connection with the Passover, and with these deeply significant words, "This is My body, which is broken for you;" "This cup is the new covenant in My blood, which is shed for you"—thus justifying and adopting the prophetic words of His great Forerunner: "Behold the Lamb of God, that taketh away the sin of the world."

Is there not enough in all this fully to justify the central position given to the Atonement in the Epistles, to say nothing at present of the guidance of the Spirit of Christ under which they wrote, and in which we recognise the fulfilment of the Saviour's promise, that what He could not say to them while He was with them in the flesh, the Holy Ghost would fully teach them after He had gone to His Father? Is there not enough in what we have from the lips of Christ Himself, to justify the instinct of the Christian Church in making the Cross the symbol of Christianity, and the Atonement, or rather Christ Himself, "Christ our Passover," "sacrificed for us," "Christ, and Him crucified,' the Foundation on which the whole structure is built? Is there not enough in all this to rebuke and condemn the cold, barren doctrine of those who make the Cross of Christ of none effect, who take away the sacrifice and leave us only an example, which apart from the grace of God none of us can imitate, and which therefore only serves to deepen our despair,—and to justify the eagerness with which all true and earnest Christians clasp to their hearts the warm, living, saving truth, which gives inspiration to words like these:—

> "Rock of Ages, cleft for me,
> Let me hide myself in Thee!
> Let the water and the blood,
> From Thy wounded side which flowed,
> Be of sin the double cure,
> Save me from its guilt and power!"

There is one more cardinal point in this concluding summary of the doctrine of Christ which we must notice ere we close. We have seen that, looked at as a whole, it fully confirms what we had already ascertained as to the nature of the Gospel according to Christ; and as we have followed it out in its several parts, we have discovered that it begins by giving the same prominence to the Person of Christ which was so marked a feature of His teaching throughout, and then proceeds to set forth the great sacrifice which had been offered up on Calvary as the sum and substance of the Gospel, the one ground on which forgiveness and salvation could be preached among all nations. And now, in closing, He points forward to the future, and fixes their thoughts upon "the promise of the Father," that is, the promise of the coming of the Holy Spirit—a promise which had been given again and again to the faithful in Old Testament times as one to be fulfilled when the Messiah should have finished His work; which had been taken up and repeated with great emphasis by John the Baptist (Matt. iii. 11; Mark i. 8; Luke iii. 16); and which, according to the testimony of St John, the Lord Jesus had repeated and enlarged on, in those tender and memorable words, spoken in the upper room, with which He comforted His disciples on the eve of His departure. Thus it is that our Lord, in this concluding summary of His teaching, brings into special *and exclusive* prominence those very doctrines which the Rationalist especially denounces and discards. The reference to the last, though, from the necessary brevity of the summary, it is in a single sentence, is yet of such a nature as to mark its essential importance as completing the third and last stage of the apostles' training and equipment for their work. The Incarnation was the great lesson of the first stage; the Atonement and Resurrection of the second; the Coming of the Spirit to endue them with power from on high was the crown and consummation of all.

In the prominence thus given to the work of the Spirit there is full agreement with the testimony of St. John, who records the parting words of Christ in the upper room. From the study of these we learn that, in taking leave of His disciples, with many things in His heart left unspoken because they could not bear them yet, He was most careful to impress their minds with the expectation that these things should be spoken in due time; that "another Comforter" was coming to continue and complete their education; and yet, while speaking of *another* Comforter, He is especially desirous to make them clearly understand that, though there must be a change in the mode of communication, there will be in reality no change of Teacher, for the Comforter is to come in His name; "He shall not speak of Himself;" "He shall take of Mine, and show it unto you;" and again and again He speaks of the coming of the Spirit as equivalent to His own coming again to continue the work He had begun on earth. It is as if He said, "Though I cannot complete My teaching and your training on earth, I shall continue and complete it by My Spirit sent to you from heaven." Let one sentence suffice for proof of this: "*These things* have I spoken unto you, being yet present with you. But the Comforter, which is the Holy Ghost, whom the Father will send in My name, He shall teach you *all things*" (John xiv. 25, 26). Thus from the lips of Christ Himself we have a guarantee that the teaching of the apostles, after they should have received the Spirit, would possess equal authority with His own; and, moreover, we are thus by Himself prepared for expecting in the writings of the apostles fuller developments of the truth which He Himself had given in germ and outline. Thus we find all consistent and harmonious, so long as we hold fast to the full-orbed truth concerning the Gospel of the Grace of God; while those who resolve it into mere ethical instruction must not only surrender the Epistles, with the book of the Acts of the Apostles and the Apocalypse, but must utterly discredit the fourth Gospel, and set aside the greater part of the words of Christ as recorded by the other three Evangelists, retaining only certain portions of the Saviour's teaching specially selected for the purpose they have in view. How dare they, after such a process of elimination and reduction, call their remainder of good counsel the Gospel of Christ!

Very much more might be advanced on this great theme; but we trust enough has been said to accomplish the object with which we set out. We think it has been clearly shown that the great truths of evangelical religion are rooted in the life and teaching of the Lord Jesus Himself, though, from the nature of the case, some of them did not attain their full development until He had ascended to His Father and ours, and His Spirit had come to guide the disciples into all the truth. We trust enough has been written to show how vain it is to try to obtain the sanction of Christ to those views of the Gospel so prevalent in our day, according to which sin is an irregularity which an honest man can set right for himself; according to which education and a little care are all that are necessary to fit men for the Kingdom; according to which, if they only admire the morality of the Sermon on the Mount, and the beauty of the parable of the Prodigal Son, and try to respond in a life as consistent therewith as their feeble nature can attain to and their unfortunate surroundings permit, they may disregard almost all else that Christ taught—enough to make it manifest that a gospel so illusory cannot be connected with the name of Christ, and that, therefore, those who are willing to risk on it their life here and their prospects for eternity, must do so on the distinct understanding that Jesus of Nazareth has no responsibility for it; that, in fact, it is heathenism pure and simple. And we trust that by our inquiry into this matter we have been led to appreciate more highly than ever "the glorious Gospel of the Blessed God," which is no bare set of rules, no dry code of laws, no mere collection of moral maxims and wise sayings, but the revelation from heaven of the Infinite Love of God in Christ His Son Incarnate for us, crucified for our offences, exalted a Prince and a Saviour to give repentance and remission of sins, and by His Holy Spirit to apply to human hearts and lives that Remedy for all our ills which is fitly spoken of by the great Apostle of the Gentiles as "THE POWER OF GOD UNTO SALVATION," by means of which we are taken "from the horrible pit and miry clay," and our feet set upon a rock; on the strength of which our sins are all forgiven, and an abundant entrance assured us into the heavenly Kingdom; by the virtue of which we are transformed, from glory to glory, into the image of the Incarnate Son of God; in the faith of which we expect triumphantly to pass through the dark valley to the scene of the full enjoyment of that eternal life, only begun here, which is God's gift to us through Jesus Christ our Lord. "Now unto Him that loved us, and washed us from our sins in His own blood, and hath made us kings and priests unto God and His Father, to Him be glory and dominion for ever and ever. Amen."

BIBLIOLIFE

Old Books Deserve a New Life
www.bibliolife.com

Did you know that you can get most of our titles in our trademark **EasyScript**™ print format? **EasyScript**™ provides readers with a larger than average typeface, for a reading experience that's easier on the eyes.

Did you know that we have an ever-growing collection of books in many languages?

Order online:
www.bibliolife.com/store

Or to exclusively browse our **EasyScript**™ collection:
www.bibliogrande.com

At BiblioLife, we aim to make knowledge more accessible by making thousands of titles available to you – quickly and affordably.

Contact us:
BiblioLife
PO Box 21206
Charleston, SC 29413

Printed in Poland
by Amazon Fulfillment
Poland Sp. z o.o., Wrocław